How to Write It, How to Sell It

Other books by Linda Palmer

Runaway! (as Linda Weintraub)
Starstruck

How to Write It, How to Sell It

*Everything a Screenwriter
Needs to Know about Hollywood*

LINDA PALMER

St. Martin's Griffin
New York

A THOMAS DUNNE BOOK.
An imprint of St. Martin's Press.

Production Editor: David Stanford Burr
Design: Nancy Resnick

Library of Congress Cataloging-in-Publication Data

Palmer, Linda.
    How to write it, how to sell it : everything a screenwriter needs to know about Hollywood / Linda Palmer. — 1st ed.
        p.   cm.
    "A Thomas Dunne book."
    Includes bibliographical references.
    1. Motion picture authorship. 2. Motion picture plays—Marketing. I. Title.
    ISBN 0-312-18726-2
    PN1996.P265   1998
    808.2'3—dc21   98-11782
                                                                            CIP

10 9 8 7 6 5 4 3 2

This book is dedicated to
D. Constantine Conte
and
Mira Waters

Contents

Acknowledgments	ix
Author's Note	xi
1. Screenwriting Is Both an Art and a Craft	1
2. Some Terms It Will Help You to Know	8
3. Screenplay Format	22
4. Screenplay "Dos" and "Don'ts"	55
5. Creating Memorable Leading Characters	73
6. Great Supporting Characters and How to Use Them	94
7. How to Build Your Screenplay	116
8. Structures: Tight and Loose	143
9. What the Megahits Have in Common and What We Can Learn from Them	160
10. The "Pitch" and the Query Letter	184
11. The "Business" of Show Business	208
12. Getting Past the Dreaded "Reader"	217
13. Surviving Rejection—"Coping" Strategies	224
14. The Birth of a New Major Studio	232
15. Recommended Reading and Viewing	250
16. The First Act of the Fox TV Movie *Marabunta*	256
A Few Final Words	299

Acknowledgments

I Am Grateful . . .

For my education at the "University of Berry Gordy" ("B.G.U."), an institute of higher learning from which—if one works very hard—one never graduates.

To Sy Weintraub for being the first person to suggest that I write this book.

To Chuck Morrell, for his immediate enthusiasm and for knowing who might want it. You are this book's "Godfather," Chuck.

To my editor, Melissa Jacobs, for going way beyond editorial duty to visit one of my classes on the UCLA campus. You have a wonderful "ear" for what an author is trying to do and your guidance has been an incredible blessing.

To Rod Amateau, the first person to hire me to write a screenplay, when I had previously only written novels, book reviews, and stories. You taught me so much about screenwriting and producing that other people hired me.

To Susan Hendler, the daughter of my heart and my personal computer expert. Thank you for patiently guiding me through a variety of technical crises, and for giving me a copy of *Windows 95 for Dummies*.

To Warren Cowan, who suggested to UCLA Extension that I teach a screenplay development course, and whose friendship I will always treasure.

To Sidney Sheldon, who has helped so many beginning writers. Whatever I know about hooks and cliffhangers I learned from you. All you wanted in return was for me to help others.

To Dr. Linda Venis, Director, Department of the Arts, Head Writers' and Literature Programs, UCLA Extension. Thank you for thinking I might be able to teach, and then giving me seminars to show me how to share what I knew. You are not only the best organized executive I have ever met, you have a talent for making people excel. You should run a country.

To Aaron Spelling, who in 1976 bought a story I wrote and turned it into two episodes of his and Leonard Goldberg's TV series *Family*. What a privilege it was to learn about story-telling from you! You gave me my first on-screen credit—and twenty-two years later I'm still getting residuals.

To those writers in my workshops who made contributions to this book: Kevin Hing, Richard Lorber, Caroline Pfouts, Elizabeth Powell, Commander Gary E. Shrout, Denise Snaer, G. Wassil—

and to my some-time writing partner, the impish and adorable Wink Roberts. You're always full of surprises.

Author's Note

As a former production vice president of TriStar Pictures, a published novelist, and a professional screenwriter and a producer, I've had the very rare experience of sitting on both sides of the desk: the buyer's side and the seller's side.

What I learned as a studio executive was immensely important to me as a writer, and I'd like to share some of that acquired knowledge with you.

You Might Be the Next Million $$$ Writer

The motion picture business is on a perpetual treasure hunt for that next $100 million-plus-grossing hit. Because no one knows from where that project magically will appear, the industry is open to *any* writer who has a script that a producer, a star, or a studio wants to buy.

In the movie "spec script" business, no one cares about a writer's gender, age, ethnicity, or looks. Creating original screenplays is perhaps the last open frontier left in America.

It's likely that at some point friends and relatives have tried to discourage you by reporting that people all over the country (and, it seems, about one in two people in California) are writing scripts, and that your script will be in competition with hundreds of thousands of other scripts.

That is true—**but it is also irrelevant.**

Those "discouragers" have the numbers right: there really are hundreds of thousands of scripts out there—which is why I believe that **one of the most important qualities a screenwriter can have is an absolute refusal to face facts.**

Now here's the good news:

Most of those hundreds of thousands of scripts out there that will be competing with you are *bad* scripts. Your real competition is the several dozen *good* scripts whirring softly from the innards of printers.

That lowers considerably the odds against your success.

All that matters to buyers of screenplays is their belief that the scripts they've discovered will make them fortunes.

The happy reality for the undiscovered writer is that those producers, production companies, directors, and stars who turn characters, plots, and dialogue into visible magic will buy scripts they like from *anyone.* The trick for the new writer is to create a script of sufficient professional quality to allow the writer to gain access to the buyers. They can't buy it if they don't know it exists!

So, after you learn how to write an appealing script, you will need to know what to do with it—how to attract an agent who wants to represent it and a production entity that wants to make the movie. Helping you develop the skills to find an agent and a buyer is the second phase of what I hope this book will help you accomplish.

It is my intention that this book will be a kind of road map for you, the beginning screenwriter, taking you from FADE IN to FADE OUT—and then, beyond that, along the mysterious "yellow brick road" that leads to the *achievable goal* of your having a career as a professional screenwriter.

Mark Twain made this comment about a friend of his: "The harder he worked, the luckier he got."

I wish you hard work and all the good luck—*and the big paydays*—that can come from that winning combination.

Now let's get to the specifics of how to write a terrific script.

How to Write It, How to Sell It

1. Screenwriting Is Both an Art and a Craft

Screenwriters need to know more than just how to write a good story. Screenwriters also need to master correct screenplay format so that their scripts look professional, learn how to develop the characters who will populate their screenplays, learn how to structure the stories they want to tell, learn to establish quickly who the leading characters are and what their stories are about, and learn the discipline that is required to tell those stories within the industry preferred length of 120 pages or less. After they've done all that, then writers need to know how to "pitch" their scripts in the marketplace, how to write effective query letters to attract the interest of agents and buyers, and how to pick their marketing targets.

In addition to all of those things listed above, writers need to learn how to stay sane and productive while enduring the pain of waiting for someone to read their work, and how to survive the agony of rejection.

It is my theory—and this theory is the basis of what I teach in my workshops—that it is important to study good movies for illustrations of what works on the screen. It can also be useful to study movies that do not work, i.e., that are not satisfying to the viewer, and analyze where that screenwriter went wrong. Studying movies to see how the best screenwriters presented and developed their characters and advanced their plots from introduction to conclusion is crucial to perfecting the skills that will be vital to your own success in the motion picture industry. Throughout the course of this book I have cited certain specific movies, scenes and examples of dialogue that I feel will be of particular help to you in perfecting your own screenplays. If it is possible, please rent or buy the videocassettes so you can see these movies in their entirety. Run them frequently enough to "decode" the secrets of their success. My recommendation is that you watch a movie for the first time simply as a member of the audience who wants to be entertained. Just surrender yourself to the experience without thinking about screenwriting craft. On your subsequent viewings, study how the movie was put together. You will, I believe, see your critical faculties develop rapidly as you begin to dissect movies for purposes of study.

Have a pad and pencil handy as you watch and study movies. Take notes as you identify what moments made you love the characters, or at least made you care what happened to them. Note how the movie is constructed. Were there any dull spots? If so, what made them dull and how would you have written that part differently? Check for variety in the action scenes. Did the screenwriter find new excitements, or repeat him- or herself too often?

Study transitions. By that I mean: how did the writer get from one scene to the next? Were the leaps in time made smoothly? Analyze moments that affected you emotionally. How did the writer manipulate your feelings? (In screenwriting—unlike in life—manipulating the feelings of others is a *good* thing.)

Study pictures you did *not* like to determine what turned you against the picture or against the characters.

Study how the star, and other important characters, are introduced into the story.

Certainly study the most successful movies of all time. As we will see when we get to that part of this guide, at their core by far the majority of the most successful films are love stories. Watch the movies on that Top 20 list. Study the little moments that made the experience of seeing the picture such an enjoyable one. Just as one example, I could discuss endlessly *E.T. The Extra-Terrestrial,* listing such priceless moments as Elliot freeing the frogs in his biology class, the boys seeing E.T. all dressed up by Gertie, E.T. touching Elliot's finger cut to heal it, bicycling across the sky—and so many other inventive gems that captivated me.

Writers have an opportunity to inspire, to elevate, and to enrich the lives of others—if they write from what is best in themselves, not from the part that is most ambitious. A generous heart is a powerful communicator. If you really love the script you're writing—if you're having fun telling the story, not just writing with the hope of earning money—that sincere quality is likely to come through to the reader.

According to newspaper articles I've read, Soviet dissident Natan Sharansky, who had been held as a political prisoner in a Moscow jail and in Russian labor camps for nine years, had been arrested just a day or two after his wedding. His new bride, Avital, quickly emigrated to Israel.

Sharansky endured terrible times in prison, but survived his ordeal because early in one of his interrogations, his interrogator made a mistake. Hoping to break Sharansky's will, the man made a remark about Sharansky's wife. That intended cruelty had just the opposite effect. Suddenly Sharansky remembered that Avital was alive and free. He knew that as long as she lived she would never stop lobbying, petitioning, imploring world governments to pressure the Soviets to release him. For Sharansky, that vision of Avital opened a window to the outside world, to the possibility of freedom. It helped Sharansky, and his sense of humor, survive.

When Sharansky was finally released and allowed to join Avital in Israel, his first words to her were an apology that he was "nine years late."

I would not trivialize what Natan Sharansky endured by comparing his ordeal to the struggles of a screenwriter. The relevance of this anecdote is that Sharansky survived because the vision of his wife symbolized the "window on the world" that gave him strength. Screenwriters can create stories that provide a similar window for audiences—that precious glimpse of *possibility* that can help people by giving them the strength to endure their circumstances and the will to change them for the better.

I love movies, which is why I write screenplays and why I teach the craft and include what I refer to as the "Hollywood guerrilla warfare" of screenwriting. I've always loved movies, even though the first movie I remember seeing precipitated an enormous upheaval in my life. I was three years old and my father took me to a horror movie. I don't remember what movie it was, except that it was in black and white, there was a beautiful woman with long hair, a monster I felt sorry for, it was scary, and I enjoyed it very much.

When we got home and my mother found out he had taken me to a horror movie, she was so furious she threw a coffeepot at his head. The coffeepot missed its target, but I never saw my original father again.

As a child in difficult circumstances it was books and movies that gave me my window to the outside world, that glimpse of *possibility* worth surviving for.

It's Tough "Out There"—but That's Part of the Fun

The world of the professional writer who works in any of the disciplines is a rugged one, but the life of a screenwriter is filled with even more traps, obstacles, and heartaches than that of the playwright, novelist, or short-story or nonfiction writer. It is a rollercoaster ride of high hopes and deep, spirit-bruising disappointments. There are many people who have the power to say no. Getting to those few who can say yes to your script is about as easy as climbing Mount Everest—but people do it! It just takes sweat and *grit*. During the hardest times, please remember this: when you do succeed, that accomplishment will be very sweet because you will know in your heart and soul that you have earned your success, *earned* what may look to others like "luck."

I have seen people destroy themselves because success came too quickly, before they believed that it was real, before they believed they had earned it. So don't despair about the disappointments and bad times; one day you will be glad that you survived them, and you will know that you earned the good times that followed.

It's time to mention something that you may have to face. Following the sale of your script, you might discover that someone you thought of as a close friend is not as thrilled for you as you would be for them if the situation were reversed. Jealousy can make otherwise good people behave unkindly. The more successful you become, the more you will learn about people you *think* you know. People tend to reveal their true characters during extreme circumstances, whether those circumstances are extremely good or extremely bad. Be grateful when people live up to your expectations. Don't let those who disappoint you diminish the pleasure of your accomplishment. Understand that life is a continuing education.

"Difficult" Is Not a Synonym for "Impossible"

Screenwriting is not for those who only want praise, or who need to write something that will remain just exactly as they placed the words on the paper. Those writers are called "poets." Screenwriters need to be strong mentally and to have the physical endurance of athletes if they want a career in the movie business.

When I meet people socially for the first time, and they learn that I'm a screenwriter and that I teach screenwriting, they will sometimes ask my advice about how to be a successful writer. My answer surprises them. I say: begin immediately—*by going into physical training.*

Some people—at first—think I'm joking, but they quickly realize that I am not. I explain that building up one's physical stamina is the best way I know to stay both sane and productive during the emotional roller coaster onto which a beginning writer is about to climb. It's a dizzying, dazzling ride full of emotional high-speed turns, the terrifying highs and lows of encouragement and rejection, the stomach-wrenching lurches between hope and despair. It's a ride that places powerful demands on the body and on the psyche; it is not for the emotionally fragile and physically out of shape.

There may be months, or even years, when "success" for a screenwriter is defined as just *surviving* with one's pride and sense of purpose intact, even if it's battered and bent. The worst blows may be dealt by people who can't create as you can, but can only criticize. Don't try to analyze the motive behind the rejection; it may be as simple as the fact that not everyone can look at the same piece of material and see its value. As for the pain of rejection, just learn to survive it, then recover from it and go on. Sylvester Stallone's Rocky Balboa was right: sometimes you win by just staying in the game, by "going the distance."

Here is a tool that will be of great help if you decide to use it. I call it "the Writer's Strength and Stamina" exercise routine. I urge you to begin your personal regimen as soon as you finish reading this chapter.

Do this routine faithfully and you will gain the strength you will need to "go the distance."

The Writer's Strength and Stamina Exercise Routine

For fifteen minutes a day, five days a week, do some kind of physical exercise that will work up a mild sweat. It can be jogging, sit-ups, knee bends, leg lifts, waist bends, running in place or on a treadmill, peddling on a stationary bike, or actual biking outdoors. It can be jumping jacks, rope climbing, rowing, scissor kicks, or arm rotations. It can be exercises with a broom handle behind your back or at a ballet barre. It can be squeezing rubber balls to strengthen lower arms and hands. It can be vigorous dancing or graceful ballet stretches. You can exercise to music, to talk radio (my favorite), or in front of the television set. You can combine exercises, or vary them according to the weather or to accommodate family obligations.

I don't care what exercise you choose—the point is that for fifteen minutes a day, five days a week, you exercise *while reciting the following:*

"I am a writer. I am exercising to be strong mentally and to increase my stamina because I need both mental strength and physical stamina to have a career as a writer."

Memorize those sentences, and repeat them at least three times during the fifteen minutes of exercise: once at the beginning, once in the middle, and once at the end, as you're cooling down or toweling off.

If you do nothing else of a physical nature, I want you to do this. Anything else you do for physical fitness or for improving your looks is fine—but that activity is separate from the Writer's Strength and Stamina routine.

No matter what one's physical limitations, there is some form of exercise that one can find to do, but if you do have some medical considerations, please ask your doctor what exercise is safe for you to do before you begin this routine.

One last reminder: It is very important that you dedicate this particular fifteen minutes of exercise to *building your strength as a writer.* So don't forgot to utter these two sentences that I've asked you to memorize:

"I am a writer. I am exercising to be strong mentally and to increase my stamina because I need both mental strength and physical stamina to have a career as a writer."

Giving voice to those two sentences *three times* is an important part of the routine.

Commit to this routine—and keep it up. One day you will be glad that you did.

2. Some Terms It Will Help You to Know

Like other industries and professions, the motion picture and television business has terminology all its own. What follows is a list, with definitions, of terms and phrases that a screenwriter should know. To make it easy to use this list, I have organized the terms and phrases alphabetically.

Above the Line: Writers, star actors, directors, producers, and composers. (This "line" is the mythical divider between the expensive talents whose names may help lure an audience and the "worker bees" who build the sets, sews the costumes, etc.)

Acquisition of Rights: When a script, book, story, outline, treatment, newspaper or magazine article, or permission to write about a living person is purchased or optioned toward the object of producing a film.

AD: Assistant director.

ADR: Additional Dialogue Replacement—words or phrases or new dialogue recorded in postproduction. It has come to include revoicing or changing dialogue already recorded. Examples of ADR would be words shouted out in crowd scenes, or muttered by people in an audience, or replacement lines of dialogue.

Air Date: The date when a given television program or film will be shown on the air.

Ancillary Rights: Additional rights arising from the production of a film or TV show, such as toys, comic books, clothing, novelization, food products, records. In other words, products derived from the story or characters created for the screenplay or teleplay. Also, spin-offs into television series or specials.

Animation: A story told in drawings, or with Claymation figures, or with any other art technology that tells a story on film without using living humans or live animals and real locations and props.

Back Story: Events that happened to one or more of the characters before the script begins.

Below the Line: Everything else on a production, including members of the crew, actors of lesser status than the stars, doubles and stunt-people, costs for locations, costumes, etc., and lower-level staff personnel.

Blue Pages: The first color inserted into the pages of the white shooting script indicating that there are dated and marked changes on those pages. PINK PAGES, YELLOW PAGES, etc. indicate additional changes to the shooting script. It is not unusual for a shooting script to look like a rainbow by the time principal photography is complete.

Box Office Gross: The money that comes into the box office from paying customers.

Breaking the Fourth Wall: This is a theatrical term, referring to the fourth "wall" of a set, which is that invisible "wall" between the story being performed and the audience watching the story. If a writer suddenly addresses the *reader,* instead of continuing to tell the story, he or she risks destroying the spell of that story. (I don't think this is a good idea because you may never get your reader back under that spell, once it's been broken.) However, if you want to have one of your *characters* (usually the star) suddenly stop and address the audience directly, this can be an effective surprise, especially in a comedy. Woody Allen used this technique entertainingly in *Annie Hall*. Another example is the comedy *Shirley Valentine*.

Buzz: The "buzz" on a project or the writer means what people in the industry are saying about the project or the writer.

Casting Breakdown: When a picture has been scheduled for production, a page is sent out to agents and managers briefly describing the film and the roles to be cast. It also lets agents and managers know where script pages can be picked up so that actors being submitted for roles can study scenes before auditioning.

Cold Reading: When an actor is asked to read aloud lines of dialogue without having had a chance to see the pages beforehand, this is called a "cold reading."

Dailies: Each day's work on a film in production that is screened on a "daily" basis by studio executives, producers, the director, and designated members of the staff, cast, and crew. (These screenings of the day's work used to be called "rushes.")

Deal Memo: A short agreement, often no more than a page in length, spelling out the terms of an agreement. (Most work in Hollywood proceeds on the deal memo. Contracts are so complex that it is not uncommon for a picture to be completed before the final contract is drafted and signed.)

Development Fund: Money used to buy, to option, or to pay for the writing of literary properties.

Direct-to-Video: This is a movie that intentionally is made for sale in video stores instead of for theatrical release.

Distributor: The studio (actually, the distribution division of a studio) that gets the movie booked into the theaters and supplies the prints.

Distributor's Gross: The percentage of box office gross that goes to the studio that releases the movie.

Distribution Fee: Fee a studio charges a production to release and distribute the picture.

DP: Director of Photography.

Exhibitor: Owner of the theater, or the chain of theaters, that play the movie.

Exhibitor's Gross: The percentage of box office gross that the owner of the theater or of the theater chain playing the movie keeps.

Exposition: Information that we need to know to fully understand and enjoy the movie we are reading or seeing. This frequently includes back story information. One movie that is absolutely brilliant at parceling out exposition (information we need to know) while the story is entertaining us is *Midnight Run,* written by George Gallo.

Fast Track: When a project is said to be on the "fast track," that means that the studio boss (the person who can say yes and authorize the spending of money) wants to make the picture and that its development has the highest priority. Sometimes a movie will be put on the fast track to beat a competing film with a similar concept to the theaters. A project also leaps onto the fast track if a major box office attraction wants to star in it or direct it.

Film Noir: Movies with "dark" situations and "dark" characters such as thieves, murderers (or those willing to murder), prostitutes, and various denizens of the night. These pictures were mostly made in the 1940s and 1950s in black and white, but *Body Heat,* in color and made in 1981, was a perfect "film noir." Some of the most skillful and memorable examples of classic film noir are *The Maltese Falcon; Touch of Evil; Sweet Smell of Success; Mildred Pierce; The Postman Always Rings Twice; Sunset Boulevard; The Third Man; Sorry, Wrong Number; The Big Sleep; Laura;* and *Double Indemnity.*

11

First Look Deal: In exchange for a development fund given to a creative entity, the supplier of this fund (usually a studio) gets the first opportunity to buy the projects developed with that money.

Franchises: Certain characters or combinations of characters prove to be so appealing to audiences that the producers or the studio discover that what they have is that most financially desirable of all creative beings: a "franchise." Some examples of franchises are the *Lethal Weapon, Die Hard,* Dirty Harry, *Star Trek, Batman,* James Bond, *Star Wars, Indiana Jones, Alien,* and *Superman* pictures. (You'll find a detailed discussion of remakes, sequels, and franchises in chapter 3.)

Green Light: This lovely phrase means you've gotten the word to GO, make the picture.

Gross "Points": The definition of gross "points"—percentage of moneys earned by a film that goes to the person (usually a star) who has a gross profits participation agreement—varies.

Guild: Another name for "union," such as the Writers Guild of America, Inc. (WGA), the Screen Actors Guild (SAG), or the Directors Guild of America (DGA).

Heat: "Heat" on a project or on the writer means that there is great interest in the industry about that project or writer.

Honey Wagon: Small trailers housing portable toilets. These are stationed near sets on studio back lots or at location sites for the use of cast and crew during filming.

Housekeeping Deal: An arrangement with a creative entity such as a writer or independent producer or star in which a studio supplies office space and plays certain overhead expenses incurred in the search for properties. In exchange for payment of these expenses, the creative entity must give the studio the opportunity to purchase what is created or developed during the period of this arrangement.

Lip-Synch: To dub dialogue to match lip synchronization in the picture.

Live Action: A story or scene utilizing real actors, props, and locations, as opposed to animation.

Log Line: A one-sentence description of a movie or of a television episode. Log lines usually appear in television listings.

Looping: Dialogue or sound replacement of existing tracks, or additions or augmentation. Looping of dialogue often requires the actors involved to lip-synch. It can also be an offscreen voice that is being added or changed.

Master Script: The final shooting script from which all other copies are duplicated for use by the actors, the crew and the staff. Any changes to this master script are dated at the top and specific changes are indicated by an asterisk (*) next to the altered lines or action.

MBA: For screen and television writers the MBA is the Writers Guild's **Minimum Basic Agreement** for fees to be paid and conditions to be honored.

Negative Pickup: An independent producer makes a film (with his own money or with money from investors) and then a studio pays the producer for the film—or "picks up" the film. The film is then released under the studio's banner. The amount of money the producer receives is subject to negotiation and varies, but it is generally the cost of the completed film plus a profit.

Net Points: Payments to a net profit participant (usually the writer or writers) begin after just about every imaginable deduction has been made against the studio's gross income on a picture. Eddie Murphy famously has described net points as "monkey points," because few people ever collect them.

Novelization: The novel version of a screenplay, usually published in soft cover and timed to hit the stores simultaneously with the release of the movie.

One-Sheet: The poster advertising the film, usually adapted for print advertising as well.

Outline: A description, running a few pages, of the major characters and major events in a screenplay.

Package: An agent or a producer puts together a combination of financially attractive elements—a star or stars and a script, sometimes including a director—and offers this "package" to financing entities. (A bit of personal history: When I was at TriStar Pictures, producer John Foreman offered me first chance to take the *Prizzi's Honor* package, which consisted of a marvelous script, Jack Nicholson as star, and John Huston as director. I wanted it desperately, but TriStar's president did not share my belief in the material and turned the package down. I had fought hard for that package, and I was a bad loser. Every time *Prizzi's Honor* got a great review, won an award, or earned good grosses at the box office I would leave the clippings prominently on my boss's desk. Luckily for me, he was a good sport and admitted that we should have made that picture.)

Period Piece: This is usually understood to mean a costume drama set in a much earlier time. Some examples are *Sense and Sensibility, Emma, Portrait of a Lady, The Madness of King George, Dangerous Liaisons, The Crucible, The Last of the Mohicans,* and the *Indiana Jones* pictures, which are set in the late 1930s, or *Schindler's List,* which was set in the 1940s, during World War II. However, for practical production purposes, a "period piece" is *any* picture set a few years earlier than the year in which the picture is produced. These productions generally cost more below the line than pictures set in "the present" because, for example, there cannot be cars on the street from a later time than the date of the story, accurate clothing from that year or earlier must be found or made, and production designers must be careful not to show outdoor advertising, landmarks, or technological innovations that came into being later than the year in which the story is set. A picture set in the future is not called a "period piece"; it is classified as "futuristic."

Pitch: As in "to pitch a story." There are two kinds of pitches. The first is the short pitch (one to three intriguing sentences) designed to get the object of the pitch to say: "I want to read that script!" The second kind of pitch is the telling of a story to a potential buyer (a producer or production company executive) in the hope that the person hearing it will pay the writer to write a screenplay, or at least a treatment, of that story.

Plot: The events in the story. "Plot" is what keeps your characters busy.

Premise: The core idea of the film. Example: A wild, almost-crazy cop who's trying to get himself killed is assigned to work with a happy family man who has everything to live for and is horrified by his new partner. This is the premise of the original *Lethal Weapon*.

Prequels: George Lucas is preparing a three-screenplay cycle—or trilogy—of movies that will predate his *Star Wars* trilogy and will be released beginning at the end of this century. These three movies will deal with the youth and early manhood of Luke Skywalker's father, and will tell the story of what happened to transform him from noble Jedi Knight into Darth Vader. *Butch and Sundance: The Early Days* (released in 1979) was a "prequel" to the hugely popular *Butch Cassidy and the Sundance Kid* (released ten years earlier, in 1969).

Principal Photography: Shooting the film with the principal actors.

Production Bonus: An additional payment given to a writer (or writers) when credits are determined. (Credits are determined after the completion of principal photography and before release to theaters or the broadcast of the film.) Example: If a writer's contract calls for a fifty-thousand-dollar production bonus, that amount is reduced according to the number of writers with whom she must share screenplay credit on the film. If a second writer is credited, then the first writer receives twenty-five thousand dollars—and so on down. Check with the Writers Guild of America, West, but as of this writing I believe the irreducible minimum credit for the writer of an original work is a shared "story by" credit. (Traditionally, there is no bonus for a "story by" or shared story credit. If a writer has received such a bonus it was due to a special agreement with the producer of the picture.)

Public Domain: A work on which the copyright has expired, or never existed, or might never have been needed. This usually means that the work can be used or adapted without payment to the original creator (author, composer, artist) or to that person's estate. Examples: *Clueless* from Jane Austen's nineteenth-century novel *Emma, West Side Story* from Shakespeare's *Romeo and Juliet,* and the enormously popular musical *Carousel* from Ferenc Molnar's 1909 play *Liliom.* It's my personal opinion (I've never seen this discussed in interviews with the filmmakers or with novelist Peter Benchley) that *Jaws* is a modern retelling of Henrik Ibsen's 1882 play *An Enemy of the People.*

Quote: A writer's "quote" is the last price he was paid for a script or for rewrite work.

Recruited Screening: Audience members selected by a research firm (often in supermarket parking lots or from lines of people waiting to see other movies) are invited to see an unreleased picture either in a theater hired for the occasion or in a studio screening room. After seeing the picture the recruited audience members answer questions about what they liked and what they did not like. One of the most famous cases of a picture undergoing radical changes after prerelease screenings was that of *Fatal Attraction.* In reaction to negative audience response, a new climax and a new ending were shot before the picture was released to the paying customers. The movie that was released made a great deal of money. Because it portrayed every straying husband's worst nightmare, *Fatal Attraction* is credited with reducing acts of adultery—for a while.

Remakes: A new version of a picture originally made at an earlier time. Two examples of remakes are *Sabrina,* made first with Audrey Hepburn, Humphrey Bogart, and William Holden, and then remade with Julia Ormond, Harrison Ford, and Greg Kinnear, and *A Star Is Born,* which was made three times. The second version starred July Garland and the most recent starred Barbra Streisand.

Rough Cut: A rough, or not-yet-refined, version of the assembled film footage. From this early version of the picture a FINE CUT is made as the director and editor discard excess footage.

Scale: The minimum payment to an artist as negotiated by that artist's guild. At the WGA the amount of "scale" for a screenplay is determined by the category of the picture's budget: whether it is a high-budget picture, or medium or low. The scale amount changes every six or so years, so consult the Writers Guild of America for the current figures.

Scene: In the language of screenplays, a scene is that action or dialogue exchange that takes place in one set or in one location. In a shooting script, each scene is given a number and shot separately from the other scenes.

Screen Credits: The list of names of the cast, staff (including writers, producers, director), and crew. Credits are determined after a movie or television show has been shot but before it is released or broadcast. The size and placement of certain credits are determined either by guild regulations or by contracts negotiated on behalf of the artists involved.

Script Assignment: When a writer is hired to write a screenplay from someone else's concept, or to adapt a piece of literary material such as a book, short story, or newspaper or magazine article.

Script Doctor: A writer who is hired to rewrite or to improve parts of an existing script that is headed for production. A script doctor may or may not get a screen credit, depending upon the amount of that writer's contribution to the shooting script.

Second Unit: Film shot without use of the principal actors, frequently shot by a second unit director and second unit cameraman. These are usually car shots, long shots, aerial views of action, or physical action scenes when the faces of the principal actors are not visible.

Sequels: New stories written to carry on the adventures of popular characters created for an earlier film. Two examples: *The Godfather* (1972), *The Godfather Part II* (1974), and *The Godfather Part III*

(1990); and *The Terminator* (1984) and *Terminator 2: Judgment Day* (1991).

Sequence: A series of connected scenes. For example, a movie "chase sequence" is a series of scenes depicting a chase, or one character (or group of characters) pursuing another. These scenes are later edited together in order to achieve an exciting action sequence.

SFX: Special Effects.

Shelving: To decide not to make a picture that's been in development. Instead of putting it in turnaround, it is put on the "shelf" to fade from memory. Completed pictures are sometimes "shelved" because it is thought by the financing company that they are not worth the money it would cost to make the prints and buy the advertisements necessary to release the pictures. Pictures aren't "shelved" very often anymore because it not only causes a loss of money, but it is also an embarrassment if the executive who said yes to the project is still with the studio. It is more common now for a picture that is deemed not worth the distribution costs to be sent directly to the video stores.

Shooting Script: The final, approved screenplay with which a director begins production. Each scene has been assigned a number. Any further revisions that occur are due to unanticipated circumstances that arise during the course of filming the movie.

Sides: Individual pages or scenes taken from a script and given to an actor to use in an audition.

Slug Line: The line in the script that precedes a scene. It is written all CAPS. Example: INT. LIVING ROOM—DAY. The three essential pieces of information that a slug line conveys are (1) whether the scene takes place in an interior set (INT.) or an exterior set (EXT.); (2) what set is to be used (LIVING ROOM); and (3) whether it is DAY or NIGHT.

Sneak Preview: Before being sent out into the theaters an unreleased film may be shown at a movie house during the regular run of an already released picture. This is to gauge audience reaction to the picture. If it is unfavorable, changes can be made before prints are made to distribute. Sometimes the theater audience knows what the film will be and sometimes it does not. Sometimes advertised sneak previews are scheduled not for purposes of deciding what changes can be made, but to build audience excitement prior to the imminent release of the picture.

Sound Crossover to: This means to carry sound or dialogue from one scene over into the following scene. How to use and how to write a sound crossover is demonstrated in chapter 4.

Spec Script: A script conceived and written on "speculation"—that is, with no promise of sale or option prior to the writing.

Spin-Off: An entertainment entity created from a part or parts of an existing entertainment entity. Examples: The character of Rhoda was taken from *The Mary Tyler Moore Show* and "spun off" into the separate series *Rhoda*. Other shows spun off from *The Mary Tyler Moore Show* were the half-hour sitcom (situation comedy) *Phyllis* and the one-hour drama *Lou Grant*. Several cop dramas were spun off from NBC's successful crime anthology *Police Story*, which was created by novelist Joe Wambaugh.

Start Date: The date when principal photography on a project begins.

Step Deal: An agreement by which a writer (or writing team) is paid for his work in stages. The first payment might be for writing the treatment, another payment for writing a first draft, second draft, etc., according to the specifics of the particular agreement. The writer can be let go after any given "step" at the discretion of the purchaser of the work.

Stet: A term taken from publishing and journalism. The genesis is Latin, and means "Let it stand." If some dialogue or action is crossed out of a screenplay, but then is restored, "stet" is written next to the crossed-out portion.

Storyboard: Sketches of scenes from a screenplay. These are usually of action sequences, which are easy to visualize.

Structure: The architectural design of your script. The most traditional choice is the three-act structure, with a clear beginning, middle, and end. An example of this is *The Godfather.* Distinctively original approaches, such as the circular, carousel-like structure of *Pulp Fiction,* can also be effective. It is the writer who decides how to tell his or her story. For a detailed discussion of contrasting structures, see chapter 7 ("How to Build Your Screenplay" and chapter 8 ("Structures: Tight and Loose").

Subplot: A subplot is a secondary story that runs parallel to the main plot. A subplot provides brief diversion or respite from the main action, or perhaps comic relief. In series television, a subplot is called "the B story."

Synopsis: A short description of a plot.

Trailer: Preview scenes run in theaters or in television spots that are designed to make the audience or the viewer want to see the picture these coming attractions advertise.

Treatment: A telling of the screenplay's story in narrative form. This is a very detailed, virtually scene-by-scene, description of the characters and the story's events. Treatment lengths vary, but in general a treatment can be ten to fifty pages long. The average motion picture treatment usually runs between twenty and thirty pages. There are three basic styles of treatment: the story point treatment, the scenario treatment, and the narrative treatment. These are discussed, with examples, in chapter 7, "How to Build Your Screenplay."

Turnaround: To have a project "put in turnaround" means that the financing entity, usually a studio, has decided not to go ahead with the project and is allowing it to be purchased by another studio for production. The second studio must then reimburse the first studio for money spent, or pay any other consideration that may be in the contract.

UPM: Unit production manager.

Writing Credits: These are determined by the Writers Guild after principal photography has been completed but before the picture is released. Writing credits can tell a little story of their own to those who know how to read them. For example, "Written by" means that the script is an *original* work, not based on any other work. "Screenplay by" means that the script *is* based on some other work, such as a book, a play, a newspaper article, or someone else's story. The word "and" between the names of the writers means that they worked separately, and the name in first position was deemed to have contributed the most to the shooting script. An ampersand (&) between names means that the writers worked as a team. The order of the names separated by an ampersand indicates only an agreement between the writers involved; it's not an indication of who wrote the most. Some teams bill themselves alphabetically; some prefer to alternate whose name comes first project by project. The industry considers that the script was written by the *team.*

3. Professional Format

Why Proper Format Is Important to Your Career

One of the things I learned as a studio vice president was how important it is that a script create an immediate good impression. A script that doesn't "look right" in its format will probably not be read past the first or second page. A script that doesn't quickly grab one's interest through setting, perceived premise and leading character will not, in all likelihood, be read past page 10.

It is my goal in this book that your script be read all the way from FADE IN to FADE OUT. (And, after you put in all the hard work of writing it, I want you to have the best possible chance to sell it.)

Nothing will get a script tossed onto the "Reject" pile quicker than one churned out by a writer who does not take the trouble to master proper screenplay format. Sloppy format labels the writer as one who does not respect the screenwriter's craft sufficiently to learn the important basics. There is little reason to respect, or to spend time reading the work of, a screenwriter who does not take the trouble to learn the proper way to write a screenplay.

Screenplay format is not some arbitrary design on the page. Every capitalization and indentation has a production raison d'être, or reason for being. Even before you understand what those reasons are, I urge you to respect and master proper screenplay format. The importance of this in the marketplace cannot be overstated.

Agents and development executives are not in the business of searching for buried treasure, that is for some writer who has talent but has not yet learned how to produce a polished work. Forget whether or not you think that agents and development executives *should be* searching for buried treasure—this is not a perfect world, and unfortunately they are not.

In the real world, a script written in sloppy format is unlikely to be read far enough for anyone to discover whether or not that writer might be talented. Professionals don't have time to wade through material from a writer who needs training. That is the simple and immutable reality. Accept it and learn what you need to know.

Many, many times I've heard this worried question from new writers:

"But don't all those slug lines just slow down the 'read'? Won't the reader enjoy my script more if I just write the story?"

The answer is no—a very firm and definite no. The reason is that anyone to whom you will be submitting the script is, by definition, a professional. The agent, producer, or production executive you're trying to impress is jerked abruptly out of the "read" by the *lack* of correct professional format. It makes a professional in the business crazy when a writer is too careless—or, worse, too uncaring—to use proper screenplay format. Professionals know what the nuances of screenplay format mean to production and, consciously or unconsciously, resent the fact that format is treated cavalierly. It must be made perfect in production to avoid costly—even catastrophic—mistakes. The earlier the script is correct the better for everyone, and especially for the beginning screenwriter.

Nothing else you learn here will be very useful if you don't accept the need to learn professional screenplay format. I urge you to take this advice seriously; it can only work to your advantage.

Now, let's learn proper screenplay format—and have some fun doing it.

Proper Screenplay Format Item by Item

The script begins:

FADE IN:

Then, after double-spacing (two lines of white space), comes the *slug line*. Example of a correct slug line:

INT. MICHAEL'S OFFICE—DAY

Like "Gaul" in the old junior high school Latin books, correct slug lines are divided into three parts (but sometimes four). The first part of the slug is: **INT.** (interior) or **EXT.** (exterior). This tells us whether the scene takes place indoors or outdoors. That's an important piece of information to the 1st AD (assistant director), who "breaks down" the script into the first rough shooting schedule.

Note: When a project has been "green-lighted," the 1st AD does the initial rough shooting schedule. Then the script is passed to the unit production manager (UPM), who does the first rough budget. After a basic budget has been agreed to by the financing entity (usually a studio), the 1st AD then takes the script and makes a "fine" shooting schedule, after which the UPM makes the "fine" budget.

Now, back to format:

The second part of the slug tells us in what *set* the scene takes place. It is vital to be specific here. In the above imagined screenplay, Michael only has one office. But if Michael has more than one office—for example, a home office as well as a company office—the slug line might read either:

INT. MICHAEL'S MEDIA WORLD OFFICE—DAY

or:

INT. MICHAEL'S HOME OFFICE—NIGHT

The third part of the slug tells us whether the scene takes place during the day, or night, or morning, or afternoon—or whatever period of the twenty-four-hour clock is appropriate to your screenplay. Try to refrain from using the designation "Magic Hour," or use it as seldom as possible. It means dawn or sunset, and getting the shot before losing the light can be a production nightmare.

Day or night, etc. is a very important piece of information to the director of photography (DP), as well as to the 1st AD and UPM. One DP told me that he even wanted to know whether it was day or night when he was lighting a scene that took place inside a fully enclosed elevator!

Because scenes are seldom shot "in continuity"—meaning that scenes appearing one after the other on the screenplay page might, in a production schedule, be shot weeks apart—it is important that each slug line be *complete*. Don't assume that just because two consecutive scenes in your script are both day that you can leave the DAY off the second slug. Each scene is shot as a separate little movie, so each slug must respect that fact. To assume is to be sloppy, and to risk problems during production.

Consider this: Suppose you got away with incomplete slug lines, and, during preproduction, someone else had to put in the necessary DAY or NIGHT—but just skimmed the script and got it wrong. That can create major problems: additional production costs for reshooting, or rewriting to explain why a character got out of a taxi during a day scene and immediately entered a building—but it was night outside the windows. Because someone who had to do the writer's work got the DAY and NIGHT wrong, the writer looks bad. And should.

The possible fourth part of the slug line follows DAY or NIGHT, and is encased in parentheses. Example:

INT. MICHAEL'S MEDIA WORLD OFFICE—NIGHT
(LATER)

or:

EXT. MEDIA WORLD OFFICE BUILDING—DAY
(2 YEARS LATER)

or:

INT. MEDIA WORLD LOBBY—DAY (1981)

This last parenthetical designation is used when there's been a big jump in time, either forward or backward. Whether you tell us the time period of the story is now taking place 2 YEARS LATER or that this scene is set back in 1981, the vital thing here is that the agents, producers, stars, or the dreaded "readers" know where they are in terms of time. Don't make us search for such vital information as we read. Don't make us wonder why your characters are calling each other "thou"—when it's easier to tell us that the story takes place in the year 1371.

In writing a screenplay, always strive for clarity. If it helps, think of a screenplay as a kind of blueprint.

Above are the simple dos of proper slug lines. Now for some major don'ts:

Professionals don't want to see a slug line that reads:

INT. MICHAEL'S HOUSE—DAY

Interior *house?* In *what room* in this house will the scene take place?! The set designer must know what room (set) to build. The set decorator must know what set to decorate. The director of photography must know what set to light. Is the scene to take place in the living room, in a bedroom (whose?), in a bathroom (whose?), in the kitchen, in the attic, in the basement? Specify *precisely* in which room you want the action to occur.

If you've imagined a house in which there is only one room, say so in the slug line, thus:

INT. ONE-ROOM CABIN—DAY

or:

INT. JENNIFER'S ONE-ROOM STUDIO APARTMENT—NIGHT

Now that we're safely inside the house or apartment, it's irritating to professionals to see a partial slug such as:

BEDROOM

or

STAIRWAY

It is true that you can purchase sample scripts in which these sloppy slugs occur. These scripts might even have been tossed off by a screenwriter who commands high prices and *knows better*. Just because an established writer is allowed to get away with careless work, with disrespect for screenplay craft, doesn't mean that a writer who does not yet have a high "quote" (the price paid for his or her last screenplay) is given the same leeway.

You may even run into screenwriting instructors who will tell you that complete slug lines "interrupt the flow of the read." In my opinion, that is utter nonsense, and probably told to you by someone who has never been in production. The truth is that lack of proper format, lack of complete slugs, is what throws a professional "out of

27

the read." A non-filmmaker might not see anything wrong with it, but professionals with production experience know that in preproduction all of that must be cleaned up, that those slugs must be complete. It is very irritating to someone with production experience to see that kind of sloppiness in a screenplay. Once you've been through a production from pre to post and beyond, you understand the importance of what may seem, at an earlier point, like nit-picking. You don't have to take this advice, but is this a gamble you can afford to lose? Is using a partial slug so important to you that you're willing to risk irritating an experienced filmmaker who knows better—and expects *you* to know better?

If you want to make a good impression on people who don't yet know your name, then *command* respect for yourself by respecting your art and craft. Take the time and the trouble to learn the dos and don'ts of professional screenwriting. (Would you want to be operated on by a surgeon who didn't bother to go to medical school because all he wanted to do was cut and sew? The principle here is the same. First learn your craft; then you will be free to create.)

Now, after FADE IN and the first slug line comes the narrative.

There are two distinct styles of narrative writing: the "literary" and the "lean." Writing gracefully phrased, near poetic narrative, or keeping your narrative spare and to a minimum is a matter of personal style. Either style can be effective, but each has its potential problems. For the writer of prose-poetry narrative, the mistake can be in saying too much. Agents, producers, and production executives don't want to wade through excessive verbiage to get to the point the writer is trying to make. There are so many scripts that they *must* read, they are unlikely to expend time and energy slogging hip-deep through a virtual Sargasso Sea of unnecessary words. On the other hand, we don't want to see narrative that tells us *nothing*. The following beginning of a screenplay is an example of telling us too little:

FADE IN:

EXT. HENDERSON HOUSE —DAY

BILL MARSHALL's car stops in front of the house. There is a
CHILD in the front passenger seat beside Bill. Bill gets out of
the car, hurries to the front door, and rings the bell insistently.

                              BILL
                     (calling as he rings)
          Hello. Anybody home?

What's wrong in the above excerpt is that the opening of this script
leaves out too much information. For example:
    What kind of a house is it? A tiny tract? Or a well-landscaped
ranch house? A two-story pseudo Tudor framed by perfectly mani-
cured yew trees? Or is it a Cape Cod deteriorating into what real estate agents tactfully refer to as "deferred maintenance"?
    And in what kind of neighborhood is this house? Lower-income?
Middle-class? Upper-income? Are there old clunker cars on blocks
outside other houses on the street, or are there expensively paved
driveways leading to each enclosed garage?
    What kind of a car did Bill Marshall drive to the house? The type
and condition of the car will tell us something about the character of
Bill.
    Paint the picture for us so we'll know where we are, so we'll feel we
are *in* the scene with the characters.
    And about that "CHILD" in the front seat—is it a boy or a girl?
Is the child two years old or nine years old? Is it his child or a runaway? What attitude do Bill and the Child display toward each other?
Do we sense a warm connection, or do we sense an awkwardness between the two of them?
    The most important question of all that's left unanswered by the
opening above is:

Who is Bill Marshall?

We can't "see" him on the page unless the writer gives us a little information. What is his physical type? Is he athletic or out of shape? What's his approximate age, or age range? (Late teens or late seventies?) Is he charismatic, or dull? Is there an air of danger and intrigue about him, or does he project an image of solid, even dull, dependability? The writer only needs a few words in which to give us a powerful impression. Our imaginations will fill in the rest.

You must tell us enough of what we need to know so that we'll have a clear idea of who and what the movie we're reading is about—and give us the flexible images, described in intriguing but not *too* precise words, we need so that we can visualize the movie in our heads as we read the screenplay.

If we have to waste time wondering what we're supposed to be seeing, it will distract us from concentrating on the unfolding story. The screenwriter's first duty is to cast a spell on the readers—to so enthrall us with characters, setting, atmosphere, and story that only an emergency will force us to put down the script until we've finished reading it.

Now, here's an example of how the above scene might have been written to supply the information that was missing in the first version:

EXT. HENDERSON HOUSE—DAY

This is a modest one-story house in a blue-collar neighborhood, built in the optimistic 1950s, when upward mobility was taken for granted. Now the paint is peeling, the lawn has been largely overwhelmed by weeds, and "optimism" is a dim memory.

A red Ferrari, looking as out of place in this neighborhood as the First Lady at a strip show, roars to a stop in front of the house. The car is driven by a very angry BILL MARSHALL, a smart, good-looking former pro quarterback, in his late 30s.

An 8-year-old boy (STEVIE) sits, pale and afraid, in the passenger seat beside Bill. Bill vaults out of the Ferrari, hurries to the front door, and rings the bell insistently.

                              BILL
                    (calling as he rings)
          Hello. Anybody home?

See how much information we have learned in *this* example, as opposed to how little we were told in the incorrect first example.

Never Let Your Reader Wonder: *Who* Is the Leading Character?

Most professionals will not read much farther into a script if, by page 10, they are in doubt as to the identity of the leading character. (On many first drafts that I've critiqued in my workshops I've written the words: "It's page 33 and I still don't know who your leading character is!!!") Establish your protagonist as soon in the script as it is possible to do so, and write a description for him or her that tells any professional that *this* is the picture's star, the most important character in the plot. Develop the technique of describing your major characters in such a way as to allow professionals the opportunity to visualize casting. This does *not* mean that in your screenplay you should suggest a specific actor to play the part. *Never do that.*

Here is an example of the introduction of the star character, the protagonist, in a natural disaster/thriller called *Marabunta* that I wrote with screenwriter Wink Roberts, and which was filmed as a Fox TV Movie-of-the-Week (MOW) for the 1998 season. Here is the introduction of the protagonist, Jim Conrad. See how much information you learn about him in a brief time through the setting in which he works and through his first few lines of dialogue.

After the scene opens with what, at first, looks like a scene from nature, the camera pulls back and reveals that we are actually:

INT. L.A. NATURAL HISTORY MUSEUM
ENTOMOLOGY LAB—DAY

The pair of Tarantulas and the Praying Mantis and her late mate
are actually in glass cases filled with replicated terrain we mistook for a scene from Nature. The cases rest on a worktable in
the lab. Reverse on the lab's glass door reads: "James Conrad,
M.D., Ph.D., Director of Entomology."

DR. JIM CONRAD, wearing surgical gloves, has been watching the Tarantulas and the Praying Mantis. Conrad is the antithesis of the stereotypical nerdy scientist: he's good-looking,
athletic, and has an irreverent sense of humor. Conrad reaches
into the case to remove for study the body of the late mate.

                    CONRAD
                 (to the Mantis)
     I'm going to put an ad for you in the Personals:
     "Young widow, hot to mate again. You won't be
     my first love, but I'll be your last."

He puts the headless body into a plastic container and sets it
aside.

Around Conrad we see that this lab contains row upon row of
stacked shelves above a work station on which stand clear glass
jars filled with assorted INSECTS soaking in Formaldehyde.

ON THE WALLS, meticulously displayed in glass cases, are
rare butterflies (some of extraordinary SIZE and BEAUTY) and
beetles of various sizes. Other cases house a wide array of exotic
bugs.

Mounted above the door to the lab is a basketball hoop.

Conrad strips off his gloves and picks up a Nerf basketball. Now
facing the hoop, he's concentrating, attempting a three pointer
into the hoop above the door. He shoots and—swish!

CONRAD
Jim Conrad for three! Yes! At the buzzer!!!

The laboratory door opens. His graduate student lab assistant, FRAN, enters, ducking automatically. It's clear she's done this before. Conrad goes for another shot, but this time misses.

CONRAD (CONT'D)
How are we for time?

FRAN
You'll never make it, Dr. Conrad.

On one of the lab tables, in a big greenery-filled fish tank, are two LARGE TARANTULAS. Conrad takes some bits from a sandwich on the table and feeds them to the tarantulas.

CONRAD
I will if you let me drive your car.

Fran reacts with horror.

FRAN
I've only had the car for a week!

Conrad gently taps the glass to attract their attention, gives them more food.

CONRAD
(re the tarantulas)
Take care of Bill and Hillary. I think she's pregnant.

FRAN
Congratulations.

Conrad makes a quick tour of the lab, picking up papers, glancing at them, stuffing them into various file folders which he hands to Fran, as Fran, receiving the folders, takes items out of her purse and hands them to Conrad.

> FRAN
>
> Here's the key to your apartment. I watered your plants. Here's your plane ticket. Your bag's in my trunk.

He hands her some loose papers and more file folders.

> CONRAD
>
> If Dr. Mason calls, what are you going to tell him?

> FRAN
>
> He'll have your article on the Rove Beetle by the tenth.

> CONRAD
>
> If Barry Richards calls—

> FRAN
>
> You've decided not to sell the beach house after all.

> CONRAD
>
> If Danielle calls—

> FRAN
>
> You died in a freak lawn chair accident.
> (looks at her watch)
> You're absolutely not going to make that plane, Dr. Conrad.

A devilish glint lights Conrad's eyes. He holds out his hand.

> CONRAD
>
> Car keys.

And we cut directly to the airport in Goodnews Bay, Alaska—with Conrad getting off the plane at his destination.

Let's examine how much we've learned in this brief scene:

The description of Jim Conrad tells any professional reading it that Conrad is the star role, yet the description is intentionally spare so that a variety of actors to whom the script might be submitted would be able to visualize themselves. We didn't choose the color of his hair or eyes, or give his exact height or weight. His age is an approximation; "early 30s" was chosen as a kind of one-age-fits-almost-all leading man generic. The actor chosen for the part was Eric Lutes, who plays Del on the TV series *Caroline In the City*.

The basketball hoop implies that he's athletic. We've established that there's nothing nerdy or "stereotypically" scientific about him, and the fact that he shoots baskets in his lab confirms this. The conversation with his lab assistant gives us the following information:

Conrad is successful (he's writing a scientific article someone's waiting to publish), he has both an apartment *and* a beach house that he's decided not to sell, that he's just broken up with a woman named Danielle, and that he's a notoriously fast driver, probably something of a daredevil.

Also, Conrad's second line (when he's shooting the basket) tells the audience what his name is. This information is reinforced when Fran calls him "Dr. Conrad." Thus the name will be impressed on the viewing audience.

Another example of Conrad's irreverent humor is that he keeps a pair of tarantulas he calls "Bill" and "Hillary." On the set there were problems with the tarantulas, so only Hillary ended up in the finished movie.

Because Fran is a minor character who appears only in this one scene, all we need to know about her is that she's young, that she works for Conrad, and that he trusts her to take care of personal business for him—and that she doesn't want him to drive her new car. The brief dialogue between them suggests that they've worked together long enough for her to know what to say to whom in Conrad's professional life and personal life.

You need to establish very quickly *which character* is the star. Don't let the person reading wonder *whom* the story is about. If you need to do it superfast because the picture opens with an action sequence, here is an example of how to do that:

In "The Adoption," an action adventure screenplay by Wink Roberts, the star role is introduced on page 1 and is described in these few potent words:

INT. CH-46 SEA KNIGHT HELICOPTER—NIGHT

Special Forces Major MIKE MITCHELL stares out of the helicopter as it speeds low over the desert of northern Iraq. He raises his dark visor and we see his face. If forced to describe Mitchell in one word, that word would be: unforgettable.

This description was carefully devised so that it could fit any male star of any reasonable age, from Tom Cruise to Sean Connery. Mitchell's intelligence and his courage are obvious from his dialogue and from his immediate actions, so those qualities in his character did not need to be included in a description.

Paragraphs of narrative are single spaced. Double-space between the paragraphs. If you have a narrative paragraph that runs more than three or four lines, my suggestion is to break it up into separate paragraphs. (I don't mean three or four *sentences,* I mean three or four lines of type.)

When I was a vice president at TriStar Pictures I gave a major ("A list") director a script I thought would be perfect for him. He glanced at the first page, saw a ten-line narrative paragraph, and handed it back to me without reading further. He said: "I don't want to see ant colonies!" Translated, that means that he had no interest in reading thick blocks of narrative. This is also true of readers, many of whom just skip thick narrative passages—and thus miss important pieces of information that are needed to understand the plot and the character motivations. Then, having skipped important pieces of information, they critique the script with a damning remark such as: "The story doesn't make sense." (It would have made sense if the person had bothered to read the whole thing!) And, if anyone relays this criticism to the writer, she will be stunned and plunged into despair wondering how she could have explained the story better!

It is a sad and vexing reality that too many people in Hollywood hate to read. Because we can't change the reality of people's behavior, we have to make a script easy on the eyes and therefore inviting to read. The objective here is to give ourselves the best chance in the marketplace, and it's worth the trouble it takes to learn how to give ourselves that best chance.

About that script I gave to the director, here's the rest of the story: I suggested to the writer that he reprint the script with narrative passages that were no more than three or four lines long. He did that, and a few weeks later I gave the reworked screenplay to the director as a "new" script. The director read it, liked it, and optioned it for his production company. In terms of the writing, this was the same script he had refused to read a few weeks earlier. (Ultimately, that picture was not made, but there was "heat" on the writer because of the director's interest. The writer got several well-paid writing assignments, and got to see his name on the screen.)

So, remember that keeping your narrative passages short, with white space in between, makes your pages inviting to the eye of the person reading the script. Agents, producers, and production executives have so many scripts to read that seeing your script, with lots of white space on the page, makes reading it an appealing experience visually. Remember that the first step in selling a completed screenplay is getting the right person to agree to read it.

You will use two spaces between the slug line and the narrative passage, and then two spaces between narrative and the dialogue "boxes."

Dialogue is indented so that the character name is centered on the page. Dialogue beneath the name is "boxed" as shown in the sample script page from *Marabunta*. There is *no space* between the character name and that character's dialogue.

If a character whom we (and the camera) are following visually leaves one set and goes into another, or exits to the outdoors into a new scene, then that action requires a *new* slug line.

There is little that is more irritating to read than a sequence with missing slugs.

The scene below is an example of what *not* to do:

INT. MICHAEL'S MEDIA WORLD OFFICE—DAY

Michael is doing knee bends while arguing on the speakerphone with Doug.

> MICHAEL
> You said the pictures would be here by noon and it's three-thirty! Did you send 'em by ship, around Cape Horn?!

> DOUG'S VOICE (ON SPEAKERPHONE)
> Come on, Mike, cut me some slack. Maybe the messenger can't read street signs.

> MICHAEL
> Maybe you don't care you just lost this account!

Michael slams his hand down on the instrument, cutting off the conversation. He grabs his jacket and storms out of the office.

Michael fishes his car key out of a pocket as he reaches his parking space, crams the key into the lock, yanks open the door, and burns rubber getting out of the lot.

Do you see the problem? *According to the last slug line, Michael is still in his office*—and yet the script has him getting into his car. Is his car parked in the *office?*

While these two scenes occur only moments apart in the script, they could be scheduled for shooting anywhere from days to weeks apart.

Now consider what could happen *without* the correct slug line, which would be:

EXT. MEDIA WORLD PARKING LOT—DAY

Without that slug, the appropriate parking lot would not be found by the location manager and the necessary city permits to shoot at that location would not be obtained. Rental fees to the owner of the lot would not be negotiated. The scene would not be scheduled for shooting and so would not be filmed.

Then, during "post" (postproduction), when the film's editor is searching for this brief—but necessary—parking-lot transition scene, which he needs for continuity, it's discovered that the scene was never shot because it was never scheduled because the writer didn't know enough, or care enough, to put in the proper slug line. With the enormous amount of work necessary during preproduction, nobody caught the writer's initial mistake. "For want of a nail the shoe was lost . . ." You get the idea.

Camera directions should be used very sparingly. Directors don't want the writer to "direct" the script on the page—and the chances are good that the director will know better than the writer where the camera should be placed and when to go to ECU (extreme close-up) and when to zoom in.

Use camera directions *only when absolutely necessary to reveal a dramatic surprise. Never* use them just because you "want to," or because you imagine the film being shot with certain camera angles. Selecting camera angles is not part of your job as screenwriter. Tell the story—and let the director direct.

It's quite possible to write the movie you see in your mind without so annoying a director that he won't read very far into your script. Here's an example of storytelling instead of directing:

INT. PATRICIA'S BEDROOM—NIGHT

The room is empty for a second—then we see Patricia, black-gloved hands first, climbing as quietly as possible up and over the front windowsill.

As soon as the girl makes it safely into the room, she pauses, listening for any sounds indicating that she's awakened her parents.

Silence. Visibly relieved, Patricia quickly removes her black gloves and sweater. As she shoves them under her bed, she notices Todd's letter lying on the spread.

Afraid that she can guess its contents, Patricia grabs the letter and rips it open, quickly scanning the contents. Her reaction tells us that her worst fears have been confirmed. The note reads: "I'm sorry, Pat. Dad says it's you or Harvard. I can't give up my future. Maybe we'll have another chance one day. Love, Todd."

Patricia crumples the letter and drops it on the floor as she rushes into her bathroom. We can hear the SOUND of her agonized RETCHING (O.S.)

The scene above does not include a single camera angle, nor does it tell the actress what facial expression to use, or how to play the scene. It simply tells the story, and it does not use the following unnecessary device:

INSERT

The note reads: "I'm sorry, Pat. Dad says it's you or Harvard. I can't give up my future. Maybe we'll have another chance one day. Love, Todd."

BACK TO SCENE

It may be necessary that we know the contents of the note—or we may be able to guess from the story that preceded this scene.

It is the director's job to decide whether to show the note in close-up on the screen and let the audience read it as Pat reads it, or whether to have the note read aloud in V.O. (voice-over) in either Pat's voice or Todd's voice. But if the script has set us up either to know or to suspect that Todd was going to abandon Pat, then we probably don't need to hear or see the exact words of Todd's painful brush-off. We saw it coming, so the exact words may be unnecessary.

Note: At this point in our imagined script, we will have been in Patricia's bedroom before. But the first time we "see" this room on the page we should be given a brief description of it. For example:

INT. PATRICIA'S BEDROOM—MORNING

It's the room of a 16-year-old girl from an upper-income family. A canopied bed, framed posters of rock stars and Georgia O'Keeffe flower prints cover the walls. There's a large color TV, an expensive stereo system, and a wall of closets with mirrored doors.

This tells us just enough to visualize the room we're in, but doesn't tell us too much. We don't need to know the color of the paint, or the print on the wallpaper, or the design of the bedspread or drapes. Don't give us more details than we require. Excess detail will only slow down the story for no positive purpose. Just let the room reflect Pat, so that, in effect, the room is a small part of her character description. Learning the difference between telling too little and telling too much is part of mastering the craft of screenwriting. If you are aware of the difference between telling too much and telling too little you will be happily surprised at how quickly good judgment becomes a natural part of your craft and writing style.

A related part of mastering the screenwriter's craft is learning what to include and what to leave out of *dialogue.* Sometimes the best "dialogue" a screenwriter can devise are the lines an audience cannot hear. If we already know what a character is about to be told, there is no need to tell us again. An important scene in *The Verdict* shows us how silence can indeed be golden.

This marvelous scene was done in a long shot, entirely without dialogue:

Jack Warden's character, Mickey, flies to New York to tell Frank Galvin (Paul Newman) that he's learned the identity of the traitor who's been damaging their case by selling their secrets and strategies to the opposing lawyers. That traitor is the woman Galvin loves, played by Charlotte Rampling.

Because we've seen Mickey discover the damning check in her purse while he was looking for a cigarette, we know what he has to tell Galvin. We don't need to hear the information we already know. Seeing Mickey speaking urgently to Galvin—and watching Galvin's body language (a slight, involuntary recoil, as though he has been struck), we know how hard Mickey's revelation has hit Galvin.

This brief scene is a perfect example of brilliant visual storytelling, and proves that there are times when the best "dialogue" is silence.

Do Not Write "SMASH CUT"

There is no such thing as a "smash cut"! Ask any director or film editor. If you're tempted to put "SMASH CUT" into your script, my advice is to resist the temptation if you want to look like a pro to the pros.

Transitions such as **CUT TO, DISSOLVE TO,** and **FADE OUT** appear on the far right side of the page, and on a separate line of their own, thus:

CUT TO:

Using proper screenplay format became much easier on the fingers when computer software developed for screenwriters came on the market. Several different programs are available. My personal favorite is Scriptware, which I have used almost from the moment it came on the market. For those of you who have not yet installed screenwriting software, let me list just a few of the advantages.

1. You can produce a proper slug line simply by typing "int." or ext." Typing just those three letters and the period will instantly transform the line to capital letters.

2. After you've once established a slug line, that setting or location (such as PICNIC AREA BY THE LAKE or ROGER'S LIVING ROOM) is stored in the computer's memory so that when you want to use it again all you have to do is type the first few letters of the slug line (EXT. PIC . . . or INT. RO . . .) and the rest of the slug line will appear automatically, saving you over the course of a 110-page screenplay valuable typing time and energy.

3. When you have once established a character saying something, that character's name will appear in the proper place over dialogue just by typing the first letter or two of the character's name.

4. Dialogue is automatically indented properly and single-spaced.

5. Narrative, also single-spaced, appears in the correct location on the page.

Screenwriting software offers many other features as well. Using a screenwriting software program is much easier on the writer than when we had to make each of those choices every time, back in the days when writers used typewriters, or when we were trying to write a screenplay using just a basic word processing program.

Scriptware, and probably other screenwriting software, also gives you the choice of writing a screenplay in the "Submit" form or the "Shooting" form. The difference between these two forms is that "Shooting" puts in **Scene Numbers** and **CUT TO** automatically. Unless you are writing for a producer who requires the work to be in shooting script form, most screenplays are written in the "Submit" form, and this is the form that I recommend. Traditionally, scene numbers are not put into a script until the project is in preproduction, so don't put scene numbers in your spec scripts.

In the "Submit" form, putting in **CUT TO** and other **transitions** is a matter of personal choice; it is not done automatically. My recommendation is to omit the **CUT TO.**

Having said that, let me add that there are some transitions that help to tell the story, but even these should be used sparingly. My favorites are

DIRECT CUT TO:

and

SOUND CROSSOVER TO:

Let me repeat that I use these two transitions very seldom, and *only* when they aid in storytelling.

Here are examples of how and where these two transitions can be used:

EXT. CENTRAL PARK RESERVOIR JOGGING
PATH—MORNING

Michael and Doug are jogging, working up a healthy sweat. Michael is still steaming from his last fight with Laura.

MICHAEL
It's impossible to talk to her. She's the most unreasonable woman I've ever met.

DOUG
Give her a couple of days. You two'll get back together.

MICHAEL
Never! I will never, ever, ever go anywhere near
Laura Mills again!

DIRECT CUT TO:

EXT. FRONT DOOR OF LAURA'S E. 64TH STREET
TOWN HOUSE—DAY

Michael, staggering under the weight of three dozen yellow
roses and a five-pound box of Godiva chocolates, rings Laura's
doorbell.

The transition **DIRECT CUT TO** is not strictly necessary, but I
think that it adds just a little richness to the storytelling. This transition is used for a sharp contrast between what a character *says* and the
completely contrary thing that character then *does*.

Because there is a very specific meaning to this transition (sharp
contrast between statement and action), if you misuse it, then that
misstep will jar the professional reading your script out of the story.
That interruption of concentration can lead someone to put your
script down and go do—or, much worse!—read something else.

Always avoid giving people a reason to put your script down. They
may never pick it up again.

The transition **SOUND CROSSOVER TO** means that the sound
track (music or dialogue) from one scene is carried over and heard
while we are watching a new scene.

Here's an example:

INT. MICHAEL'S MEDIA WORLD OFFICE—DAY

Michael and Doug examine the mock-up of their new "hot
body" magazine, *Stems & Sterns*. The cover photo shows a top-
less woman with a fabulous figure wearing very skimpy shorts
made of military camouflage material. The UZI she holds just
covers the middle of her breasts.

MICHAEL
I think we should save the General Colin Powell
centerfold for the Christmas issue.

DOUG
We could put him in a Santa hat—or—picture
this! Reindeer antlers!

MICHAEL
You gonna tell a man who knows where to get
rocket launchers to wear reindeer antlers?

DOUG
We got six months to worry about it. We need to
find Connie Malone by tomorrow morning.

SOUND CROSSOVER TO:

EXT. CENTRAL PARK CAROUSEL—DAY

MICHAEL'S VOICE
Give it up, Doug. She doesn't want to be found.

This small pocket of 19th-century charm is filled today with
CHILDREN ages 2 to 10 and their NANNIES and MAIDS.
No one who looks like an actual father or a mother is visible.

DOUG'S VOICE
She doesn't know we're looking for her. I'm sure
she's in New York.

CONNIE MALONE, ten years older than the high school
yearbook picture Michael has of her, but still angelically beautiful, watches carefully as a little BOY of 5 plays "cowboy" on a
Carousel horse. Connie wears a pale gray maid's uniform and
glasses she does not need.

MICHAEL'S VOICE
New York is 5 boroughs and 10 million people.

DOUG'S VOICE
Forget Brooklyn, the Bronx, Queens, and Staten
Island.

As Connie waves at the little boy, and smiles at him encouragingly, she glances around furtively, trying to discover if she's being watched.

MICHAEL'S VOICE
That leaves Manhattan—8 square miles and 3 million people. Didn't anybody ever tell you about needles and haystacks?

This above sample shows you one way to use the sound crossover. Another is to carry music from one scene—perhaps a song playing on a radio in one scene—over into the next, so that we continue to hear the music under the new visuals.

Now, let's go back to the other side of the script page, the far left side. For those of you who, like me, have trouble with left and right, that's the side with the three holes.

If you are including a **FLASHBACK,** a **DREAM SEQUENCE,** or a **MONTAGE** in your screenplay, those designations go on the far left side of the page, directly above the **INT.** or the **EXT.** of the scene or scenes to follow. Example:

FLASHBACK

EXT. JUNGLE IN VIETNAM—NIGHT

Then write whatever scene is in your flashback. When the scene, or the series of scenes or images, concludes:

END FLASHBACK

And then return to whatever set you were in when the flashback began. Example:

END FLASHBACK

INT. MICHAEL'S BEDROOM—NIGHT

Michael awakens deeply shaken and sweating profusely from that devastating FLASHBACK. He gets out of bed and heads for the living room.

INT. MICHAEL'S LIVING ROOM—NIGHT

Michael goes to the liquor cabinet and pours himself a tumbler of Scotch. He drinks it down in one gulp, without tasting, as though it were medicine.

When you have concluded a flashback, a dream sequence, or a montage it is necessary to designate in proper form that this diversion is over, as here:

END DREAM SEQUENCE

END MONTAGE

Introducing Characters into the Script

The first time a character appears in the screenplay, put his or her name in capital letters. *But only the first time.* Capitalizing the character's name on his or her first entrance tells the professional reading the script that this is the character's entrance into the plot. Some professional screenwriters like to capitalize a character's name again, especially in action sequences, but if this is a style which you use to write a scene, be aware that this capitalization is only used on the far left side of the page, as though you were designating a flashback, a dream sequence, or a montage. Example:

The clock on the bell tower directly above Michael and Connie CHIMES suddenly, sending reverberations of sound echoing through the subway station.

Connie clings tightly to Michael, afraid to breathe lest that faint rush of air give their position away to the gunman lurking somewhere in the shadows of the pillars. Then, without warning, Michael and Connie hear the sound of a HEAVY FOOT CRUSHING GLASS. Instantly—

MICHAEL

Shoves Connie into the alcove behind him, draws his Beretta, and FIRES into the darkness!

The above sample illustrates how one can capitalize a character's name after that character's introduction into the story—but save this style for action scenes. Don't overuse it, or the effect on the page will be distracting and jerky and, rather than heightening the tension, this style will feel abrupt and discordant.

When you first introduce your major characters and important supporting characters, tell us *just a little bit* about them so that we will be able to visualize them as to basic physical type and to get an *impression* of who they are. Unless there is an important plot reason for doing so, *do not* give your characters specific ages.

In our screenplay, *Marabunta,* Wink Roberts and I say that Jim Conrad is "early 30s" because there is a plot reason for that. The second male lead in the script, Sheriff Jeff Croy, is on the edge of 50, and we wanted the contrast of a younger and an older man.

I don't know if there's some strange virus in the air that attacks only writers who have not yet made their first sale, or if some person or book is teaching them *wrong,* but I have seen many first drafts in my classes where the screenwriter has given everyone who appears on the page an exact age: 32, 47, 54, 62. Even elevator operators, clerks, messengers, and receptionists who have only one line are given exact ages. Not only is there no good reason to do this, all of those needless ages are annoying to read. In a professional screenplay, a detail like that suggests the character has some importance, but when it's quickly apparent that this glimpsed bit player is not a meaningful part of the story, then giving an exact age becomes one of the hallmarks of an inexperienced writer.

The exception to this matter of exact ages occurs when children appear in a script. For production reasons it is important to know whether a "child" is an infant, 2 years old, 6 years old, or 10 to 12 years old. Not only are those important distinctions as to what they can do in a scene, but work rules—and hence budget considerations—must be allowed for.

When a "teenager" comes into a script two things must be stated immediately:

1. Is the teenager a male or a female? (Unless one can tell by the character's name. I don't want to hear about "A Boy Named Sue"!)
2. What is the teen's age? There's a big difference between a thirteen-year-old and a nineteen-year-old. For one thing, there are no work restrictions other than those imposed by SAG (the Screen Actors Guild) once an actor comes of legal age at 18.

There is no young actor more beloved of a producer or director than the "emancipated" sixteen-year-old, especially if he or she is small and can "play younger." Emancipated minors are those who have gone to court and proved their maturity and responsibility to a judge, and are thus allowed to work adult hours.

If there are children and young teens in your script, as the professional reads it he or she will be taking into consideration such things as the number of children and how much time they must be on-screen. A screenplay in which heavy story responsibility falls on actors under eighteen years of age has special problems in scheduling. An underage actor comes to the set with a state-mandated tutor and a chaperone, the fees for whose services come out of the production budget. The young actor's restricted working periods must be allowed for in the scheduling of scenes to be shot, which can lead to logistical complications and budget escalations.

(O.S.) vs. (V.O.)

If the scene you're writing involves a character we can hear but cannot see immediately—one who is on the premises of the set but out of sight, or nearby in another room or on the other side of a door—then you must put (O.S.) next to that character's name. Example:

DOUG (O.S.)
Pour me another drink. I'll be there as soon as I
find my other cuff link.

(O.S.) means offscreen. (O.C.) means off-camera, and is used in teleplays, not screenplays.

The difference between (O.S.) and (V.O.), or voice-over, is sometimes a fine one, and it needs to be understood.

(V.O.) is used when a character's voice is narrating a scene from another time, such as when that character is telling a story that happened at an earlier time, even if that time wasn't very long ago.

(V.O.) is also used when we hear the voice of a character reading a note or letter that he or she has written while we are watching someone else read it.

Another use of (V.O.) occurs when we see the character writing the note and hear the voice in his/her head speaking the words as the character writes.

Here's a pop quiz.

Imagine this scene:

On the screen we see a car driving on a road or a highway. We hear the voices of the two people inside who are talking to each other as someone drives. Is this written (V.O.) or (O.S.)?

The answer is (O.S.), because the characters are *physically present in the scene at that moment,* it's just that they temporarily are not visible to us, the audience.

If we saw that same scene (the visual) and heard a conversation between those same two people—but the conversation took place in the past (in the memory of one of the characters, for example) then the dialogue would be written as (V.O.)

Watch the Location of Your Page Breaks

When writing your dialogue, make sure that you don't let the name of the character appear at the bottom of the page and the actual dialogue begin at the top of the following page. *Always keep character name and dialogue together.* To let them be separated by a page break is unprofessional and jarring. It breaks the spell you're trying to weave over the reader.

When dialogue is interrupted by action and the same character speaks again, it is best to put (CONT'D) or (continuing) after the character's name. This states to the professional that some intervening dialogue spoken by another character was not dropped accidentally in the typing.

Below is an example of the *correct* way to interrupt dialogue with action:

MICHAEL
Give me that gun!

Paul pulls the trigger just as Michael drops to the floor and smashes the footstool into Paul's knees. Paul screams in pain and loosens his grip on the gun enough so that Michael is able to grab it.

> MICHAEL (CONT'D)
> You've got exactly 3 seconds to tell me where Connie is.

Now, in contrast, the example below demonstrates the *incorrect* way to interrupt dialogue with action:

> MICHAEL
> Give me that gun!

Paul pulls the trigger just as Michael drops to the floor and smashes the footstool into Paul's knees. Paul screams in pain and loosens his grip on the gun enough so that Michael is able to grab it.

> (continuing)
> You've got exactly 3 seconds to tell me where Connie is.

Every speech that's interrupted by narrative must have a character designation above it, *unless* the action is described in a brief parenthetical, such as in the following illustration:

> MICHAEL
> Give me the gun!
> (smashing Paul's knees with footstool,
> grabbing gun)
> You've got exactly 3 seconds to tell me where Connie is.

Just as you should not have a character name at the bottom of a page with his dialogue at the top of the following page, you should not have a SLUG LINE at the bottom of the page with the narrative appearing at the top of the following page.

However, if you have enough room at the bottom of the page following the SLUG LINE, the space between and at least two sentences of the narrative, that is all right. After at least two sentences of narrative, the rest of the narrative can be continued at the top of the following page.

This same statement does *not* apply to dialogue. Even if you have room at the bottom of the page for the character name and for two or more lines of dialogue, it is still not a good idea to split up a speech. It is far better to have a shorter page, with more space at the bottom, than to break up a character's block of dialogue. The exception to this is the *very long speech* which cannot be shorter for dramatic reasons. If it goes for a third of the page before the break and then continues on for several more lines, it is acceptable to break the speech and continue over onto the next—with a new character name above the continuation of the speech. One caution: if you have written a very long speech, *be sure that you really need all those words.* Patton needed all those words for the dramatic and effective opening in the movie *Patton.*

In movies that revolve around trials, lawyers sometimes need long speeches. Just be sure that your character's long speech is dramatic and/or entertaining—and that the character isn't just talking so much because the screenwriter doesn't know how to edit himself.

4. Screenplay "Dos" and "Don'ts"

Here are some of the fine details you will want to attend to in your screenplay. The higher you aim the more professional you will become.

Don't narrow the margins to try to squeeze too much on your pages in order to keep your page count under the industry-preferred top length of 120. Nor should you use a smaller typeface to create an artificial length of 120 pages. These two strategies will not only fool no one, but seeing pages with margins too narrow and type too small will only create a feeling of hostility in the reader! Not only is the writer trying (ineptly) to trick the reader, but he or she is making the script harder on eyes that are already strained to the limit.

Part of the overall good look of a script page is *correct spelling*. In these days of "spell check" there is no excuse for gross mistakes. But there is also no excuse for the careless use of "there" when you meant "their" or "they're."

Because he kept using "your" when he meant "you're" I once asked a very talented screenwriter in one of my workshops to write the following twenty-five times:

You're = you are (a contraction)
Your = "This is your pen." (possessive)

He was a good sport about it, turned in the page of twenty-five "you're = you are" and hasn't made that mistake since. He's also still speaking to me.

Attention to correct spelling is important because it illustrates that the writer respects her craft.

Another example of a writer who respects her craft is one who never gives someone a script that has blank pages in it, pages that have been badly Xeroxed, or pages that are out of order or—horrors!—missing. NEVER give anyone a copy of your script unless you have personally checked *every page* to catch what I call "the dreaded 3 M's." Translated, this means to make sure that nothing in the script is *mis*placed, *m*angled, or *m*issing.

With most screenplay software there is no longer the problem of improper margins, but if you are writing scripts on a nonscript program, or one of your own devising, make sure that the dialogue boxes are of the proper width on the page. A common (but no less annoying) mistake before screenplay software was dialogue that ran almost the width of the narrative, or was not centered under the character name.

I know that by the time your (not "you're") script is ready for submission to an agent or a producer you've read it so many times that you think you can't possibly read it again. But read it again you must—to check for typos.

If you're (not "your") fortunate you might know someone who's a good proofreader, and will help you out. Wink Roberts and I are lucky to have his friend, Chad, whom we've nicknamed "Mr. Typo," read our scripts before they go out into the world. While I'm an excellent proofreader for others—as writers in my workshops have learned through the merciless wielding of my infamous red pen—I still find typos in my own work. Many writers who try to proofread their own work discover that they're "reading" what their minds tell them *should* be there, and don't see the mistakes their flying fingers have made.

Use one typeface or font style in your screenplay. Just one. Don't use **boldface** or *italics*—and don't use any of the more exotic fonts. Stick to Courier, or something similar. Choose a font that is easy to read, and *no smaller in size than 12*. Remember, if you want your screenplay to be read by an agent or a buyer, it must be inviting to the eye.

"Mom" and "Dad"—or "mom" and "dad"?

Memorize the difference between Mom and Dad—and mom and dad.

Mom and Dad take the capital M and capital D when they are used as names, as in a sentence such as:

> JESSICA
> I didn't come home when I was supposed to, so
> Mom grounded me for a week.

If mom or dad is referred to by their familial status—as in "my mom" or "my dad," or "his mom" or "her dad"—then the m and the d are in lowercase, as:

> JARED
> It's not just that my dad wants me to work with
> him - I really want to study law.

While quotation marks appear around dialogue in books and short stories, they are not used in screenplay dialogue unless your character is quoting someone, as in:

> SUSAN
> "That which does not kill me makes me stronger."

JESSE
You're brilliant, Suz!

SUSAN
That's not me, it's Nietzsche.

Never try to pass off a quote that you know belongs to someone else without proper attribution. It will make you look like a thief and it will make the reader wonder if other memorable lines in the script are your original work, or that of someone else you're quoting without attribution. If you've heard or read a famous line but don't know to whom it should be attributed, do some research (if your character would be precise about knowing the source of the quote), or let your character say he or she has heard it or read it but can't remember where. The chances are good that at least one of the professionals who read your script *will* know from what source the line you're quoting comes. I know that people quote without attribution in everyday speech all the time, but in using a quote in your work I suggest acknowledging that it is not original with you. If your producer or director chooses to eliminate the attribution, then so be it. You will have done the honorable thing.

How to Write a Montage

A montage is a series of shots, of fragments of scenes, that cover the passage of time, from hours to months to years. Montages can be written in one of three ways: each fragment of time can be designated with a numeral (1, 2, 3, etc.) or with a letter (A, B, C, etc.) or with no designation at all. Just be consistent in the style you choose. Example:

MONTAGE

1. Mark & Garcia, sweating in the Summer heat, search the back alleys of the West 70s, rousting addicts and winos.

2. Mark questions an Upper East Side doorman as Fall leaves drop.

3. Garcia, bundled in a sheepskin coat against the Winter snow, shows Laura's picture to men outside Harold's Show Spot on W. 47th Street.

4. It's Spring again. Mark & Garcia are sweating in an office, searching through overflowing boxes of files.

If you need to show brief glimpses of faces or activities—reactions or actions—that take place simultaneously or within a narrow period of time, that is called a SERIES OF SHOTS and is written like this:

SERIES OF SHOTS

Jack recoils as Gino tells him the bad news.

Rico's mother and aunt, wearing black, prepare the body for burial.

Matty and the Priest hurry toward the house.

Alone in his cluttered back bedroom, Jack loads his .357.

One of the most memorable examples of this storytelling device occurs in *The Godfather*—in the famous intercutting of the series of assassinations that take place during the christening of Connie's and Carlo's baby in the cathedral.

Ration Your Parentheticals!

There are three types of parentheticals used in dialogue boxes. Two of them are good, and the third is very, very bad.

The first good parenthetical is one that clarifies the meaning of dialogue, as when the character speaking means something other than the words that are spoken. Example:

> MIRIAM
> (she hates it)
> Love your new haircut!

The second good parenthetical conveys an action the character is in the midst of as he or she speaks. Example:

Julie shivers inside their one thin blanket.

> TOM
> (lighting the sticks in the fireplace)
> We have just enough wood to last one night.

> JULIE
> What happens if we're not rescued by then?

> TOM
> (joking to keep her spirits up)
> We get to know each other an awful lot better.

In that brief exchange we have a parenthetical involving an action (lighting the fire in the fireplace) and a second one that clarifies what Tom really means (joking to keep her spirits up).

The third type of parenthetical is one that is so ill-advised that there should be a computer program that prevents its use! That is the parenthetical beneath the character's name that tells the actor how to act. Example:

> ELIZABETH
> (angrily)
> I wouldn't go to the party with you if you begged
> and crawled naked across broken glass!

It's clear from what she's saying that the character is angry, or it would be from the tone of the entire scene. If she was being playful and teasing—while using those same words—that would also be clear in the full context of the scene in which that speech appears. So there is no good reason to tell the actor to say that speech "angrily."

Just as directors hate being told how to direct, so do actors hate being told how to act—and for much the same reason: because they're better at it than you and I. They resent being told something—"angrily"—that should be obvious from the line itself, or from the line's context in the scene. Ask any good actor you meet and he or she will tell you that the first thing they do when they get a part is to strike out any parenthetical that tries to give them an emotion. They particularly dislike (laughingly), (chucklingly), (giggling), (tearfully), (smiling), and being told when to roll their eyes or lift their eyebrows—and other such presumptions.

When you think you absolutely must use a parenthetical below a character's name, ask yourself the following question:

Is it worth *$100* to tell the actor how to speak that line?

I think you'll find that few parentheticals will pass the "$100 Test."

Now for an example of a parenthetical that *does* pass the $100 Test. In my summer 1997 workshop at UCLA Extension, a talented writer and actor named David Fields was writing a comedy screenplay set against the background of a supermarket tabloid newspaper. On the same page he used two parentheticals—one was correct and one was not. Here they are:

1.   DARLENE
                          (taunting)
             Why don't you just go in, Tommy?

2.   DARLENE
                          (mockingly)
             I think that's Barnes, isn't it?

Example number 1 is *correct,* because "taunting" makes the meaning of the line clear. The words are a *challenge* to Tommy, not a suggestion.

Example number 2 is *incorrect,* because "mockingly" tells the actor how to say the line, and that the writer should *not* do.

Don't Underline That Word—If It's in *Dialogue*

Another thing that actors hate is dialogue in which the writer has underlined words to indicate which one should be stressed in speaking the line. Again, the average actor knows far better than the average writer how to say that line.

Some writers in my workshop have tried to resort to trickery to get around my stated aversion to "directing" an actor's performance. Instead of underlining words to tell the actors how to say the lines, they have tried putting words they want the actor to stress in **boldface,** in *italics,* or in CAPITAL LETTERS. However they try to sneak in an unwelcome line-reading instruction, the effect is the same: it makes the actor hostile. Underlined, CAPITALIZED, **boldfaced** and *italicized* words in dialogue are very irritating to read, and feature-film professionals know that actors dislike this.

Having come out strongly against underlining words in dialogue, I want to give you an example of one of the rare times when it is correct to underline a word, and explain why in this example it is correct.

To refer again to the David Fields screenplay which uses a supermarket tabloid newspaper as its setting, in one scene a secondary character is on the telephone and asks the question:

PATTY
Well, what does your psychic say?"

In the above sentence, underlining the word "your" was correct because there are two possible meanings to Patty's question. Patty could have been asking the other person what her (the other person's) psychic had to say. If that had been the case, then there would have been no underline. But what the writer meant—and the gist of the joke—was that *both* Patty and the person on the other end of the phone conversation had psychics, and that they were comparing the opinions of their separate psychics. Underlining "your" made clear the meaning the writer intended.

By dissecting that line, I've managed to remove the laugh. Please believe me that the line I quoted was, in the context of David Fields's scene, laugh-out-loud funny.

Whose Voice? *What* Sound?

Here is an example of a line NOT to use in your screenplay:

> Michael was roused from sleep by a VOICE in the darkness, followed by a loud SOUND from the direction of the kitchen.

If we were in a theater or at home watching the movie we could hear whether the "VOICE" was male or female, and whether the "SOUND" was a crash, or a clatter, or a dog barking, or glass shattering, or the stove exploding. But we cannot hear a screenplay, we can only read it, so the writer must tell us the gender of the voice and the kind of sound the character in the scene heard O.S. Don't make us guess! And capitalize the sound effects. Here's how that narrative sentence *should* have read:

> Michael was roused from sleep by an unfamiliar WOMAN'S VOICE in the darkness, followed by a loud sound of GLASS SHATTERING from the direction of the kitchen.

If the woman's voice that we heard in this scene was the voice of a character we have already met, then this voice should have been identified. Example:

Michael was roused from sleep by CONNIE'S VOICE in the darkness.

Then, if other information is needed, add it to the narrative.

A Few Words About Good Writing

One of the best things writers can do at the beginning of their careers is to buy a *Roget's Thesaurus.* There may be other thesauri on the market, but I've never encountered a better one than Mr. Roget's. Don't depend on the thesaurus in your software; the ones I've seen don't have nearly the selection of synonyms and antonyms that good old Mr. Roget's provides.

The reason I encourage new writers to get a *Roget's* and study it is to foster in them the habit of finding *active* verbs to use in their narrative passages, and to enrich their vocabularies so that their characters can be written with a greater variety of expression. In life, not everyone speaks alike, so your characters—unless they are robots—shouldn't all speak alike.

As a test, go through your script and count the number of times you use the word "walk." (She walked into the room. He walked to the window. They walked to the car. He walked to the bar. She walked to the TV set, etc.) Find and use verbs with some spirit to them. Some of the alternatives for "walk" are: stroll, step, hurry, scurry, creep, slither, undulate, amble, march, stomp, stalk, promenade, saunter, parade, tramp, hike, tread. That's just off the top of my head. You can come up with others.

Study the English language (or the language in which you write), revel in its (not "it's") rich opportunities for imaginative expression. Learn its quirks and nuances.

It's been my unhappy lot to observe that too many new writers have what I call a *hearing* vocabulary, as opposed to a *reading* vocabulary. By that I mean too many writers have grown up with television instead of books as their primary source of at-home entertainment. They type "faze" (to confuse or disturb) when they mean "phase" (aspect or condition) or think that "two," "to," and "too" are interchangeable. They are not! Don't be among those who confuse "enormity" (an atrocity, monstrousness) with "enormous" (huge, immense), or "it's" (the contraction of it is) with "its" (the possessive), or "dessert" (sweet—hot or cold) with "desert" (not so sweet and *very* hot during the day if a noun, or meaning "to leave" if a verb). Let's not forget "tale" (story) and "tail" (that appendage on the hind end of a dog—or, in detective literature, slang for "follow"). And how about council, counsel, and consul?

Is it any wonder English is considered a difficult language for foreigners to learn?

Consider these crazy-makers: "raze" means to tear down, while "raise" means to elevate, bring up, increase. Or "hare" (rabbit) and "hair" (tresses), or "tear" (weeping) versus "tier" (level). Then again there is "tear" (spelled the same, but pronounced to rhyme with "wear")—meaning to rip or to shred. How about "pallet" (bed), "palate" (taste), and "palette" (an artist's tray of paints)—all pronounced the same. Also pronounced the same are "core" (as in an apple, or the center of a nuclear reactor) and "corps" (as in Marine Corps or Corps de Ballet.) On the other hand, there is "corpse" (body)—pronounced the way any sane newcomer to English would assume "corps" is pronounced, but isn't. Then there's "led" (as in "He led the marching band") and "lead" (the mineral) and "lead" (pronounced "leed") as in "To lead the marching band was a great honor." Don't forget "down" (the nether direction) and "down" (baby-soft feathers).

Let the "who are they" of your characters dictate the state of their grammar, but be sure to use good grammar in your narrative so your readers will know *you* know the difference.

One last pair (not "pare") that I usually have to look at twice to be sure I've got it right is "effect" and "affect." My mnemonic trick is this phrase: "Effect" means *consequence,* "affect" means *change.*

"Cool as a Cucumber" to "the Bitter End" Under "a Blanket of Snow"

Avoid clichés in narrative. If you use a cliché in dialogue, be sure that it's consistent with your character's personality to speak in clichés. On pain of having your surge protector disconnected, *don't* use this tired, tired, tired narrative description: "like a deer frozen in head-lights." I have read that line in at least half of the scripts by new writers who enroll in the classes I teach—and every one of them thought that he or she was the only one using this image. (They didn't think that for long!)

Go through your screenplays with a can of Raid (or a bottle of White-Out) and eradicate such dreary phrases as:

at his mercy
bite the bullet
the proof is in the pudding
quiet as a church mouse
leaps and bounds
countless hours
a bird in the hand
his days are numbered
innocent bystander
up by his bootstraps
by hook or by crook
play it by ear
trust implicitly
powers that be
nip in the bud
eyes like stars
moment of truth
sickening thud
tongue in cheek
broad daylight

bored to tears
thick as thieves
it goes without saying
easier said than done
rape and pillage

Don't use that last one even if you know what "pillage" means without looking it up.

See how many more you can add to this list, and then take an oath you'll never use any of them—unless it's in the dialogue of a dunderhead. (Note: even though I discourage the use of clichés in writing, some familiar phrases make excellent titles.)

Courageous former first lady Betty Ford has rehabilitated thousands of alcoholics and drug abusers. If I've cured even a few writers of "cliché abuse," I will die happy. (Not "happily.")

Find a fresh way to convey images to the reader. Stretch yourself mentally. The result will be well worth the effort.

Right ways to Write a Phone Call

There are four types of phone calls that we see in the movies:

1. The one-way call, during which we see only one party to the call on the screen, and hear only one side of the conversation.
2. The one-way call in which we see only one party to the conversation, but we hear the unseen person's voice.
3. The two-way (or more-way) call, where we see both (or all) of the participants in the call.
4. The split screen, where we see both (or all) of the parties on the line simultaneously.

The one-way (one visible character) phone call is written with the ellipsis (the three dots . . .) appearing in the speech to designate when the person we see is listening to words we cannot hear. (So do not use "pause" or "beat" to indicate when the character is listening.) Here is the proper way to do it:

> NANCY
>
> I'm sorry, Mom, I meant to call but I got so busy . . . No, I'm not upset . . . Aunt Molly's got a big mouth . . . Sorry, I mean there are times when Aunt Molly says more than she should . . . Okay, Mom . . . Yes, I'll be there on time. Love you, bye.

Between the lines "I got so busy" and "No, I'm not upset" the ellipsis tells us that Nancy's mother said something to her that we could not hear. If by the time this conversation occurs we know something about Nancy, her mother, and their relationship, we will know what Nancy means by what she says, and we can guess what her mother is saying.

If we had been able to hear what was said on the other end of the line (while still only seeing one character on the screen) the scene would be written like this:

> HOLLY
>
> Hello.

> DAN'S VOICE (ON PHONE)
>
> Is this Holly Weintraub?

> HOLLY
>
> Yes. Who's this?

> DAN'S VOICE (ON PHONE)
>
> Don't you recognize my voice?

> HOLLY
>
> Look, I don't have time for games—

> DAN'S VOICE (ON PHONE)
> I'm watching you, baby. I can see what you're
> doing, what you're wearing—I even know what
> color panties you put on.

Because this exchange contains an implicit threat to Holly, a sense of menace, it will probably go on for a full page. Be sure that if all we can see is one party to a phone conversation that we have something visually interesting to look at while we're listening. What is Holly doing while she's listening? Does she quickly scan the room for hidden cameras? Or does she take the phone over to the window to look outside?

In the third kind of movie phone conversation, we see both parties, and so me must establish two separate slug lines, for the two separate sets. Then, instead of going back and forth, alternating slug lines, most writers prefer the following technique:

INT. MELANIE'S HOSPITAL ROOM—DAY

Melanie is alone, attached to an IV drip and surrounded by at least a dozen flower arrangements. The phone on the night table RINGS. She reaches past the bottle and glass on the table and picks up the receiver.

> MELANIE
> Hello.

INT. SARDI'S/PHONE BOOTH IN LADIES'
ROOM —DAY

Belle is alone at the wall phone next to the makeup table.

> BELLE
> Hon—Tony's here, with that blonde bimbo he
> swore he didn't know!

INTERCUT AS NEEDED BETWEEN

> ### MELANIE
> No "hello"? No "what'd the doctor say, Mel? Are
> you going to die next week or next year"?

> ### BELLE
> You said you wanted me to find out for sure. If
> you didn't mean it, then I'm sorry, but what good
> does it do to fool yourself about Tony-the-bum?

> ### MELANIE
> Maybe because it makes me happy.

> ### BELLE
> You need to talk to "Dr. Laura"!

This technique leaves up to the director and the editor the choice of which actor to feature at which moment in the conversation. If you want to end this phone conversation and continue in one of the two sets with one of the two characters, the conclusion of the conversation is written like this:

INT. MELANIE'S HOSPITAL ROOM—DAY

Melanie is still alone.

> ### MELANIE
> (lying)
> Sis—Nurse Ratchet just came in to take some
> more blood. Talk to you later, okay?

Melanie quickly replaces the receiver, but she doesn't lie back down. She thinks for a moment, then carefully extracts the IV needle from her arm and eases herself out of bed.

Then continue with this scene in Melanie's hospital room, or go to another slug line and proceed to another set, such as Sardi's main room, where we see Tony and the bimbo, or go to any other scene appropriate to your plot.

If you want to rejoin Belle in the ladies' room, that requires a new slug line, because Melanie has said good-bye, breaking the phone connection. *Anywhere* we go after this hospital-room scene concludes requires a new slug line.

The fourth way to create an on-screen phone conversation involves the use of a split screen for multiple simultaneous images of people or happenings in separate locations. This is how to do it:

INT. CHARLENE'S BEDROOM—MORNING

Charlene, toweling herself dry after a shower, hurries out of the bathroom to answer the RINGING phone.

CHARLENE

Talk fast, I'm dripping wet.

As she picks up the receiver—SPLIT SCREEN to show both sides of the conversation simultaneously:

INT. JACK'S PRIVATE GYM—MORNING

Jack, wearing only gym shorts, hangs upside down from his stretching bar as he speaks into his palm-sized cell phone.

JACK

I'll be right over.

Specify SPLIT SCREEN *very rarely* in your screenplays. It's one of those creative decisions usually made in the editing room during post-production.

End a split-screen scene with a new slug line. By that I mean either choose one of the split-screen locations on which to concentrate attention for the last few seconds of the sequence, or go to another location entirely.

The same principle applies to ending an "INTERCUT" telephone conversation.

End on *one* of the speakers by giving a new slug line designating *that speaker's particular location,* then complete the scene and go on to the next.

This may seem like a great deal to remember, but these correct screenplay techniques quickly become as automatic as all the little details you mastered when learning how to drive a car.

5. Creating Memorable Leading Characters

Very few people will be able to remember details of a movie's plot after a few weeks or months, but even years later they'll usually be able to tell you about emotions, or about personality quirks and qualities that made certain characters unforgettable. That's because people stay in our minds and in our hearts longer and with greater clarity than do situations.

These are the first questions you must ask when developing your screenplay:

Whom is your story about? From that answer comes the next question:

What kind of trouble is he or she in?

The characters we create should have some contradictions—just as do our friends and enemies, our loved (and not-so-loved) ones. Just as we do. As a woman friend of mine once told me: "I can have an affair with a married man, but I could *never* open somebody else's mail!"

What your characters do and what they say through you, their storyteller, will resonate with emotional honesty if you know your characters thoroughly. You don't need to know them, or to have known them, in your real life, but you'll sometimes take bits from people you've known. Then, like Dr. Frankenstein, you'll sew them together into a "creature" of your own design.

In writing a "star part" for a spec script, understand that you are writing in a vacuum, and that "tailoring" of the part will be done when it's cast. Many "star parts," especially in action pictures or detective stories, can be played by a range of actors, from Will Smith (late twenties) to Sean Connery (a sexy sixty). In between are Denzel Washington, Brad Pitt, Tom Cruise, John Travolta (thirties), Mel Gibson, Liam Neeson, Samuel Jackson, Bruce Willis (forties), and Harrison Ford and Michael Douglas (fit and fifty) to name only a few major stars for whom most writers would be eager to tailor a starring role.

What follows are the questions you should answer as you develop your major characters. You will not use all of the answers in your script—perhaps not even very many of these specifics—but knowing the answers will allow you to create characters that agents and buyers are looking for: those unforgettable "people" who seem to leap off the page. You will write them with the sureness and the authority that comes from knowing your creations very, very well.

A Short "Character Questionnaire" to Jump-start Your Imagination

1. What does a stranger notice first about your character?
2. What does your character notice first about other people?
3. Of what is your character most afraid? This could be anything from a minor humiliation to being vaporized by hostiles. (There was a study that discovered that more people fear speaking in public than fear *death*.)
4. What person, living or dead, does your character most admire?
5. Who, living or dead, does your character consider most despicable?

6. What does your character like best about him/herself?
7. What does your character like least about him/herself?
8. What does your character like about his or her looks?
9. What does your character dislike about his or her looks?
10. What does your character regret?
11. What would your character do all over again if given the chance?
12. What would your character not do all over again?
13. What was your character's worst day?
14. What was your character's best day?
15. If your character had to pursue a different occupation, what would it be?
16. What is the human quality that your character most admires?
17. If there were such a thing as reincarnation, as what would your character choose to return?
18. Does your character have a personal creed or motto?
19. What is your character's dearest material possession?
20. How would he or she like to be remembered?

Is your brain exhausted yet? I hope the answer is no because:

Now, here's the "long form" that will take you even more deeply into the heart and soul of your creations.

I urge you to answer every question. Your writing will benefit from all this hard mental labor.

1. Who Is Your Protagonist?

Gender?
Age?
Religion?
Politics?
Race?
Place of birth?
Birthplace of parents?

Birthplace of grandparents?
Brothers? (How many and how old?)
Sisters? (How many and how old?)

2. What Does He/She Look Like?

Appearance:
  Body type
  Hair color and eye color
  Vision? (Glasses or contact lenses?)
  Style of dress?
  Personal hygiene? (Immaculate? Or needs a bath
    and a shave?)
  Style of movement? (Graceful? Awkward? Fast?
    Slow?)

Speech:
  Accent?
  Style of speech? Breathy? Fast? Soft? Loud?

Financial category?
  Low income?
  Lower middle class?
  Middle class?
  Well-off?
  Very rich?

3. What Does He or She Want?

Money?
Power?
Respect?
High social status?
Awards?
Love?
Children?
To own a home?
To become a partner?
To own a business?

To get a job?

To go to Europe?

4. How Far Will He or She Go to Get It?

Lie?

Cheat?

Steal?

Betray? (Who: Spouse? Employer? The Government?)

Sabotage?

Kill?

5. What Does the Character *Need*?

Food?

Clothes?

Shelter?

Love?

Companionship?

Social status?

6. What Will Your Character Do to Fill That Need?

Lie?

Cheat?

Steal?

Betray?

Sabotage?

Kill?

7. For Whom Would He or She Break the Law?

Spouse?

Child?

Parents?

Siblings?

Friends?

Lover?

No one?

8. How Far Would Your Character Go to Keep His or
   Her Deepest Secret Hidden?

> Lie?
> Steal?
> Bribe?
> Betray a stranger?
> Betray a friend?
> Betray a loved one?
> Give up material possessions?
> Leave everyone familiar and assume another name
>   and life?
> Kill?

9. How Does Your Character Evolve?

> What does he or she learn in the course of your story?
> How does he or she change because of what is
>   learned or experienced?
> Does this knowledge add to his or her happiness?
>   Sense of self-worth?
> Does this knowledge have a negative affect?

10. What Obstacles Are in the Path of Your Character's
    Objective?

11. For Whom—or for What—Will Your Character Make
    Sacrifices?

> A friend?
> A lover?
> A child?
> A parent?
> A principle?
> A religion?

12. What *Does* Your Character Sacrifice?

> Material wealth or possessions?
> Personal safety?

Self-respect?
The respect of others?
Freedom?
His or her life?

13. Why Does Your Character Make This Sacrifice?

14. Is Your Character Inspired by a Real Person? (Even a Little Bit?)

Someone in your own life?
Someone in your past?
A historical figure you've studied?
The image of an actor or actress?
A character in a book, movie, or play you've read or seen?
The public persona of a person in the news?
Yourself—or *aspects* of yourself?
The "you" you wish you were?

15. Who Is the Most Important Person in Your Character's Present Life?

Wife or husband?
Child?
Parent or parents?
Boss?
Friend?
Lover?

16. Who Was the Most Important Person in Your Character's Back Story?

Parent or parents?
Authority figure?
Object of your character's passion?
Object of your character's obsession?
Wife or husband?
A child?

17. What Is Your Character's Religion?

> Does he or she go to the services of that denomination?
>
> If he or she attends services, is it regularly or irregularly?
>
> Is religion important to his or her behavior?

18. How Does Your Character Grow?

> How does he or she change?
>
> What does he or she learn?

19. What Difficult Decision Must Your Character Make?

20. Has Your Character Been "Labeled" by Others?

21. Does Your Character Have a Sense of Humor?

> Does he or she play practical jokes?
>
> Does he or she have a quick verbal wit?
>
> What strikes him or her as funny?
>
> Who's your character's favorite comedy figure or comedian?
>
> Does he or she have a favorite cartoon or cartoon character?

22. Who's Your Character's Best Friend? (Is This Person in the Script?)

23. Does Your Character Keep Up Friendships?

> Write letters?
>
> E-mail?
>
> Make phone calls?
>
> Send gifts for occasions? (Christmas, birthdays, Valentine's Day, etc.)

24. List Your Character's Favorite Leisure Activities

> Drinking?
>
> Gambling?

Being with friends?
Pursuing a hobby?
Reading? (If so, what does he or she like to read?)
Museums?
Movies?
Athletics? (Tennis? Jogging? Swimming?)

25. What Is Your Character's Favorite Music?

Classical?
Broadway?
Rock?
Motown?
Pop?
Heavy metal?
The newest (whatever that is)?

26. What Accidents Has Your Character Had?

Any visible signs of past accidents?
Any physical limitations due to accidents?

27. To What Is Your Character Most Vulnerable?

Plight of loved ones?
Plight of animals?
Plight of strangers?
Appeals to his or her sense of honor?
Appeals to his or her sense of guilt?

28. About What Does Your Character Feel Guilty? (Even If It's Long in the Past)

A cruelty?
A serious lie?
A betrayal or infidelity?
Not being able to prevent a tragedy?
Not believing someone until a tragedy happened?

29. What Is Your Character's Career or Job?

> Is he or she happy in this work?
> Would he or she rather be doing something else? (If so, what?)
> How did he or she come to this job or career?

30. How Much Money Does Your Character Have?

> Approximate amount
> From what source? (Earned it? Won it? Inherited it?)

31. What Would Your Character Do with an Unexpected Windfall?

> Of $500?
> Of $1,000?
> Of $10,000?
> Of $1 million?

32. Has Your Character Ever Been the Victim of a Crime?

> Burglary?
> Robbery?
> Assault?
> Battery?
> Rape?

33. What Kind of a Car Does Your Character Own?

> Is it the kind he or she really *wants* to own?
> How well does he or she take care of it?
> Who taught him or her to drive?
> What kind of a driver is he or she?
> What's in the trunk of the car? (The necessities—or a lot of junk?)
> Does your character eat in the car? Or drink coffee while driving?

34. Does Your Character Have a Pet?

> What kind?
> How many?
> What was his or her favorite pet?
> What animal does he or she like best?
> What animal does he or she like least?

35. How Does Your Character Feel About His or Her Environment?

> Does he or she litter?
> Does he or she recycle?
> Give money to environmental organizations?
> Have environmental bumper stickers?
> Is he or she a "country" person or a "city" person?

36. Which of the Following Words Describe Your Character? (Choose As Many As Are Appropriate.)

> Cheerful?
> Dour?
> Enthusiastic?
> Witty?
> Energetic?
> Outgoing?
> Talkative?
> Taciturn?
> Serious?
> Shy?
> Charming?
> Abrasive?
> Smooth?
> Happy?
> Morose?
> Daring?
> Cautious?

Generous?
Suspicious?
Truthful?
Brutally honest?
Tactful?
Kind?
Thoughtful?
Selfish?
Courageous?

37. How Does Your Character Feel About the Death Penalty?

For it
Against it
Deeply conflicted
Hasn't given it much (or any) thought
Felt one way once and has since changed mind (If so, why?)

38. What Are Your Character's Personal Quirks?

Is he or she usually on time or usually late?
Emotionally mature or immature for his or her age?
Collect unusual objects?
Superstitious?
Any peculiarities about the food he or she will or will not eat?

39. What Would His or Her Friends Like to Change About Your Character?

Is he or she judgmental?
Stubborn?
Unreliable?
Does he or she have a temper?
What makes him or her angry?
Is he or she inclined to be impetuous?

Does he or she form opinions quickly?

Impatient?

Does he or she swear to excess?

40. What Kind of Trouble Does He or She Get Into?

Romantic trouble?

Legal trouble?

Family trouble?

Is he or she in mortal danger?

Does he or she take on someone else's troubles?

Does he or she take big risks?

Does he or she stop to weigh the consequences, or
plunge into danger?

Track your character's emotions during the course of the story. Be sure that your character's behavior is consistent with what she's feeling. How does your character react to what's happening in the plot? Is your character on a consistent through-line, true to who she is—or does the character *wobble* according to what you want her to do in a given scene?

Now there may be a rare occasion where a character must behave *out of character* for plot purposes. If you are faced with this situation, then *address the fact that the character behaves "out of character" in dialogue.*

A perfect example of writers needing a character—for an important story reason—to behave "out of character" occurs in *Casablanca.*

Sydney Greenstreet's character, Ferrari, owner of the Blue Parrot nightclub and a competitor of Rick's, is the only person in the script who could tell Lazlo and Ilsa that Rick probably has the Letters of Transit they need in order to escape from Casablanca and Major Strasser. But giving away information that valuable is not the kind of thing a man like Ferrari is likely to do. Yet Lazlo and Ilsa *must* learn that Rick has the papers so that the plot can move forward, so that first Lazlo and then Ilsa will be forced to go to Rick—but the only character in the story who could conceivably convey this information is a selfish, greedy man who never appears to do anything unless he has something to gain from it.

The solution the writers devised is contained in the following exchange between Ferrari and Lazlo:

> FERRARI
> (re Ilsa, with admiration)
> I observe that you in one respect are a very fortunate man. I move to make one more suggestion. Why, I do not know because it cannot possibly profit me. Have you heard about Senor Ugati and the Letters of Transit?

> LAZLO
> Yes, something.

> FERRARI
> The Letters were not found when Ugati was arrested.

> LAZLO
> Do you know where they are?

> FERRARI
> Not for sure, monsieur, but I venture to guess that Ugati left those Letters with Monsieur Rick.

> LAZLO
> Rick . . .

> FERRARI
> A difficult customer, that Rick. One never knows what he will do, or why, but it is worth a chance.

Lazlo and Ilsa thank Ferrari and leave.

As most of the civilized moviegoing or video-renting world knows, when Rick does not give Lazlo the Letters of Transit, Ilsa goes to Rick later that night. This is the action which results in the reconciliation of Rick and Ilsa, and creates the suspense as to which man will board the plane with Ilsa: Rick or Lazlo. This device—the "I don't know why I'm telling you this, but"—is a writer's technique of last resort, and is a perfect example of the credo "If you can't hide it, paint it red!" The ideal situation in a script in which a major character needs a piece of information that is crucial to the forward progress of the plot, is for the writer to create a character who can convey that information through a logical motivation. One of the most frequent examples of this is found in "cop" movies and TV shows in which leading characters are able to coerce by threat, or to induce by camaraderie, some supporting character to give them the important little piece of the puzzle they need in order to progress toward the solution of the mystery they are trying to unravel.

By now you should have a pretty clear vision of the characters you want to share with the audience. Here is a Character Development Checklist. Use it as a test against which to measure the special people you've created for your screenplay.

Creating vivid, memorable characters is *absolutely essential* to your success as a screenwriter. After completing the Character Questionnaire in order to give yourself a vivid mental picture of your major characters, go through this checklist to see if you know all that you need to know.

1. What does your main character (or main characters) want? (And is it good for him, her, or them?)
2. What do they *need?*
3. What are their personalities, intelligence, aptitudes?
4. How far will they go to get what they want?
5. Do they discover that there is a line they will *not* cross? Or do they discover there is no line they will not cross to get what they want or need?
6. What will they give up for the one they love? (In *A Tale of Two Cities,* alcoholic lawyer Sidney Carton goes to his death in the place of the husband of the woman Carton

loves. He once told her that he would do anything to keep her safe, or to keep safe those she loved. He proves he means that by placing his neck in the guillotine so that her husband can escape that death.)

7. Give the star of your story moments that actors look for. (Example: Frank Galvin in *The Verdict*—that pause before he drinks the glass of whiskey in the morning. Galvin knows he is throwing his life away, but at that point he has no compelling reason not to. Later, in the hospital, he looks at the girl on life support—really looks at her—and knows that he has to win the case for her—and for himself, while there is still a tiny spark of Frank Galvin left.)

8. What is your star's personal style? (Examples: In *The Odd Couple* Oscar is the ultimate slob and Felix is a total "neat freak." In the TV series *Remington Steele* Pierce Brosnan's Steele never gets dirty, while Stephanie Zimbalist's Laura does all of the running, sweating, and getting bedraggled.)

Here's an exercise for you:

Think about some of your favorite movies or TV series, write down the characters' names, and then describe the personal style of the main characters. List the *particular things* that are most noticeable about them, most distinctive.

Learn to watch for memorable details. You can use them as a model when you create your own original characters.

Now answer these questions:

How Does Your Star Character Behave to Weaker People?

In *Pulp Fiction,* Bruce Willis's character, Butch, is kind to his not very bright girlfriend, even though she left behind his father's watch in their motel room. That watch is so precious to Butch that he risks his life to go back for it. In *Sea of Love,* Al Pacino's character can not arrest a felon in front of the man's little son; instead, he lets him go. And the audience loves him for it. In *The Godfather,* violent Sonny Corleone is gentle, tender, and protective with children and with the women in his life: wife, mother, sister, mistress. That protectiveness is the part of his character that makes us care what happens to Sonny, and grieve when he is murdered. In *Casablanca,* Rick orders his own roulette wheel "fixed" so that a young refugee can win enough money to get himself and his wife out of Casablanca, which means that the young woman will not have to sleep with the police captain in order to obtain their exit visas. When Rick sends his drunken ex-girlfriend, Yvonne, home in a cab under the protection of his bartender, Sasha, he orders Sasha to return immediately, making it clear that Yvonne is not to be taken advantage of in any way.

What in Your Star Character's Background Drives Him?

In *Midnight Run* it is Robert De Niro's character's loss of his job as a cop, at which he was good and honest. His character, Jack Walsh, wouldn't be corrupted, and so he was framed with planted drugs and thrown off the force. He lost his wife, his child, and what he regarded as his mission in life: getting the bad guys. Now he works as a bounty hunter to earn enough money to buy a little diner and get away from all the ugliness he sees.

What drives Clint Eastwood's character in *In the Line of Fire* is that he has not forgiven himself for being unable to stop President Kennedy's assassination.

What Is Your Star Character Afraid Of?

There are so many dramatically rich possibilities. Loss of control? Loss of money or status? Helplessness? Loneliness? Humiliation? Loss of family or community respect? How does he face his fears? How has he avoided facing those fears? How does he face his real or imagined personal or professional failures?

Be Sure You Know *Who* Your Story Is About

Keep the star character front and center in all, or most, important scenes and sequences.

Examine your screenplay page by page and apply this test: If your major character has nothing to do in a scene, then it's possible that he or she shouldn't be there, or the scene should be rewritten to make your star a meaningful part of it. The third possibility is that the scene should be cut. Consider all three, and make your decision.

Don't leave your stars out of major scenes, or allow your stars to be passive bystanders. If you make this mistake you are unlikely to get a star to commit to the project.

When several things have to be done in a scene, give your star the most important task. This is especially important in action pictures. Remember: Stars save people; supporting characters save equipment.

Do as much research as necessary to make your characters sound as though they know their professions. Take the trouble to learn the "terms of art" and use them appropriately. Having your characters use the right vocabulary and references for their professions helps us believe your characters. If your star is a cop, find out how long it takes to run a ballistics test, or to do an autopsy, or to check license plate numbers—or whatever else that character will need to know in your script. If an important character is a photographer, learn enough about cameras and lenses and lighting so that he or she will seem real, and not phony. If your star is a doctor or a nurse, learn about whatever medical procedures and tests are part of your story, and how long they take and what the mechanics of such things are.

Be sure your characters belong—seem realistic—in the period in which your story is set. Don't use contemporary references in a script set in an earlier period. Be conscious of the possible differences in speech patterns, forms of address, manners, and customs when you're writing of an earlier period. Read enough background material so you'll know what was going on in the larger world around the characters in your story. Great reference works are *Timelines of World His-*

tory and *Timelines of American History*. They are available in most bookstores and libraries and will tell you what music and entertainment was popular in almost any year, as well as what was invented and discovered in that year and who the famous political, literary, scientific, and sports figures were then—as well as many other useful and interesting details.

Be so thoroughly inside your characters that you will know what they will do in practically any situation. People frequently alter their behavior depending upon whom they are with and according to what's going on around them—but they will remain consistent within themselves, to the core of whoever it is they are. However, a change in a person is dramatically interesting. If a character must behave inconsistently in a scene, then address this fact in dialogue.

Be audacious. You can say things through your characters in their "reel" lives that probably you would seldom dare say in "real" life— and you can get away with it.

A Word About "Character Arcs"

The word is: *You don't have to have them.*

Surprised? Think about it for a moment. The term "character arc" means that a character is changed by the circumstances of your plot. He or she begins the story with one attitude, or set of attitudes, and later, because of what the character goes through in your story, those attitudes are altered in some material way.

But not all characters change.

In fact, refusing to be changed by circumstances can be the most appealing point about some characters. Take, for example, the character of Dirty Harry. No matter what goes on in the plot of a Dirty Harry movie, Inspector Harry Callahan of the San Francisco PD does not change. He's a near vigilante. At the beginning of each movie he is a man with a low tolerance for criminals and a vivid way of demonstrating that fact, and by the end of the movie he is still a man with a low tolerance for criminals and a high propensity for violence.

To illustrate another series of popular cop pictures in which a star character does have an arc, let's take *Lethal Weapon*. Detective Martin Riggs (played by Mel Gibson) undergoes a significant change, or "arc," in his character. When the audience is first introduced to him, Detective Riggs is a near madman, an emotionally damaged character racing toward self-destruction. Then he becomes the partner of a happily married family man, Danny Glover's Detective Roger Murtaugh. After a while, and due largely to the influence of his partner, Riggs—while still remaining a daredevil—stops trying to kill himself. The isolated cop who thought he had nothing to live for is absorbed into the loving family of his partner. He stops trying to kill himself when he realizes there are people who care about him, and that he has come to love. With something to live for, dying stops being so appealing to Riggs. Interestingly, the point of relative stability at which Riggs arrives is the point from which the *Lethal Weapon* sequels take off.

Both of these successful series, Dirty Harry and *Lethal Weapon,* are in the same action genre, both star fearless cops who make cleaning up the bad guys their mission. But Callahan and Riggs and Murtaugh are three very different men—and audiences love all three of them.

Two men who are very similar, but appear on the surface to be quite different, are Rick in *Casablanca* and Jack Walsh in *Midnight Run.*

Humphrey Bogart's Rick Blaine is cool, polished, urbane, probably well educated, and wears a dinner jacket as though he was born in it.

Robert De Niro's Jack Walsh is tough, gritty, hotheaded, and thoroughly "street."

Both men are honest and incorruptible—and have suffered for those qualities. Both had their hearts ripped out of them by the loss of what mattered most. For Rick it was the sudden, cruel, unexplained abandonment by Ilsa. For Walsh it was the loss of his job and family.

At the point we meet them, both Rick and Walsh, although functioning effectively in their new lives, have built a concrete wall around their hearts. Rick now owns a popular, elegant nightclub; Walsh has become a skilled bounty hunter. Both have sworn that they will never again let another human being get close enough to hurt them.

Then, through the course of their separate stories, both men have their respective walls slowly torn down. By the end of *Casablanca* and *Midnight Run* both have emerged as the men they used to be, before they lost what mattered to them most.

You don't have to have a "character arc" if you've chosen to create a character who is not changed by the circumstances of the plot.

If it is right dramatically that your character grow or change as a result of the challenges you've put him through, then that's the correct choice.

Be true to the character you have created. Don't let someone dictate to you that your character must have an "arc" if that's not true to your story.

It's entirely possible that the character Harry Callahan had an "arc" before we met him—circumstances that turned Harry Callahan into "Dirty Harry"—but that was not the story the writers chose to tell.

What story to tell is the writer's choice. *Your choice.* Use any guidelines that work for you, and only those that work for you.

6. Great Supporting Characters and How to Use Them

Great supporting characters are those who are so well thought out, so carefully crafted and specific in their beliefs and attitudes, in their humanity (or lack thereof) that conceivably they could "star" in some other script, just as the supporting characters in our own lives—postmen, store clerks, doctors, mechanics, accountants, colleagues—are the "stars" of their own life stories. Supporting characters "support" and enhance your stars in vital ways that we will discuss here.

In this chapter I am going to describe some great supporting characters—and then explain the *function* of the characters in the movies in which they appear. Study these characters and how they are used in their separate stories so that you can utilize the supporting characters you create to their fullest potential. All of the movies I mention here are available on videocassette. Even if you've seen these pictures before, I strongly suggest that you rent these videos so that you can study the movies, and especially the scenes I will bring up here.

The Bishop's Wife and The Preacher's Wife

The Bishop's Wife is a romantic comedy released in 1947 starring Loretta Young in the title role of Julia, David Niven as her husband, Henry, an Episcopalian bishop, and Cary Grant as Dudley, the angel sent to earth in response to Henry's prayers for help with a problem.

This movie was remade, and considerably altered, in 1996 as *The Preacher's Wife*. In this nineties incarnation it became more of a romantic drama, with some brief moments of comedy and several opportunities for Whitney Houston, as Julia, to sing. Courtney B. Vance plays Henry (now a Baptist preacher) and Denzel Washington is the handsome and charismatic Dudley. I won't do a detailed comparison of the two pictures here, except to talk about a wonderful supporting character from the original who was, oddly, I think, left out of the remake. I believe the creative team responsible for *The Preacher's Wife* missed a marvelous romantic opportunity by abandoning Sylvester, the elderly cabdriver, and cutting down to a fraction the famous—and absolutely enchanting—ice-skating scene from *The Bishop's Wife*.

The basic situation in the two movies is the same, although details and subplots differ. The similarities are that Dudley's miraculous appearance to Henry, and Dudley's explanation of his being an angel sent to help Henry, are first greeted with suspicion, and then with moderate appreciation as Dudley provides some help to Henry. But Henry soon becomes concerned that Dudley has more than an "angelic" interest in the lovely and unhappy Julia. Even though Henry's intellect tells him that nothing can happen between Dudley and Julia, fear of this "other man"—the possibility of losing Julia's love—helps to bring Henry back to being the fine, caring man of the people Julia originally fell in love with and married.

Because Julia is a married woman—and married to a clergyman at that—Samuel Goldwyn's *The Bishop's Wife* needed to keep her pure, but the filmmakers still wanted the commercial appeal of a romantic triangle. They could not have a traditional love scene between Julia and Dudley without damaging the spirituality of the movie. They wanted a romantic sequence that would leave no bad "aftertaste" with the audience and harm the commercial prospects of the picture. I haven't been able to find a copy of the original screenplay, but someone—and as a writer, I hope with all of my heart that it was the screenwriters—came up with the idea of creating a character who would act as a kind of chaperon in the movie's one romantic Julia-Dudley sequence. This is the function of Sylvester the cabdriver.

It is Christmastime, and it is night. Julia and Dudley are returning home by cab from a visit to Henry's old parish church, a visit Henry was too busy fund-raising to make himself. They begin talking to the elderly cabdriver, Sylvester. As they are going through the park they hear music and see the ice-skating rink, sparkling with lights and swirling with skaters. Impulsively, Dudley asks Sylvester to stop the cab and invites both Julia and Sylvester to go skating. Out on the ice, it is clear that Dudley is a wonderful skater. As Sylvester is putting on his skates, Dudley begins a lovely, graceful waltz on the ice with Julia. She is awkward and unskilled at first, but in moments, in Dudley's arms, she becomes a beautiful skater, too. Then Sylvester makes his way onto the ice, slipping and falling and comically clinging to a post. Dudley leaves Julia, skates over to Sylvester, and helps the old man up. Under Dudley's spell, Sylvester begins to skate like a champion. Julia and Sylvester are joyous at their newfound skill on the ice. Dudley, Julia, and Sylvester link arms and skate together in an exquisitely choreographed, graceful series of glides and turns around the skating rink. This scene is magnificently lighted and photographed, and it's one of the sequences that prove there are times when black and white can be far more beautiful than color.

Because elderly Sylvester is part of this romantic "dance on ice," the scene retains its innocent beauty. It is not something for which either Julia or the audience need feel guilty for enjoying.

In my opinion, the creation of Sylvester the cabdriver for the trio's ice-skating scene was a brilliant concept for a sequence that combined romantic appeal for the audience and innocent fun for the participants.

Body Heat

Before our workshop's film-clip nights I go through my own collection of videocassettes and cue up the movies to the beginning of the scenes I want to show that evening. Whenever I unpack the *Body Heat* video I can see male eyebrows go up in happy anticipation of visual treats to come. I quickly squelch this hope by announcing:

"Sorry, guys—I'm not showing one of *those* scenes." If anyone wants to see Kathleen Turner naked—certainly a beautiful sight—he will have to get his own copy of *Body Heat*.

The scene I show runs less than four minutes, and it is the only scene in which actor Mickey Rourke appears. He plays a young man who was once an arsonist and bomb maker, and who was a former client of the male star, the sleazy lawyer Racine, played by William Hurt.

Racine has gone to The Arsonist for instructions on how to commit arson. The Arsonist explains the basics of the process, but The Arsonist doesn't like doing it. I believe there is only one reason this scene is in *Body Heat*—and it's not to give Racine instructions on how to burn a place down. Racine could have told Matty in one sentence that he'd found out what he needed to know about arson from a former client. I believe this scene is in the picture because it gives us a glimpse of an aspect of Racine that we, the audience, have never seen. It's evidence that he is at least partially a good man, that he's helped another human being without reward to himself. That glimpse is of a man who is worth our worrying about. It gives us an emotional reason to root for Racine to get out of the mess his lust for Matty has gotten him into.

Here is a brief excerpt from their well-written exchange:

THE ARSONIST
. . . These are mag chips. If you want a little more,
splash a little accelerator around.

RACINE

So just regular gasoline?

THE ARSONIST

Regular, unleaded, supreme, whatever you like,
Counselor. I wanna ask you something. Are you
listening, asshole? 'Cause I like you. I got a serious
question. What the fuck are you doing? This is not
shit for you to be messing with. Are you ready to
hear somethin'? I want you to see if this sounds familiar: "Any time you try a decent crime you got
50 ways to fuck it up. If you can think of 25 of
them then you're a genius—an' you ain't no genius." You remember who told me that?

Racine doesn't answer. He takes a pack of cigarettes out of his
shirt pocket and starts to light one.

THE ARSONIST

Hey, no smokin' in here. Why don't you let me do
it for you? Gratis. I'll do it for nothin'—I wouldn't
even be on the street if it wasn't for you.

RACINE
(declining the offer)

Thanks.

THE ARSONIST

I sure hope you know what you're doing. You better be damn sure 'cause if you ain't sure, then don't
do it. Of course, that's my recommendation anyway. Don't do it . . .

The Arsonist likes and respects Racine, which is why he offers to
do the job for him—no questions asked. He's willing to risk getting
caught and sent back to jail, willing to risk his own life for Racine.

Racine thanks him, but declines the offer, which is another reason we now have to like Racine. I also want you to study the dialogue in the above exchange to see how a scene that has a hidden purpose is made entertaining by the personality of The Arsonist. He is crude but sincere, witty but serious. The Arsonist is a very good small part, not just a vehicle for conveying information the writer wants us to know. That is accomplished by the attention that was paid by the writer to giving this one-scene character a distinct personality and style of expression. This is the difference between *typing* and *writing*.

Now, I want to be sure you are clear about what the scene with The Arsonist accomplishes for Racine. Remember that all we have observed of Racine prior to this scene is a character with a dubious to poor reputation as a lawyer who is so besotted by Matty that he's agreed to kill her rich husband so that they can be together and live happily ever after on the husband's money. This is not an admirable fellow. The beautiful, sexually uninhibited Matty, who eagerly betrays her husband and wants to have him murdered, is not exactly a sympathetic leading lady. She tells Racine that she's afraid of the husband, but we've seen no evidence at all that the husband is either abusive or dangerous. With the given protagonists, we can enjoy this Technicolor "film noir" for the steamy sex scenes and for the amusing performance of Ted Danson, as the local prosecutor, but there is no one for whom we can root. We have no real emotional investment in the story.

The Racine we see through the eyes of The Arsonist adds an important dimension to our enjoyment of the movie, and it makes the ending—when Racine realizes how he's been used—more powerful and poignant than it would have been without the scene that shows us another, better Racine than the man caught in Matty's lethal web.

In this respect, I think *Body Heat* is an even more satisfying movie than the classic picture it so resembles in premise: *Double Indemnity.* But *Double Indemnity,* as we are about to see, has its own special pleasures.

Double Indemnity

A classic film noir, *Double Indemnity* was released by Paramount in 1944. The screenplay was written by Billy Wilder and Raymond Chandler and adapted from a successful novella by "novel noir" writer James M. Cain. Among Cain's novels was another erotic immorality tale, *The Postman Always Rings Twice.* In *Double Indemnity,* Fred Mac-Murray plays Walter Neff, the insurance man who, like William Hurt's sleazy lawyer, Racine, in *Body Heat,* falls in love with an unhappily married woman and agrees to kill her wealthy husband so that they can be together. Barbara Stanwyck plays the wife, Phyllis Deitrickson, and Edward G. Robinson is Barton Keyes, the brilliant claims manager at the insurance company, and Walter's immediate superior.

Double Indemnity, like *Body Heat,* which was made thirty-seven years later, had the same problem of having a protagonist who murders the husband of the seductive, and deliciously no-good, woman he loves. This is, innately, a character for whom it's hard to root.

The solution in *Double Indemnity* was the presence of the character Barton Keyes, an incorruptible man who is so good at spotting phony claims that he is a powerful adversary. So what we have in *Double Indemnity* as the protagonist's adversary is the picture's only "good guy." It is an unusual story configuration—and it works.

Keyes is a short, pudgy, rather sloppy genius who hates to wear jackets and frequently spills things on himself. He lives for his work, complaining about it as he revels in the pleasure of uncovering deceit and saving his company from paying false claims.

A scene in the second act demonstrates to the audience what an expert Keyes is in his field. His speech about suicide is a masterful kind of verbal aria without music. It illustrates Keyes's expertise while being entertaining about it.

Norton, the not-too-bright head of the insurance company (he's an inept man who inherited the business from his smarter father) is trying to avoid paying off the "double indemnity" claim on a life insurance policy taken out by Deitrickson, the murdered husband, two weeks before his death. Norton's idea is that he can avoid paying the claim by proving that the man's death was not accidental, but was really a suicide. Hardly taking a breath, Keyes recites to Neff and Norton statistics on suicide. Read it carefully so that you can appreciate how cleverly worded it is, how this speech both entertains the audience while it is establishing that Keyes is a very smart antagonist:

> KEYES
> Come now, you've never read an actuarial table in
> your life, have you? Why there are ten volumes on
> suicide alone: suicide by race, by color, by occupa-
> tion, by sex, by seasons of the year, by time of day.
> Suicide: How committed: by poison, by firearms,
> by drowning, by leaps, suicide by poison, subdi-
> vided by types of poison: such as corrosive, irri-
> tant, systemic, gaseous, narcotic, alkaloid, protein
> and so forth. Suicide by leaps, subdivided by leaps
> from high places, under the wheels of trains, under
> the wheels of trucks, under the feet of horses, from
> steamboats. But, Mr. Norton, of all the cases on
> record there's not one single case of suicide by leap
> from the rear end of a moving train. And do you
> know how fast that train was going at the point
> where the body was found? Fifteen miles an hour.
> Now how can anybody jump off a slow-moving
> train like that with any kind of expectation that he
> would kill himself? No, no soap, Mr. Norton.
> We're sunk and we'll have to pay through the nose,
> and you know it . . .

Walter is tremendously relieved that Keyes does not suspect what really happened, that the deceased man was murdered. Keyes, with his years of experience and his keen instinct, was the only person that Walter was worried might foil their scheme.

That night, Phyllis calls Walter from a booth around the corner from his apartment. She's happy that they've fooled the insurance company and now she wants to be with Walter. He tells her that she can come over, but be careful that she's not seen. Seconds after Walter hangs up the phone, his doorbell rings. Knowing that Phyllis couldn't have gotten there that quickly, he opens the door to find Keyes.

Walter tries to act calm, but his heart is racing with fear because he knows Phyllis could arrive at any moment. If Keyes sees her, they will be exposed. Keyes has come to tell Walter that "the little man" in his stomach—Keyes's instinct for detecting fraud—has been acting up. Keyes tells Walter that he now knows that the man they insured was murdered. In this brief excerpt, Keyes explains to Walter Neff how he has come to that conclusion:

> KEYES
> . . . Now look, Walter, a guy takes out an insur-
> ance policy that's worth $100,000 if he's killed on
> a train. Then two weeks later he is killed on a
> train. And not in a wreck, but falling off some silly
> observation car. You know what the mathematical
> probability of that is? One out of—oh, I don't
> know how many billions . . .

Now that Keyes has figured out that the dead man was murdered, he is determined to find out who committed the crime. Naturally, because she is the beneficiary of the insurance policy, Keyes suspects the dead man's wife.

The entertaining "good guy" character of Barton Keyes gave the killers, Walter Neff and Phyllis Deitrickson, an adversary who was smart and therefore dangerous to them—and it gave the audience a good person to like.

In the 1940s, when *Double Indemnity* was made, there was a powerful "code of morality" under which the studios operated. That code controlled what could be shown on movie screens. Some of the rules were ridiculous; for example, most married couples in movies had twin beds, and if both husband and wife were in the same bed, one of them had to have at least one foot touching the floor. There was no nudity in American movies, and no swearing. Sexual relations were implied, but adults in the audience knew what was going on between Phyllis Deitrickson and Walter Neff when cameras cut away to open windows, ocean waves, or stars in the sky. Very good movies were made in spite of these tight restrictions.

Movie buffs know that there was a major clash involving *Gone with the Wind* and producer David O. Selznick's absolute insistence that Rhett Butler be allowed to use his exit line from the novel, which included the word "damn." He finally won that fight, but it was a big one. Another of the most strictly enforced "code" rules was that characters who committed a crime must pay for that crime on-screen. So while everyone who went to the movies knew that the "bad guys" wouldn't get away with their crimes, the fun was in finding out how they would be caught, or how they would otherwise be made to pay. No one who went to see *Double Indemnity* believed that Phyllis and Walter would live happily ever after, even if they hadn't read Cain's novella, but they enjoyed the skill of the writers and the actors in bringing the story to the screen. Audiences knew that the murderous pair would pay for their crimes; the suspense came in wondering *how* they would be made to pay.

Mrs. Miniver

I cannot think of a movie that is less like *Body Heat* and *Double Indemnity* than is *Mrs. Miniver,* which starred Greer Garson as a middle-class Englishwoman, the wife of an architect, trying to hold her home and family together during the years of terrifying World War II German bombing raids over England. Yet in spite of the differences between these two pictures, the scene I show from *Mrs. Miniver* fulfills a function similar to that of the Mickey Rourke scene in *Body Heat:* It helps to shape our opinion of the leading character.

Mrs. Miniver begins just before the start of World War II in Europe. We meet Mrs. Miniver as she is boarding a commuter train to return to her suburban home after an extravagant day of shopping in London. She shares a train compartment with the local clergyman and with Lady Beldon (the richest woman in the area, a domineering old lady) and Lady Beldon's meek and mousy secretary-companion. Our impression of Mrs. Miniver in these early scenes is that she's lovely, but somewhat frivolous.

When she gets off at her destination, she's greeted by Mr. Ballard, the elderly stationmaster. It's clear that Mr. Ballard has been waiting for her, because he remarks that she's returned on a later train than the one he expected her to be on. Mr. Ballard tells her that he wants to show her something, and asks if she could come into his office for a moment. Even though she's in a hurry to get home, she agrees. Once inside, Mr. Ballard proudly shows her a magnificent red rose that he, an avid amateur gardener, has bred.

Mrs. Miniver genuinely admires its stunning beauty and lovely scent and congratulates him. Mr. Ballard asks her permission to name the rose after her, to call this, his proudest achievement, "The Mrs. Miniver." He gives as his reason the fact that he's known her and watched her over the years, that she's never been too busy to stop and talk to him, and that he's seen other examples of her kindness and of her fine personal qualities. Mrs. Miniver is charmed and flattered, and expresses her great delight in having a rose named after her.

This short scene tells us that Mrs. Miniver is a woman of character and quality—before we've had a chance to see this for ourselves. The subtle importance of this scene is that it sets us up to believe the quiet courage and endurance she shows soon after this, during the terrible years of the war. It shows us the woman of quality beneath the essentially carefree, rather self-indulgent life she leads before her pleasant world is turned upside down by circumstances beyond her control.

Quiz Show

Quiz Show is based on the true story of the spectacular rise and fall of Charles Van Doren, a young man who was hailed as the "intellectual Joe DiMaggio." Van Doren, a college instructor from a distinguished literary family, got caught up in the glamour and the seductiveness of the celebrity that came to him as a week-after-week winner on the TV quiz show *Twenty-One,* which was a great popular rage with the American public in the late 1950s. Van Doren was finally exposed as a fraud. He disgraced himself and his family name when it was revealed that he was given the answers to the questions in advance. Ralph Fiennes plays Van Doren. David Paymer plays Dan Enright, producer of *Twenty-One.* His associate, Al Freedman, is played by the amazingly versatile Hank Azaria. (It's worth renting *The Birdcage*— the American remake of the French hit *La Cage aux Folles*—just to see Hank Azaria as Robin Williams's and Nathan Lane's exotic "maid," Agidor.)

This scene from *Quiz Show* illustrates how having *two* supporting characters "double-teaming" the star can enable you to get across to the audience a lot of important exposition information while being entertaining.

Early in the story producer Dan Enright believes that his current champion of *Twenty-One,* Herbert Stempel, has peaked as far as public interest is concerned and sets out to look for a new television hero. The film clip I show begins when Enright's associate, Al Freedman, spots the handsome WASP Van Doren as he's auditioning for a less important TV quiz show that Enright also produces and realizes that he's found their man!

Enright and Freedman, sitting together opposite Van Doren, question him about his family, his ambitions, how much he earns as an instructor at Columbia University—and point out how much less Van Doren's eighty-six dollars a week is than the salary of TV's Chuckles the Clown. While passing questions and answers back and forth between themselves, they circle in on Van Doren, finally asking how Van

Doren would feel about being an *assured* winner. The way they put it to him, what they are suggesting is just entertainment.

> FREEDMAN
> When Gregory Peck parachutes behind enemy
> lines, you think that's really Gregory Peck?

> ENRIGHT
> That book that Eisenhower wrote? A ghost-writer
> wrote it. Nobody cares.

> FREEDMAN
> It's not like we'd be giving you the answers. Just
> because we know you know, you still know.

> ENRIGHT
> It's not like putting Al or me on the show, pre-
> tending to be an intellectual.

In this scene we learn exactly what is going on at *Twenty-One*. If an attractive young man from a celebrated family, like Charles Van Doren, were to be the show's champion it would spike the ratings and keep them high. They suck Van Doren into the scheme by first convincing him that America needs an "intellectual Joe DiMaggio," a hero who would make kids want to do their homework and grow up to be smart and well educated like Van Doren.

Because of writer Paul Attanasio's clever concept of using Enright and Freedman in a two-against-one assault on Van Doren's principles, we learn what we need to know about the quiz show scam in a very entertaining, fast-paced scene. It's a skillful example of the "spoonful of sugar" that "makes the medicine (exposition) go down."

Heaven Can Wait

The sequence I show from *Heaven Can Wait*, starring Warren Beatty, James Mason, and Julie Christie, with great support from actors Dyan

Cannon, Charles Grodin, Jack Warden, Buck Henry, and others, illustrates how use of multiple supporting characters can get us through several exposition-filled short scenes that provide us with the information we must have in order to enjoy the movie, and entertain us while we are learning what we need to know.

The situation is that Joe Pendleton, a rising young pro football player on one of his strenuous exercise routines, bicycles into a tunnel. He is unaware that a train is coming from the other direction.

Joe awakens to find himself in a misty "way station" where he is urged to get on a plane that will take him to Heaven. He protests loudly that he's not supposed to be dead! The commotion he causes prompts the arrival of Mr. Jordan (James Mason), a higher-level afterlife executive. Mr. Jordan has the records checked and discovers that Joe is correct—he isn't due to arrive up there for another fifty years. It seems that his tenderhearted new escort (played by writer-actor Buck Henry) removed Joe from the tunnel just *before* collision with the train, because he wanted to spare Joe pain. Mr. Jordan sternly reminds the escort that the rule is escorts must wait for the "outcome" and not enter the scene prematurely. Mr. Jordan apologizes to Joe for the error and tells him that they will return his spirit to his body immediately.

When Joe and the escort arrive back on earth it is at the scene of Joe's funeral—and they discover that Joe's body has been cremated! Back up at the way station, Mr. Jordan assures Joe calmly that they will find another body for Joe's soul to occupy. Joe insists that this new body must be as good as his old body—which was in perfect condition because he was about to become the Ram's starting quarterback.

Mr. Jordan shows Joe a variety of athletes in the moments before their deaths—and Joe rejects them all for one reason or another.

The film clip I chose begins as Mr. Jordan, growing frustrated, urges Joe to "not so much lower as broaden" his standards. Mr. Jordan next takes Joe to a lavish estate in Beverly Hills.

The first man Joe sees he immediately rejects as a replacement body, but Mr. Jordan explains that that man is Tony Abbott (played by Charles Grodin), personal secretary to the owner of the mansion, and that the very agitated woman he's trying to prevent from taking a drink is the rich man's wife, Julia (Dyan Cannon, in a performance that should have won her an Oscar).

Upstairs, in the master bathroom, Joe and Mr. Jordan see—although the audience does not—a man named Leo Farnsworth who has been drugged and is slowly sinking under the water to his death. Mr. Jordan tells Joe that they are watching a murder, that Farnsworth's secretary and his wife are trying to kill him. Mr. Jordan urges Joe to make up his mind quickly because as soon as Farnsworth's body is discovered it will be too late to put Joe's soul into that body. Joe, thinking he can save Farnsworth's life, begins racing through the house, trying to attract the attention of any of the maids or butlers, but they can neither see nor hear Joe, and he must accept the fact that there's nothing he can do to save Farnsworth's life.

While Joe is trying to find some way to save Farnsworth, into the house comes Betty Logan, a lovely young Englishwoman (played by Julie Christie) who insists on seeing Farnsworth. She is determined to prevent him from destroying her small village for the profit of his corporation.

Joe is touched by Betty and her problem, and wants to help her. Mr. Jordan tells him that the only way he can do that is to become Leo Farnsworth. Joe asks if he could become Farnsworth "just for a while." Mr. Jordan tells him that can be arranged.

Upstairs, Joe, now in Farnsworth's body (although we, the audience, see only Warren Beatty) hears Farnsworth's butler knocking on the bathroom door, calling to Farnsworth. Joe doesn't believe he can fool anybody, but Mr. Jordan assures Joe that while Joe will look and sound like himself to himself and to Mr. Jordan, everyone else will see and hear Leo Farnsworth.

In the next few seconds, as Farnsworth's valet dresses him in a polo outfit, complete with mallet and helmet, we—and Joe—learn that Farnsworth was more than a ruthless businessman, he was also a pompous fool. Joe looks at the immaculate and expensive costume he's wearing and asks the butler if he (Farnsworth) plays polo. The butler's simple reply of "Not really, sir" tells us plenty about the late Leo Farnsworth's pretensions.

Farnsworth's imperturbable butler, Fisk, and his stoic valet—and the brilliant comic actors Dyan Cannon and Charles Grodin as Farnsworth's high-strung wife and his hilariously bland secretary—entertain us while we're learning the "rules" of this otherworldly movie: who can see Joe Pendleton and who can only see Farnsworth, and that while Joe now looks like Farnsworth, he's retained his own personality, his decency and genuine desire to help people. We learn what a rat Farnsworth was and why the wife and secretary want him dead.

We also learn a little fact that will turn out to be crucial—that Joe will not remain for the rest of his earthly life in Farnsworth's body. Wondering when Joe will have to give up Farnsworth's body and life adds tension and poignancy to Joe's falling in love with Betty Logan. We worry about when Joe's agreement is going to separate these two likable people—and how they will ever find each other again.

In creating your own great supporting characters, remember that it is the reaction of your supporting characters to your star that helps to *define* your protagonist for the audience. In *Heaven Can Wait* the reactions of these characters tell Joe—and tell us in the audience—who Leo Farnsworth was.

Well-crafted supporting characters allow the audience to see a hidden aspect of the leading character, or help to clarify the leading character's motivation. They can convey exposition in an entertaining way. They can provide light moments or heavy-duty comic relief. They are some of a screenwriter's "best friends."

Certainly one of the most strongly held beliefs among professionals is that there is no place in a modern script for what some producers and directors call "Max the Explainer." Max (and his fictional brothers and sisters) were staples of mystery stories early in this century. This Max character was someone who arrived in the story for the first time in the third act and explained things to the other characters (and sometimes to the audience) that they didn't understand. Max the Explainer wrapped up the loose ends. As audiences became more sophisticated, they no longer were willing to accept this easy but emotionally empty, and oftentimes jarring, form of lazy story construction.

In general, I agree that modern audiences have moved beyond Max, but there remain the occasional, rare, instances when the best way to tell the story requires a modern Max the Explainer.

Absence of Malice

Absence of Malice illustrates that there is no such thing as an immutable rule when it comes to writing. In this very good movie is one of the rare artful examples of Max the Explainer.

This Explainer is the character of James J. Wells, played by that wonderful actor Wilford Brimley. For those of you who have not seen *Absence of Malice* (and I urge every writer to see it) here is a brief synopsis of the story:

Michael Gallager (played by Paul Newman) is a legitimate businessman, but his late father was a bootlegger and his uncle is still involved in some illegal activities. Elliot Rosen (played by Bob Balaban), in charge of Miami's Organized Crime Task Force, tricks local reporter Megan Carter (Sally Field) into printing a story that makes it look as though Michael Gallager is a suspect in the disappearance and probable murder of a popular labor leader. Rosen's motive for this is to force Gallager to help the task force find out who killed the labor leader in exchange for clearing Gallager's name. The plan backfires tragically when Gallager's best friend, Teresa Perone (Melinda Dillon), goes to Megan and tells her that Gallager could not have had anything to do with the labor leader's death because he was with Teresa at the time, out of state. They were together because Gallager—the closest thing she has to an older brother—accompanied Teresa to get an abortion and stayed with her until she recovered from the aftereffects. (The baby was not Gallager's.) Teresa begs Megan to keep what she has told her in confidence because Teresa is a Catholic who works in a Catholic school. In spite of Teresa's plea for confidentiality, Megan prints the story, which exonerates Gallager and includes the story of Teresa's abortion, which is Gallager's alibi. To protect Teresa, Gallager had refused to tell anyone where he was at the time of the labor leader's disappearance. The terrible humiliation of the information about her abortion being made public drives the emotionally fragile Teresa to commit suicide.

Gallager, grieving for sweet, gentle Teresa and furious at the people he holds responsible for her death, hatches a plot to punish them.

When Gallager's trap has been sprung, it is necessary that the people he wants to get back at know that Gallager was the one who brought about their downfall, and why he did it. Enter James J. Wells, assistant attorney general for the Organized Crime Division of the United States Department of Justice.

Wells is the one man with the power to gather all of the people Gallager has entrapped together in one room. He is the one man who can make the guilty pay. In the course of the single sequence in which Wells appears, he forces—by threat of a subpoena and a grand jury appearance—each of the people involved in the plot to ruin Michael Gallager to admit what they did. As they answer questions they, and Wells, suddenly realize the truth, which they will not be able to prove: that Michael Gallager has successfully destroyed their careers. The closest Gallager comes to admitting what he has done is his quiet mention of the name Teresa Perrone.

This climactic third-act scene is a verbal "shoot-out." Because of what he learns through Gallager's machinations, Wells forces the district attorney to resign and fires Elliot Rosen, head of the task force. Wells issues a statement to the press that publicly disgraces Megan Carter for having been tricked by Rosen into writing inappropriate news stories. She decides to quit her job on the paper and to leave town for a while.

Without Wells forcing them to own up and then to pay the price, the people who were responsible for pushing fragile Teresa Perone to kill herself would have walked away unpunished for the human devastation their actions set in motion. Wells is a wonderful character, and the movie is a richer dramatic experience for having this Max the

Explainer in it. Because of its well-drawn characters and lively dialogue, *Absence of Malice* should be on every screenwriter's "must see" list.

Another vital function of a supporting character in a script is to be the person who does or says something to the star that launches the plot into its forward trajectory.

Tootsie

It was Larry Gelbart, one of this great movie's screenwriters, who focused the development of *Tootsie* by voicing what he felt the script was really about: "It's the story of a man who dresses up like a woman and becomes a better man." The director of *Tootsie,* Sydney Pollack, appears in two scenes as George Fields, the agent of actor Michael Dorsey (Dustin Hoffman.) Pollack, a former actor, was so good in the role it prompted one major reviewer to suggest that Pollack be required to perform in all of the movies he directed in the future.

While *Tootsie* offers many pleasures in its writing and its performances (Jessica Lange won her Oscar for Best Supporting Actress in this picture) it is the supporting character, agent George Fields, who speaks the line that hurtles the plot onto its main track, in which the male lead is compelled to impersonate a woman.

Michael Dorsey bursts into his agent's office, interrupting Fields, who's on the phone, with a tirade about not getting a chance to audition for a part because Fields sent another of his clients instead.

Fields tries to reason with Michael, tries to explain that he couldn't set the audition for Michael because Michael has been labeled "trouble." When Michael responds hotly that the man Fields just cited is "an idiot" Fields is forced to be more candid in this lively exchange:

> FIELDS
> They can't all be idiots, Michael. You argue with
> everybody. Nobody in this town, Michael—
> nobody will hire you.

MICHAEL

Are you saying that nobody in New York will work with me?

FIELDS

Oh, no, that's too limited. Nobody in Hollywood wants to work with you either. You played a tomato for 30 seconds—they went half a day over schedule 'cause you wouldn't sit down.

MICHAEL

Yes, it wasn't logical.

FIELDS

Michael! A tomato doesn't have logic! A tomato can't move!

MICHAEL

That's what I said! So if he can't move, how's he gonna sit down, George? I was a stand-up tomato, a juicy, sexy beefsteak tomato.

FIELDS

Michael, I'm trying to stay calm here. You are a wonderful actor.

MICHAEL

Thank you.

FIELDS

But you're too much trouble. Get some therapy.

MICHAEL

Okay, thanks. I'm going to get $8,000 and I'm gonna do Jeff's play.

Michael, you're not gonna raise twenty-five cents.
No one will hire you.

It's that pronouncement from Michael's agent—"No one will hire you"—that drives the actor into a woman's wig, makeup, and clothing to land a part on the soap opera for which Michael had earlier coached his girlfriend.

The girlfriend, played by Teri Garr, didn't get the part, but we saw Michael working hard with her, and carefully explaining the role. Because it was clear that he was doing his best to help her, later, when Michael himself wins the part, we feel no twinge of distaste, no nagging feeling that somehow Michael "stole" the part from the actress.

Michael's prior knowledge and understanding of the role the soap opera's director and producer are trying to cast help us believe that Michael Dorsey would be able to come to that audition and do the part so well he would win it.

That's another example of expert professional storytelling craft, which can be reduced to an easy-to-remember rule: If you want us to believe something extraordinary or outrageous, *lay a foundation for it early*. Then we, the readers and the audience, will willingly make that leap of belief with you when the time comes.

To carry this point about laying a foundation a bit further:

A good visual example of this can be found in *Outrageous Fortune,* the comedy that stars Bette Midler and Shelly Long as two wildly different women who discover to their horror that simultaneously they have been having an affair with the same man.

At the beginning of the movie we see Shelly Long in a ballet class. She's a little too mature for a career in ballet, and not a very good dancer, but the one thing she can do is leap. We *think* this brief ballet class scene is just setting up the type of comic character she is—but during the climactic chase in the movie's third act, that subtly established ability to leap saves her life and sets in motion the chain of events that leads to the capture of the bad guys. We were set up for this, but—as in the best-laid foundations—we were not aware at the time that a foundation was being laid. That's clever storytelling.

Midnight Run

When George Gallo, writer of *Midnight Run,* visited one of my classes as a guest speaker, among the things he shared with us was the fact that his marvelous supporting character Marvin Dorfler—who functions in the story as both a crude contrast to and as an added complication for Robert De Niro's character, Jack Walsh—was killed off in the original screenplay. During production, when the filmmakers saw how wonderful actor John Ashton was in the role, they decided to let Dorfler live. George rewrote the script so that when Dorfler is captured by the bad guys in Las Vegas, he's left handcuffed to a motel toilet instead of shot dead.

The fact that Dorfler was still alive then presented George with the opportunity to bring him back into the story for one last sequence. The result was that the exciting climax in Las Vegas's McCarren Airport was made even better by the unexpected complication Dorfler provides by showing up and bumbling into the middle of the action, almost ruining everything for the good guys.

You'll find a detailed sequence breakdown of George Gallo's *Midnight Run* in the next chapter, "How to Build Your Screenplay." I use it to illustrate how to write a story point treatment, which is a skill you will need to develop in order to "build" your own screenplays from concept to completion.

7. How to Build Your Screenplay

You've watched movies and TV shows all of your life. You're certain you can write better dialogue than a lot of what you hear coming from highly paid screen and television writers. You have ideas for exciting stories. You've studied professional screenplay format so that you know all about slug lines and transitions, the dos and don'ts of screenwriting, and how to create interesting, complex leading and supporting characters.

Now: How do you put the various parts of the screenwriter's craft together to create a script so well constructed that it grabs the attention and keeps the interest of the agents, producers, directors, and stars to whom it will be submitted?

That is the subject of this chapter.

Very few writers are able to just sit down and write a screenplay from FADE IN to FADE OUT without having first worked out the details of the story in the form of a treatment. Personally, I don't know any screenwriters who skip the treatment step of the process without soon finding themselves in a kind of creative quagmire. Imagine if you will carpenters building a house without working from a blueprint. It's entirely possible that the result would be a second story that is larger than the first, or some other structural catastrophe. It would then take longer to rip out the structural mistakes and rebuild properly than it would have if the builder had taken the time to design a blueprint first. A treatment is the screenwriter's blueprint. It is in the treatment that you work out the storytelling problems, so that when you begin the actual script you have the confidence of knowing what you are doing. This is not to say that, in the actual writing of the script, you won't decide to depart in places from the treatment. Departing from original conceptions is part of the creative process when better ideas occur, but having a detailed blueprint keeps the writer from going so far afield that the structure collapses.

Writers at the beginning of their careers are sometimes intimidated by the idea of doing a treatment because they either don't know what a treatment should look like, or don't fully understand that there is more than one kind of treatment from which to choose.

There are three types of treatment, and this chapter will demonstrate them all:

1. The **story point** treatment. This is a list of sequences that tell the story in skeletal form. I have found that this is the least intimidating type of treatment because it is not "writing," it is "list making." Anyone can make a list—right? Besides, this type of treatment is just for the use of the writer—no one else will ever see it, so you don't need to worry about proper spelling and grammar, and you don't need to use complete sentences as long as you know what you mean. (Caution: If you do intend to show this style of treatment to other people, then you should definitely use proper spelling, grammar, and complete sentences.)

2. The **scenario** treatment is a miniscript. It contains all of the slug lines, a brief synopsis of what each scene accomplishes and what characters are in it, but there is no—or very little—dialogue. This is the most difficult treatment to write, but if you choose to do your treatment in this style it will enable you to write the script in a matter of *days*. Before you sit down to type FADE IN you will have worked out the locations and settings and the intentions of the scenes, so all you have to do now is fill in the dialogue.

3. The **narrative** treatment. In this type of treatment the characters are described and the plot is related in a kind of long short story.

Now here is a paradox, for those of you who enjoy a good paradox:

If you are hired to write a screenplay on assignment and the producer or executive hiring you requires that you deliver a treatment first, the narrative treatment is usually what they mean. When a treatment is *requested,* the screen story told in narrative is what is meant, unless another form is specified. However, if you prefer (as do I) to write a spec or an assigned screenplay from either the story point or the scenario-style treatment, then I recommend you suggest this to the person who will be paying you.

There is hidden danger in writing a narrative-style treatment, and it is a danger to both the writer and to the entity paying the writer. By that I mean, certain events can be made to sound simple to execute when they are written in narrative story form, but they can later prove to be difficult to dramatize in the screenplay. You might want to discuss this in your meeting, prior to beginning work.

If a narrative treatment is required, it is probably because that document must be shown to a third party by the producer or the executive for whom you are executing the script. If you agree—or if you *prefer*—to write a narrative treatment, please remember that those pages will be regarded as a kind of writing sample. Unless you use all of your prose skills to tell the story in a compelling manner you may find that your employer, even though she likes your characters and your plot, decides that your writing skills are not up to delivering a polished screenplay. The result may be that you are cut off after payment for the treatment. Don't waste time complaining that this is not fair—it is a reality of the business. Accept this reality and get into the habit of writing anything that you plan to show to an employer at the absolute top of your creative ability. There are two benefits to doing that. Not only will you make a good impression by not letting anyone—ever—see something that is less than your best at that moment, but setting high performance standards will be much better for you as a writer. I can't imagine that I will live long enough to be as good a writer as I want to be, but every day that I try to the best of my ability will move me a little closer. And I have found that there is an almost spiritual joy in doing my best with each stage of every assignment.

Examples of the Three Styles of Screenplay Treatment

To illustrate the story point treatment I have chosen *Midnight Run,* a film that you can either rent or buy on videocassette to study. The straightforward, linear screenplay was written by George Gallo. The film stars Robert De Niro and Charles Grodin, and was directed by Martin Brest.

As you will see, in *Midnight Run* every scene either deepens our understanding of the main characters or moves the story forward, or both. Contrary to what you may have heard elsewhere, it is not necessary that *every* scene move the story forward. A scene that enlightens us about the characters, that helps to involve us emotionally with the people in the story, is just as worthy of inclusion in the screenplay as a scene that propels the plot toward the conclusion. But each scene should do one or both of those things. If, in developing your screenplay, you find that you have scenes that perform neither of those tasks, it is likely that those scenes should be deleted.

An important reason that I use *Midnight Run* as an example of a film to study is that it provides a superb example of how to parcel out exposition in the form of entertainment. Working exposition (that is, information we need to know) into a screenplay is one of the most difficult skills a screenwriter has to learn.

Before I demonstrate the story point treatment by listing the sequences in *Midnight Run,* it's important for you to understand the underlying motivation that drives the actions of Jonathan Mardukas, the character played by Charles Grodin. Being aware of this will allow you to understand more clearly how to write a story point treatment of your own.

Mardukas was an innocent accountant who did not know that he had been working for the mob. When he discovered that he had been lied to and that actually he was in the employ of ruthless Las Vegas crime lord Jimmy Serrano, Mardukas disappeared with $15 million of Serrano's money, most of which Mardukas promptly gave away to charities.

Four separate entities are after Mardukas: Walsh, working on behalf of Eddie Moscone, the bail bondsman, who will be wiped out unless Mardukas is returned to police custody within five days; Marvin Dorfler, the second bounty hunter that Moscone, in his panic, has put on the case; mobster Jimmy Serrano; and the FBI. (The FBI wants Mardukas because of what he knows about Serrano's operations. They want Mardukas to help them bring criminal charges against Serrano that will put him behind bars.)

Mardukas knows that he will be murdered directly by Serrano's thugs if they get him first, and that he will be murdered by people paid by Serrano if he ends up in either police or FBI custody. His only chance to survive is to get away from Walsh and disappear again. Mardukas is no match for Walsh physically, so he first tries to bribe Walsh, but we learn that Walsh doesn't take bribes.

Mardukas realizes that his only hope for survival is to persuade Walsh to let him go, but Walsh is a consummate pro at his job; he's not about to let the fleeing felon he's caught get away. So Mardukas tries to break through the cement wall Walsh has built around his feelings, to get Walsh to see him (Mardukas) as a good man in trouble. Mardukas hopes that if the two of them can make a human connection Walsh will not deliver Mardukas into the hands of his killers. Walsh doesn't want to get to know Mardukas—the accountant is just a job for him, the last job Walsh plans to do as a bounty hunter. But Mardukas won't be discouraged. He begins to dig and pry and drag out personal information from Walsh. That is what Mardukas's constant questioning of Walsh is all about: Mardukas is desperate to reach Walsh on a human level. He knows it's his *only* chance to live. And yet none of this is ever stated in so many words. George Gallo's skill was in letting us figure out from his behavior what is going on inside the head of Jonathan Mardukas.

A Story Point Treatment for *Midnight Run*

1. In the opening sequence Jack Walsh is in the hallway of a slum building, stopping at a particular door to pick the lock—and almost getting blasted by a shotgun fired at him through that door. Walsh bursts into the room, sees a man fleeing out the window, and chases him down into the alley. Before he can catch the running man, a car comes along and the driver opens the door—smashing the running man in the stomach and knocking him to the ground. The driver steps out. Walsh recognizes the driver as Marvin Dorfler, and we learn that Walsh and Dorfler are competitors. Dorfler grabs the man he's knocked to the ground and tries to take him away from Walsh. Walsh tricks Dorfler, knocks him out, handcuffs the man he was after, and drives away with him in Dorfler's car, saying to Dorfler that he'll bring the car back.

2. At the police station, where the man Walsh caught is being booked, we learn that the man is a felon who jumped bail and that Walsh is a bounty hunter. (Most important: In these two sequences we see that Walsh is thoroughly professional at his job, that he uses only necessary force—nothing excessive. In contrast, Dorfler is rough and crude and would rather knock his prey unconscious.)

3. In Los Angeles, Walsh goes to the office of Eddie Moscone, the bail bondsman who hired him, to collect his fee. (Here we meet Moscone, and his assistant, Jerry.) Moscone tries to get out of paying Walsh the $1,200 he promised, but Walsh won't take less than what was agreed to. Moscone invites Walsh over to the nearby Chinese restaurant where he wants to talk to him—and where he'll give Walsh his money.

4. At the Chinese restaurant Moscone asks if Walsh has read about the mob accountant, Jonathan Mardukas. Walsh has. Moscone says that he didn't know who Mardukas was until after he bailed him out for $450,000. Now Mardukas has disappeared, and if he's not back in police custody in five days, Moscone will lose the money and be out

of business. Through Moscone's dialogue, we learn that Walsh was a cop in Chicago but lost his job because the mob boss from whom Mardukas embezzled the money (Jimmy Serrano) was the same man who ran Walsh out of Chicago. Walsh agrees to find and return Mardukas before the deadline for $100,000—it will be his last job. He wants to get out of the bounty-hunter business. Reluctantly, Moscone agrees to the fee. And the story "clock" is running.

5. Walsh goes to the police station, where a friend of his lets Walsh examine the booking slip made out when Mardukas was arrested. Walsh sees that Mardukas called a New York City phone number. (On the way into the station we see the first visual reference to the watch Walsh wears that doesn't keep the right time. This will be a running bit and pay off at the end of the story.)

6. Outside the police station Walsh meets Alonzo Mosely, FBI agent, and some of his agent underlings. Mosely wants to know if Walsh is going after Mardukas, and tells him to stay out of it, that the FBI wants Mardukas so they can bring down Serrano. Walsh is uncooperative, and makes fun of the sunglasses that the FBI men wear. Angry, Mosely has Walsh ejected from the FBI car—and as they drive away, we see that Walsh has lifted Mosely's FBI identification.

7. On a plane to New York, Walsh carefully replaces Mosely's picture on the ID with Walsh's own picture.

8. At a telephone booth in the New York airport, Walsh calls someone and gets the address for the phone number on Mardukas's booking slip. Off the phone, Walsh is accosted by two of Serrano's thugs, who also think Mardukas is in New York. We learn more about Walsh's past with Serrano in Chicago here. (Serrano now operates out of Las Vegas.) The thugs offer Walsh a million-dollar bribe, which Walsh refuses. One of the thugs (Tony) gives Walsh a book of matches with his phone number in Vegas on it, tells him to call when he's ready to make a deal.

9. In a car outside a New York town house, Walsh waits until a woman returns to the house and goes inside. He sets a tape recorder and calls her from a nearby phone booth. When she hangs up, he re-

turns to his car and sees that the little machine is recording the number *she* calls.

10. That night, outside another town house, Walsh waits until it's late, then picks the locks and enters quietly. (We have no trouble believing how he found Mardukas because, earlier, he got an address from a phone number. We just assume that's how he did it this time, since the foundation for the belief has been laid.)

11. In the house, Walsh identifies himself as Mosely from the FBI, cuffs Mardukas, and takes him away.

12. Driving in the car, Mardukas realizes they are not going to the FBI offices, but to the airport. Walsh explains he's not one of Serrano's men, he's a bounty hunter hired by the man who put up the bail for Mardukas. Walsh refuses Mardukas's offer of a bribe. Mardukas protests that he can't go on an airplane because he's afraid to fly.

13. From the airport, Walsh calls Moscone, tells him he has Mardukas and they'll be at the Los Angeles airport late that night. We learn here that the FBI is tapping Moscone's phone and has heard the call.

14. At the FBI office, Mosely is told that Walsh has Mardukas and they'll be back in Los Angeles in a few hours.

15. In Moscone's office, Jerry says he's going out for doughnuts, but calls Serrano's men from the corner phone booth to tip them off.

16. Here we meet Serrano, the villain, as Serrano is told that Walsh and Mardukas will arrive by plane in Los Angeles in a few hours.

17. On the plane as it prepares for takeoff, Mardukas throws a "fear-of-flying" fit and Walsh and Mardukas are thrown off the plane.

18. Walsh, furious, boards the train with Mardukas—and says he'll still make the deadline of Friday night with fourteen hours to spare.

19. In Los Angeles later Mosely discovers that Walsh and Mardukas were not on the plane, and that Walsh is using Mosely's name and ID.

20. In Vegas, Serrano learns that Walsh and Mardukas weren't on the plane.

21. On the train, Mardukas, trying to dig personal information out of Walsh, learns that Walsh plans to buy a coffee shop with the money

he makes from returning Mardukas to custody. Mardukas, ever the accountant, warns Walsh about the riskiness of such an investment.

22. In Los Angeles, Moscone learns Walsh and Mardukas weren't on the plane, panics, and has Jerry call Dorfler, who's in Pittsburgh.

23. In a motel room in Pittsburgh, with his own felon handcuffed, Dorfler takes the deal Moscone offers, $25,000. (Moscone told him that's what he promised to pay Walsh.) Dorfler never heard of Mardukas, but he looks in his book, calls a credit card company pretending to be Walsh, says he lost his card, and asks where was the last place he used it. The card company says "Amtrak, in New York City." Dorfler then cancels the card and lets his own felon go.

24. Walsh and Mardukas have dinner on the train. Mardukas criticizes what Walsh eats, offers to work out a low-cholesterol diet for him. Mardukas learns about Walsh's ex-wife and his daughter, that Walsh hasn't seen them in nine years. Mardukas learns more about Walsh—and tells Walsh he (Mardukas) will die if he goes to jail, so he'll have to give Walsh "the slip." Then he criticizes the size of the tip Walsh leaves, correcting Walsh's mistake in mathematics.

25. Dorfler gets on the train, finds Walsh, and tries to steal Mardukas. Dorfler and Walsh fight; Walsh wins, and tells the porter to alert the police to arrest Dorfler at the next stop.

26. Mosely learns Walsh and Mardukas are on the train, and orders the jet to be made ready.

27. Mosely and his agents meet the train and discover Walsh and Mardukas are gone.

28. From a phone booth in Ohio, Walsh calls Moscone. He's angry that Moscone put Dorfler on the case, and tells Moscone they're getting on a bus. The FBI stakeout overhears the call. When Jerry goes out to call Serrano's men, the FBI men see Jerry calling from the corner phone booth.

29. At the bus station in Ohio, Walsh learns his credit card's been canceled. He uses the money he has left and what Mardukas has in his wallet and buys tickets for them to Chicago.

30. Dorfler's in police custody. Mosely arrives and questions him about Walsh.

31. On the bus to Chicago, Mardukas tries to get Walsh to quit smoking. Mardukas suggests they look up Walsh's ex-wife and his daughter when they stop over in Chicago. We learn Walsh's ex married a Chicago police lieutenant.

32. Back in the police station, Mosely is informed Walsh is on the bus. He leaves Dorfler and tells the police to let Dorfler go.

33. On the bus, Mardukas digs at Walsh for more information.

34. In Vegas, Serrano meets with his lawyer, who's very worried about what Mardukas knows. Serrano assures him "Everything will be all right in a few minutes."

35. Serrano's men arrive as the bus pulls into the Chicago depot. There are snipers on the roof. As they get off the bus, Walsh and Mardukas are captured by the FBI. Serrano's men attack. In the shoot-out between the FBI and Serrano's men, Walsh and Mardukas escape in Mosely's FBI car.

36. In the car, Walsh discovers the log book and learns that the FBI has a tap on Moscone's phone.

37. In Vegas, Serrano's men report Walsh and Mardukas have escaped. Serrano goes ballistic, says he should have killed Walsh back in Chicago years earlier.

38. Walsh and Mardukas abandon the stolen FBI car. As they leave it, Walsh puts his own sunglasses on the steering wheel as a kind of signature. Because he made fun of the FBI sunglasses, Walsh knows Mosely will know that Walsh has left his sunglasses there to tweak Mosely.

39. Walsh and Mardukas take a cab to the home of Walsh's ex-wife, Gail. He meets Gail's son by her current husband and asks to borrow money. There is a lot of unfinished business and hostility between Walsh and Gail, and we learn that Gail has married a crooked cop who's now a captain. As Mardukas tries to make peace, Walsh's twelve-year-old daughter appears in the door. He's deeply moved by the sight of her, but hardly knows what to say. Gail only has $40 in cash, but she gives Walsh the keys to her station wagon so they can get away.

40. As they are about to leave in the station wagon, Walsh's daughter runs out of the house and tries to give him the $180 she has saved

in baby-sitting money. Walsh thanks her, but he won't take her money. (We sense this is because he's not sure he's going to live long enough to pay it back—although this is unspoken.)

41. Walsh makes a phone call from a booth to Moscone, demanding money and telling Moscone about the tap on Moscone's phone. Walsh tells him to go to the Chinese restaurant and he'll call Moscone there in five minutes.

42. Moscone races to the restaurant phone. Walsh tells Moscone to wire them $500 to Western Union in Amarillo, Texas—as far as they will be able to get with Gail's $40.

43. In Moscone's office, Moscone instructs Jerry to wire the money to Walsh in Amarillo—and to get Dorfler.

44. As Walsh drives, Mardukas digs more of the back story out of Walsh. We learn that when Walsh wouldn't take bribes in Chicago, a big drug dealer planted drugs on Walsh, which got him kicked off the force. The dealer was Serrano. This explains why Walsh is now a bounty hunter.

45. In Amarillo, at a diner, they only have enough money left for a cup of coffee for Walsh and tea for Mardukas. It's ten minutes before 9 A.M. Walsh tells Mardukas that they will have the money in ten minutes, when Western Union opens, and then he'll buy Mardukas anything he wants for breakfast. Mardukas tells Walsh how much he knows about Serrano's businesses—and that he was about to put that information on computer disks, but didn't have a chance. He tells Walsh that he didn't know he was working for the mob, but when he found out, that's when he took the money to give to charity and ran. He tells Walsh again that he (Mardukas) will be killed in jail by Serrano's men—that there's no way he won't be found in the witness protection program—that his only hope to stay alive is to disappear again.

46. Serrano's men arrive and wait outside Western Union. As Walsh and Mardukas arrive, Serrano's thugs grab them. Dorfler arrives and takes Walsh and Mardukas from Serrano's men. As Dorfler smashes the thugs, Walsh handcuffs himself to Mardukas and throws the key down a sewer grate, so Dorfler must take them both in Dorfler's car.

47. In the car, Walsh tells Dorfler that Dorfler's just knocked out mob guys and learns Moscone put Dorfler on the job. Suddenly a helicopter starts shooting at Dorfler's car. In the ensuing car chase, Dorfler's vehicle crashes. Walsh unlocks Mardukas's cuff (Walsh actually threw a car key down the grate, not the handcuff key) and pushes Mardukas into the river to get him out of the line of fire. Walsh gets a gun from Dorfler and shoots down the helicopter, which crashes. Walsh hits Dorfler and handcuffs Dorfler to the door of Dorfler's car, then jumps into the river after Mardukas.

48. In the river, Walsh and Mardukas fight the strong current, trying to get to shore. Mardukas makes it to safety first and offers to help Walsh out of the river if Walsh promises to let Mardukas go. Walsh promises, but once out of the river takes Mardukas back into custody.

49. The police find Dorfler handcuffed to the car.

50. Mosely learns of the escape of Walsh and Mardukas.

51. Walsh and Mardukas, hungry and tired, walk and talk about food. A truck driven by and full of Native Americans comes along, gives them a ride in the back.

52. In Vegas, the thugs return. We learn the helicopter gunship that Walsh sent down in flames carried Serrano's men.

53. The truck takes Walsh and Mardukas to a tiny town populated by Native Americans. It has no phone. Mardukas spots an old prop plane and escapes in it. Walsh discovers that not only is Mardukas not afraid to fly, he's actually a pilot. Walsh grabs at the plane, hangs on, hits Mardukas, and drags him out of the plane before it is fully airborne.

54. Walsh wants to take an old rattletrap truck for transportation. He has no money, so he trades Mardukas's watch for it.

55. Traveling in the truck, Walsh and Mardukas argue about who lied to whom first. Walsh's ulcer starts acting up, but they have no money to buy milk to soothe it. Mardukas promises that in the next town he'll get milk for Walsh.

56. In the next town, using Mosely's FBI badge, Mardukas, with Walsh's help, cons a bar owner out of several $20 bills he says are counterfeit.

57. Walsh and Mardukas buy food with the scammed money—then run to catch a freight train that's starting to move.

58. The bar owner sees these two "FBI men" running for the train and makes a phone call.

59. Mardukas tries to keep Walsh off the train, but Walsh gets on and recaptures Mardukas.

60. Dorfler is in police custody and Mosely arrives again. Mosely gets word of the $20-bill scam and that the fugitives caught the freight train.

61. On the train, knowing time is running out for him, Mardukas tries again to connect with Walsh. He makes jokes, makes Walsh laugh, digs out more of Walsh's personal story. Here we learn the meaning of the watch Walsh wears that doesn't keep time: It was a present from ex-wife Gail, who set it a half hour early because Walsh was always a half hour late. Walsh confesses that he used to think that they would get back together some day. Mardukas suggests that since it doesn't look as though Walsh and Gail will ever get back together, it's time Walsh got another watch.

62. As Dorfler is given back his personal effects by the police, he learns that Mosely and the FBI men went to Flagstaff, Arizona.

63. The next morning, on the train, Walsh tells Mardukas they are somewhere in Arizona. Mardukas tells Walsh that he's going to die in custody, at the hands of the man—Serrano—who ruined Walsh's life.

64. Walsh and Mardukas jump from the train before it pulls into the next stop.

65. FBI and the police wait for the train. Dorfler arrives in his car as it pulls in. No Walsh and Mardukas.

66. Walsh and Mardukas are in a small town. Walsh hot-wires a truck and steals it.

67. Local police start following the stolen truck with Walsh and Mardukas.

68. Mosely is told where Walsh and Mardukas are. He orders a helicopter.

69. Police cars chase Walsh and Mardukas in the stolen truck. Dorfler in his car and Mosely in the helicopter follow.

70. Walsh suddenly tears across country in a scene of wild off-road driving. Cop cars follow and both the truck and the cop cars crash. The helicopter and Dorfler still follow.

71. Walsh and Mardukas escape on foot. They are recaptured by Dorfler, who knocks Walsh down and takes Mardukas.

72. Walsh is alone in a diner when suddenly a pair of sunglasses come sliding down the counter to stop in front of him. He turns to see Mosely and his men. Mosely has returned Walsh's glasses to him as a "gotcha" to Walsh, echoing Walsh's leaving the glasses on Mosely's steering wheel, continuing the running gag with the sunglasses. Walsh is taken into custody by Mosely.

73. Dorfler takes Mardukas to a small private airport and knocks him out.

74. At the FBI office, Mosely questions Walsh and allows him to make a call. Walsh calls Moscone.

75. Moscone tells Walsh he has only five hours left to deliver Mardukas. Walsh is surprised—he thought Dorfler had taken Mardukas to Moscone. Moscone tells Walsh that Dorfler doesn't have Mardukas.

76. Walsh hangs up, thinks, figures out what happened, and finds the matches Tony (Serrano's thug) gave him with his telephone number. Walsh calls the thug and discovers that Dorfler is now working for Serrano.

77. Walsh tells the thug to tell Serrano that Walsh has the computer disks with all of the information on Serrano's illegal business dealings. He will trade the disks to Serrano at McCarren Airport in Las Vegas for custody of Mardukas. Walsh hangs up and tells Mosely that he wants to make a deal. Walsh tells Mosely he will deliver Serrano to the FBI (and lists the charges on which they can get Serrano) if Mosely will let Walsh take Mardukas back to Los Angeles and Moscone so that Walsh can collect his bounty money. He'll explain his plan on the way, but now they've got to get to Las Vegas's McCarren Airport in two hours.

78. Dorfler has Mardukas handcuffed in the bathroom of a Vegas motel. He takes a Polaroid of Mardukas holding that day's paper.

79. On the plane to Vegas, Walsh and Mosely work out a plan to catch Serrano at the airport.

80. Serrano's thugs meet Dorfler, who shows them the Polaroid of Mardukas, but demands $2 million dollars for him. Tony knocks out Dorfler when he sees the name of the motel on the towels in the picture of Mardukas. They go to get Mardukas.

81. Serrano makes plans to get the computer disks from Walsh, and then kill both Walsh and Mardukas. He and his men leave for McCarren.

82. FBI cars follow Serrano's car.

83. Mosely has a "wire" put on Walsh. Walsh remarks that it makes him feel like a cop again.

84. Outside McCarren, in a car, Serrano meets Mardukas and tells him he'll die that night, and then Serrano will find and kill Mardukas's wife.

85. Inside McCarren: The FBI is ready, listening to the "wire" on Walsh. Serrano approaches Walsh and demands the disks. Walsh won't give them until he has Mardukas. Serrano tries to bait Walsh, but Walsh won't blow up. Mardukas arrives and Walsh puts Mardukas behind him. Dorfler shows up at the airport to buy a ticket to Los Angeles, sees Mardukas, and rushes into the middle of Walsh's plan. He interrupts the exchange. Walsh's wire goes bad. Serrano snatches the disks from Walsh, but the FBI can't hear Walsh telling them to move in on Serrano. Walsh shouts it out, and there's a melee. Serrano and the thugs are caught by the FBI. Dorfler is taken in by the FBI and Walsh takes Mardukas back to Los Angeles.

86. A silent scene between Walsh and Mardukas on the plane to L.A.

87. At the Los Angeles airport, Walsh calls Moscone and tells him he has Mardukas and has made it back before the deadline.

88. Moscone tells Walsh that the feds arrested Jerry.

89. Walsh lets Moscone hear Mardukas's voice, then tells Moscone that he's letting Mardukas go and hangs up.

90. Walsh completed the mission, getting Mardukas back in time.

But Walsh knows Mardukas is right, that he will be killed if he's taken to jail. Walsh tells Mardukas that it would have been a nice coffee shop . . . Then Walsh gives Mardukas a souvenir of their five-day adventure, the watch that Gail once gave Walsh. Mardukas has a gift for Walsh, a money belt with $300,000 in $1,000 bills. It's not a bribe, Mardukas explains, because Walsh already let him go. Walsh is persuaded and accepts the gift. Walsh turns away for a moment, and when he turns back, Mardukas has vanished.

91. Walsh can't find a cab that can change a $1,000 bill. He starts walking . . . FADE OUT

I suggest you watch *Midnight Run* again to see how the individual scenes are written and played.

As you can see by studying the foregoing list of story points, we learn Walsh's back story as the present-day plot is moving forward. Let's review briefly how two little bits that are planted early in the story pay off effectively by the end.

1. Mardukas tells Walsh he was planning to put the information that would convict Serrano on computer disks but didn't have time before he was arrested. Later, Walsh uses that by *pretending* to Serrano that Mardukas actually made such disks. This is the trick he uses to get Serrano to give him Mardukas, as well as the lure he uses to trick Serrano into committing crimes on federal property (McCarren Airport) for which the FBI can then charge him.

2. The watch Walsh wears that never has the right time. We learn why Walsh wears it, and what it means to him. At the end, when Walsh gives the watch to Mardukas as a souvenir, we understand that Walsh has finally accepted the loss of Gail and is going to move on.

The Scenario-Style Treatment

The scenario-style treatment is really a mini-screenplay. To be more precise, it is a screenplay in everything except dialogue, dynamic narrative writing, and atmospheric details. In the scenario-style treatment, each setting is included and under each slug line there is a brief synopsis of the scene which includes these three vital elements:

1. Who is in the scene
2. What actions occur
3. What information is conveyed

Remember that while scenario-style treatments take the longest amount of time to write, when one is finished, writing a screenplay from that type of treatment is very fast. The writer has already worked out many storytelling problems, so most of what is left to be done is filling in dramatic narrative and adding the dialogue. Because it is very difficult to imagine exactly how this style of treatment should look by describing it, here is an example.

What follows are a few scenes from a scenario-style treatment that I wrote, working from a story by writers Rod Amateau and Harold Nebenzal. The title of the script is *The Diamond Traders*.

FADE IN:

MAIN TITLE AND STAR CREDITS ARE SUPERIMPOSED OVER:

EXT. SCHWECHAT AIRPORT, VIENNA—NIGHT

An AUSTRIAN AIRLINES' EUROBUS lands and PIERRE LATOUCHE deplanes. He's a very attractive, charismatic man who carries a jeweler's case that has been fitted with a high-security lock.

Two female flight attendants closely follow Pierre as he crosses the tarmac to the terminal. They are attracted to Pierre and would like to connect with him, but he is paying no attention to them.

INT. AIRPORT VISITOR'S AREA—NIGHT

Pierre is looking for someone he does not find. One of the female flight attendants offers him a lift into the city. Pierre declines, explaining that his wife is meeting him. The two women express disappointment that he's both married and faithful. Suddenly two men with badges approach, identify themselves as Customs Officers, and insist that Pierre accompany them. The female flight attendants hurry away in fear.

END CREDITS as Pierre is politely but firmly led away.

INT. CUSTOMS OFFICE—NIGHT

Customs Officers examine Pierre's passport, question him about his being in Antwerp for the previous three days. He's impatient, concerned that his wife won't be able to find him. The Officers insist he open his briefcase. He's reluctant, but is told things will go faster if he cooperates. He agrees and we see that Pierre is carrying a magnificent collection of Diamonds. The Officers immediately confiscate the diamonds in the name of the Tax Bureau. Pierre, knowing he's innocent of wrongdoing, protests and telephones his lawyer, Dr. Tranck. The Officers give him a receipt for the diamonds and tell Pierre to report to the Tax Bureau next morning.

EXT. AN ELEGANT OLD BUILDING IN
VIENNA—NIGHT

Pierre's office is here. Establish and describe.

INT. ELEGANT OLD BUILDING—NIGHT

Pierre arrives at his 4th-floor office to discover a dozen Tax Officials searching it. Pierre's attorney, Dr. Tranck, a wily old fox, is there. Tranck is angry but controlling himself. He's relieved to see Pierre arrive. The Tax Officials take diamonds from the premises and give Pierre a receipt. Pierre is shocked to discover that this receipt doesn't look like the receipt he was given at the airport. The Tax Official in charge examines the two receipts and gives Pierre some bad news: the receipt he got at the airport is fraudulent. Pierre realizes he has been robbed of a fortune.

EXT. STREET OUTSIDE LATOUCHE HOME—NIGHT

Establish one of the most beautiful residential streets in Vienna. His house and grounds are magnificent. Pierre and Tranck arrive in Tranck's car, get out, and go inside the house.

INT. GRAND FOYER/LIVING ROOM OF LATOUCHE HOME—NIGHT

Another horrible shock for Pierre: His house has been stripped of paintings and furnishing. His immediate reaction is terror that something has happened to his wife, Barbara, and their children. Pierre's houseman and cook give Pierre more bad news: Barbara has taken the children and their valuable possessions and left voluntarily in the company of an American man. The description of the man they give Pierre makes him realize that his wife and children have departed with an American gangster named Joe Di Franco.

EXT. TRANCK'S APARTMENT BUILDING IN VIENNA—LATE NIGHT

Establish a splendid old building. As Pierre and Tranck arrive we learn in brief (V.O.) dialogue that Tranck blames himself for persuading Pierre to put Pierre's business and bank accounts in Barbara's name.

INT. TRANCK'S LIVING ROOM—LATE NIGHT

Full of ancient art, museum-quality antiquities. Tranck and a despondent Pierre drink and talk. Pierre is in so much emotional pain that the more he drinks the more sober he becomes. In this conversation we learn that Pierre doesn't blame Tranck for putting his wealth in Barbara's name, that he saw the tax benefits for himself. He loved and trusted Barbara. Tranck observes that women are "God's dirty joke on Man." We learn that Joe Di Franco was Barbara's first husband, whom she divorced just before he went to prison for a long sentence. He should still be there. Tranck observes: "Americans are peculiar. They let bad men out of prison years early for 'good behavior.' And the first thing this one does is steal everything that was yours." Pierre tells Tranck that Di Franco vowed he would destroy Pierre. Now, suddenly, with no warning, Pierre has lost his diamonds and his family, and is about to go to jail on a false tax-evasion charge. Against Tranck's official advice as his lawyer, but with Tranck's unofficial blessing as his friend, Pierre decides to flee the country.

In the above example of the scenario treatment we have quickly established the protagonist (Pierre) as very attractive to women but loyal to his wife. This was done by creating the two pretty flight attendants who would like to tempt him, but whom he resists. Then we quickly throw one shock after another at Pierre. These losses are so serious that he must flee his country to avoid false imprisonment. If you want to sprinkle a little sample of dialogue in—I like to—do it by placing the few spoken sentences inside quotation marks.

The Narrative-Style Treatment

The most traditional type of treatment is the narrative-style treatment, which tells the story that will become a screenplay in descriptive prose, as though you were writing a longish short story. This narrative style treatment is the one you are most likely to use if you are writing a treatment as part of a screenwriting assignment for which you are being paid. This treatment describes the characters and the events of the story, and, if it includes some bits of dialogue, that dialogue is written as it would be in a novel, with quotation marks around the spoken words. Here is a sample, excerpted from the treatment for the screenplay version of my first novel, *Runaway*.

Thirteen year old Freddie Robinson, I.Q. 167, was alone in his perfectly decorated bedroom in San Francisco, working out the last details of his kidnapping. He was already halfway through a pile of old magazines and newspapers as slowly, one word at a time Freddie clipped, pasted, and completed his ransom note. He was wearing a pair of his mother's white cotton beauty gloves so that he wouldn't leave his fingerprints on the paper.

As Freddie worked he fantasized the scene when the FBI man came to the house:

"These people will want the $500,000 in small, used bills, Mr. Robinson. No consecutive serial numbers. If you'll have your bank prepare the cash, I'll take it to General Delivery in Dallas." Suddenly the FBI man noticed the dubious expression on the father's face. "What's the problem, Mr. Robinson?"

"I'm not sure we should pay the money."

"What?! But you must! It's for your son!"

Freddie's father was squirming, but holding firm. "You see, I don't really know the boy very well. Is he worth half a million dollars? I mean, it's hard to get liquid right now. Do you know what happens when you try to sell in a falling market? Now, if this could just wait a month or two—"

The FBI man grabbed Freddie's father by the shoulders and shook him roughly. "I'm going to get the money for the ransom myself, Mr. Robinson. We have a miscellaneous fund at the Bureau for emergencies not covered by the rule book. I'm going to get Freddie back, and when I do I'm going to start legal action to adopt him. He's just the sort of son I've always wanted!"

"Aw, hell," Freddie said, shattering the fantasy. The last word was glued into place and the note was finished.

Freddie slipped the note into a plain envelope, opened the door, and slipped silently down the hall to his mother's empty bedroom. It was time to commit grand larceny.

Three thousand miles across the country, in a diner near to the Harrisburg, Pennsylvania, bus terminal a beautiful fifteen-year-old light-skinned black girl named Sara Lee and a very thin, mute eight-year-old white child named Gailie were eating the most delicious doughnuts they had ever tasted. The few coins that remained in Sara Lee's pocket had only been able to buy them two large Cokes, but the middle-aged waitress with the faded bruised-peach looks had brought them two big glazed doughnuts apiece when she brought the Cokes.

"These are on me, ladies," she told them. "If they stay on the counter any longer I'll eat them myself and blow a month of Weight Watchers meetings."

It was the first time in her life that anyone had ever given Sara Lee a present.

"Thanks," Sara Lee mumbled, trying to keep her voice from betraying the depth of her feelings. She quickly glanced around the diner, checking to see if Authority was watching them. "You won't get in trouble, will you?"

"Not if you two eat up the evidence." The waitress, whose name tag identified her as "Lou," looked at Gailie so intently that Sara Lee went cold inside with fear.

"Your little friend's about the skinniest kid I ever seen," Lou said. "She been sick?"

In a narrative-style treatment, the text is double-spaced and dialogue is enclosed in quotation marks. The characters and locations are described just enough to give one a quick mental picture and the plot unfolds in story form.

As you build your screenplay it is important to keep the following topics in mind.

Surprise Endings

If you plan a surprise ending to your script, here are several movies you should study because they spring their surprises so skillfully:

No Way Out (1987), starring Kevin Costner and Gene Hackman. The end of this movie sent people out of the theater arguing about whether or not they liked the final revelation. The good news for this successful movie was that audiences talked about it for quite a while.

A Big Hand for the Little Lady (1966), starring Henry Fonda, Joanne Woodward, and Jason Robards, and with a wonderful group of supporting players, almost all of whom have starred in other movies. The final revelation in this movie was not only skillfully set up, but the ten-minute sequence after we find out what certain of the characters were up to allowed us to know why they did what they did and to enjoy their triumph with them.

The surprise at the end of *Carrie* (1976), starring Sissy Spacek and Piper Laurie, with John Travolta in a supporting role, was a visual one, not a "story" surprise as exemplified in *No Way Out* and *A Big Hand for the Little Lady.* The unexpected visual at the end of *Carrie* was meant to make you *gasp,* not to make you *think.*

The Crying Game (1992) sprang its stunning surprise not at the end of the picture but in the second act. I don't think there's anyone reading these words who doesn't by now know *what* that surprise was, but this movie is well worth seeing again to study how this shocker was accomplished. If you haven't seen it I'm not going to spoil it for you. Rent the movie.

Know Your Genre and Watch Your "Tone"

After you've constructed the blueprint for your screenplay by writing your treatment in the style with which you're most comfortable, you are now ready to write the first draft. Please remember to be true to the genre of your story and to write dialogue and narrative in the correct "tone" for that genre.

In the *Lethal Weapon* pictures the villains may be outrageously powerful and armed like small countries, and Mel Gibson and Danny Glover joke with each other, but the action is serious, and if those men get shot, they bleed.

In a cliff-hanger homage like the *Indiana Jones* movies, the villains "Indy" faces and the trouble he gets into top the Outrageous Meter. In this category (genre) of picture the tone of the dialogue should reflect the cartoon lightness.

At this point, it would be a good idea to watch the *Indiana Jones* films again, just to study their "tone." You will see that Indy (like James Bond) may get dirty, may even get bruised or have an occasional tiny cut near his hairline, but he's never seriously hurt, no matter what ordeal he goes through. This is the spirit of the superhero genre, and consistent with the tone of cartoonlike suspended disbelief.

Remember that dramas, even the most serious, can have light moments, might be even more powerful for the welcome relief of humor, but here light moments must come from a place of truth inside your characters. Faced with identical challenges—whether serious or humorous—different characters behave in different ways, according to their own specific individual natures. This is true of living humans and it should be true of invented characters.

Comedies can have serious moments, but these moments should be within the spirit of a comedy. For example, someone might die in a comedy and the aftermath (even the events of the death itself) can be funny. But it is *not* funny—in a comedy—suddenly to see something bloody and gross, like a graphic, brutal killing. Gore and brutality are a violation of a comedy's "tone." It would not have been funny in, for example, *Sleepless in Seattle,* for us to have witnessed a bloody death.

On the other hand, *Pulp Fiction,* which is a comedy, is filled with gore, but that gore is true to the tone of the old "pulp fiction" stories that Quentin Tarantino was celebrating.

Having chosen a genre for your screenplay, it is important that you stay within that genre at least while you are writing that particular script. You can write in as many different genres as you like to see, but you should not mix genres in the same script.

If your current script is a farce, then don't take an abrupt left turn into satire and expect the reader to follow you without confusion. A romantic comedy can have its farcical moments, but a satire is a different comic creature altogether. Satire is the most difficult form of humor to execute successfully because it is the farthest away from reality, from even the stretched reality of comedy. Parody, which is close to satire in style, makes fun of reality. In simple terms that I use to guide my own work, I divide the styles this way: the best comedy has some heart. A farce should have at least a little heart somewhere among the quick-firing, relentless laughs. The best satires and parodies of which I am aware are without heart. The are funny, but with a slick, hard, impenetrable surface. You will laugh, if it's skillful work, but your emotions will not be engaged. This is laughter without "nourishment," without the recognition we feel when some quality in a character speaks to a similar spirit within us.

Here are some examples of the various genres. View them again to get a better understanding of their differences:

Sleepless in Seattle (Tom Hanks and Meg Ryan, with a script by Nora Ephron and David S. Ward and Jeff Arch) is a classic romantic comedy featuring characters most of us would like to know, and laughs with heart, humor that comes from the individual foibles and vulnerabilities of those characters.

The Apartment (Jack Lemmon and Shirley MacLaine, with a script by I. A. L. Diamond & Billy Wilder) is a darker romantic comedy. The leads in this story are nice people who are each doing something that they are ashamed of—she's having an affair with a married man and he's lending out his apartment to executives in his company for their extracurricular trysts in order to foster his career. In getting to know each other these two people find the will to declare their freedom to live more honorable lives. It is at times both very funny and deeply touching and has become a classic because we fell in love with these two characters and wanted them to be both happy and together.

A Fish Called Wanda (John Cleese, Kevin Kline, and Jamie Lee Curtis, with a script by John Cleese & Charles Crichton) is a farce. It's an absurd story told at high speed. The characters are immensely appealing in their antics. It careens between the wicked and the tasteless, but it manages to make us care about the people.

The Nutty Professor (especially the Eddie Murphy remake) is an excellent example of farce with some tenderness beneath the hilarity.

Airplane! (Robert Hays, Julie Hagerty, Leslie Nielsen, and famous faces in cameo appearances, with a script by Jerry Zucker, Jim Abrahams & David Zucker) is a parody, spoofing big budget "disaster" pictures like *Airport*. There is no underlying tenderness, as there is in Eddie Murphy's *The Nutty Professor*. There does not need to be; this is the writer's choice.

Other successful examples of parodies are the *Naked Gun* pictures, starring Leslie Nielsen. These movies manage to spoof everything and do it with good-natured affection. "Lampoon" and "spoof" are other labels used for parodies. For this type of movie these terms are interchangeable.

Network (William Holden, Faye Dunaway, Peter Finch, written by Paddy Chayefsky) is categorized as a satire. Personally, I've always considered it a documentary, but for the purpose of this discussion I won't argue with the satire label. The movie is Chayefsky's indictment of the television industry. It is entertaining because of Chayefsky's great talent as a writer, but horrifying if one takes the time to think about what Chayefsky is saying about television's decision makers and their frequently heartless agendas.

One of the most brilliant satires I have ever seen is *Wag the Dog*, starring Robert DeNiro and Dustin Hoffman, directed by Barry

Levinson with a screenplay by Hilary Henkin and David Mamet. It was released in late December 1997. This is a must-see for every screenwriter.

Now that you know how to write the three types of screenplay treatments, and you have decided on the genre and tone of your script, let's turn to the next chapter and talk about structure.

8. Structures: Tight and Loose

Structure is to a screenplay what a skeleton is to a human body: It supports the flesh and blood and sinew.

A tightly structured screenplay is one that is sharply focused and tells a straightforward story from Fade In to Fade Out, with no digressions. A loosely structured screenplay tells a story of wider scope, usually covering a longer time span and with digressions into subplots or back story.

We will examine tightly structured films first.

Casablanca is an excellent example of a tightly structured film that has a three-act structure. It covers just two days in the lives of its principals. The film begins on the night that Ilsa Lund and Victor Lazlo walk into Rick's café in Casablanca and it ends forty-eight hours later when Rick, making the decision for the emotionally torn Ilsa, puts the woman he loves on the plane to safety with her heroic husband and then disappears into the mist with his friend Louie to fight for freedom. As we see his trench-coated figure vanish in the distance, Rick famously predicts: "Louie, I think this is the beginning of a beautiful friendship."

A less discussed example of a tightly structured three-act film is another classic, *Bad Day at Black Rock*. Made in the 1950s, starring

Spencer Tracy, *Bad Day at Black Rock* is a thriller that every screenwriter should see, and it's available on videocassette. The story takes place over a span of just twenty-four hours. One morning at 10 A.M. a cross-country train makes an unscheduled stop in the town of Black Rock. This stop, the first in four years, and the arrival of a stranger on unknown business sends the local residents into various states and forms of panic. The story concludes at 10 A.M. the next morning, when the train makes a second unscheduled stop to pick up the visiting character, played by Spencer Tracy.

In that intervening twenty-four hours, Tracy's character, against enormous odds, survives attacks on his life, solves an old and tragic mystery, and triumphs over a vicious gang of bad guys. In escaping death and righting a terrible wrong, Tracy's character discovers that he has a powerful reason to go on living. The plan that the character had for himself, before stopping off at Black Rock, comes as a shock to us, and gives what we have experienced with the character a far greater depth than had the story been a simple thriller. *Bad Day at Black Rock* is a "must see" for writers who want to learn tight structure and how to reveal a character a bit at a time. It's available in most video stores.

Having described two tightly structured films that cover short spans of time, let me point out that a short time span does not necessarily guarantee a tight structure. *Pulp Fiction* ends in the same scene with which the film began, scrolling backward only a few minutes. While the stories told in the movie cover approximately twenty-four to thirty-six hours in total time, the structure is loose. Other examples of loosely structured films that we will discuss in detail later are *Fried Green Tomatoes, The Godfather Part II* and *The Searchers.*

Whether a structure chosen by the writer is going to be tight or loose, the best screenplays start as *deeply into the story as possible.* By that I mean they don't begin with the main character getting up, dressing, and having breakfast unless those activities are relevant to your plot or to our understanding of *who you star character is as a human being.* Because adult characters have lived for some decades before we meet them in the script, there is usually something that happened to them in the past (called "back story") that is relevant to the present story. Don't be tempted to start "back there" if you main story begins some years later.

Casablanca does not start the day before Ilsa and Lazlo come into Rick's, not a week before, when Rick presumably broke up with the French girl, Yvonne, that he had been seeing, nor several years before, when Rick and Sam arrived in Casablanca and Rick opened the café.

The Godfather, although it covers several years in time—from 1945, when Michael arrives at his sister's wedding, a marine hero just discharged and still in uniform, until approximately 1950—does not start a day before the wedding, or when Michael was awarded the Navy Cross for heroism. It begins when Michael returns to his family home and is caught up in events that change the course of his life. Even though it covers at least five years in time, *The Godfather* is an excellent example of a three-act film.

While it is usually advisable to start a movie as deeply into the story as you can, there are times when there is something important that must be done first. *Midnight Run* does not begin its story with Jack Walsh accepting the hundred-thousand-dollar job of recapturing Jonathan Mardukas. It starts a few hours before, with a scene of Walsh capturing another bail jumper. This scene is necessary because it establishes the kind of man Walsh is: a professional who does not use excessive force to do his job. The contrast between Walsh and the much more primitive Dorfler, who'd just as soon render a bail jumper unconscious and drag him in by the scruff of the neck, is an effective way to show Walsh immediately as a good man.

Act Breaks

There are those who believe that Act One of *The Godfather* ends when Michael is in the hospital with his wounded, helpless father and whispers: "I'm with you, Pop." I disagree. I think the first act ends earlier, in the wedding scene, after Michael has told Kay about how his father and Luca Brazzi got Johnny Fontane out of his contract with his first manager, using the line that has become part of our language:

"He made him an offer he couldn't refuse." At the conclusion of that story, Michael says: "That's my family, Kay. That's not me." I believe that is the real end of the movie's first act because from that point on, circumstances begin to prove to Michael how wrong he is. It's as though God heard Michael's statement and whispered: "That's what you think, Michael Corleone."

I think most people will agree that Act Two ends with the death of the Godfather, Vito Corleone.

Here is a simple formula for creating your own three-act structure:

Act One sets up *who* the story is about, what kind of people your main characters are, and lays the foundation for the events to come, or gives us an idea of the obstacles they will face.

Act Two plunges your main characters into major plot events and increases the size and number of obstacles between your stars and their goal. Act Two ends with some event that will change the course of the story and catapult your star or stars toward the climax.

Act Three takes your characters into bigger challenges, leading to the climax, which is the pinnacle of the action. Quickly after the climax comes the resolution, when the story comes to its conclusion, or implies what will happen to the characters after the fade-out. Put into Hollywood shorthand, the three acts consist of the Who, the What, and the Big Bang.

In the real world of the professional screenwriter, there are only two times when you need to know the exact location of your act breaks:

1. When you are writing for network television and the act breaks are required to come at certain mandated intervals so that the commercials can be inserted.
2. When your producer or your production executive asks you to tell him.

No one else in the professional arena is likely to ask this question because if you have written a story that establishes your characters, keeps the interest of the reader or the audience, and builds to a conclusion, it is unimportant where someone thinks the act breaks come.

This is true whether you are writing a tightly structured three-act screenplay or are telling your story in a distinctively original way. In terms of structure, if you tell a compelling story that does not let the attention of the audience wander, then there are no absolute rules that you must follow slavishly as to how you must tell that story.

The writer can get whatever back story we need to know into the script through the use of dialogue with or about the star character that tells us briefly what we need to know, or through flashbacks. Generally speaking, it is not a good idea to use flashbacks unless they are a vital part of the storytelling design, or unless there is absolutely no other way to reveal what we need to know.

In *Midnight Run* there are some very important things we need to know about the personal history of De Niro's bounty hunter, Jack Walsh, but there is not even one flashback in the movie. The writer worked that information in through his dialogue.

I had never met writer George Gallo when he heard through a mutual friend that I was using his movie as an instruction tool in my classes. We spoke on the telephone and he asked if he could come to the class as a guest. As you can imagine, I was very happy to have him there.

George Gallo arrived early and stayed to the end. He was warm, funny, unpretentious, *very* candid about being a writer in the movie business, and generous in answering every question. He is an altogether delightful human being, the living refutation of drama critic and member of the Algonquin Round Table Alexander Woolcott's famous comment: "Great writers should be read and not met."

Now that we've discussed the three-act structure, let's go to the other side of the room, to those wonderful movies that follow the beat of their own separate hearts.

The "Irregular Weaves"

Four very different, and very successful, movies that have highly irregular structures are *Fried Green Tomatoes, The Godfather Part II,*

The Searchers, and *Pulp Fiction.* These are excellent examples of loose structure, movies that I call "irregular weaves."

I have chosen to discuss these four movies because they represent four separate types of loose structure that achieve four different dramatic objectives.

Fried Green Tomatoes is really two separate stories that take place several decades apart. The setting for both stories is Alabama.

The first story, which takes place during the course of a year in present time, features sweet, shy, overweight Evelyn Couch (Kathy Bates). Evelyn, with her husband, Ed, comes to a nursing home to visit Ed's miserable Aunt Vesta. But the aunt is such a mean old lady she throws things whenever she sees poor Evelyn. In the waiting room, while Ed visits his aunt, Evelyn meets an eighty-two-year-old widow, Mrs. Ninny Threadgoode (Jessica Tandy), who is warm and outgoing.

In the course of their conversation, Mrs. Threadgoode begins to tell Evelyn a story about relatives of Ninny's who lived in the nearby small town of Whistle Stop, Alabama, sixty-some years earlier. Mrs. Threadgoode functions as what I call a "bridge character" connecting the two eras. The central figures in the enthralling story Mrs. Threadgoode relates are daring, independent wild-child Idgie (Imogene Louise) Threadgoode and gentle, ladylike Ruth Jamison. The story begins in 1920, shortly before Idgie's adored older brother, Buddy, who loved Ruth, was struck by a train and killed. It will cover a period of eighteen years, until Ruth's death in 1938, and will include the arrest of Idgie and her employee, Big George, who are put on trial for killing Ruth's viscious and physically abusive husband.

The story that Evelyn hears in serial fashion over several months has a profound effect on Evelyn Couch's life. Evelyn goes from being an almost comical embodiment of the kind and thoughtful, but unassertive and habitually ignored, southern woman who can't understand why people don't treat her with respect to a modern version of Idgie's "Twanda, the Avenger!"

Through learning about the problems Idgie and Ruth endured

and triumphed over, Evelyn reinvents herself as a stronger, healthier woman who can focus her energy in positive ways. The new out-of-her-shell Evelyn thoroughly unsettles her husband, Ed, as she tries to bring him into new habits with her. He doesn't like the low-fat diet, but at least he finally has dinner with *Evelyn* instead of the television set.

Evelyn loses none of her innate kindness as she gets stronger and attains confidence in herself as a person. The changes she has made in herself allow her to keep loving Ed, she explains to him. She is gently adamant with Ed about including Mrs. Threadgoode in the circle of their family when Evelyn discovers that the older woman will have no place to go when she is released from the nursing home.

Fried Green Tomatoes is well worth studying. It was not only a great financial success, it was as much loved by men who go to boxing matches as it was by women who go to museums, and by teenagers as much as by older people. I think the reason for this was that the major characters in the story possessed a universal humanity. So many people could identify with some part of the story, or at least one of the characters, or felt some of the same powerful emotions: love, generosity, and personal sacrifice. The broad appeal of *Fried Green Tomatoes* proves that good stories are not the property of one gender or another, or of any one generation. Humanity reaches out to humanity. In this case it rang up big grosses at the box office.

The *Godfather Part II* is also structured so that it tells two stories that are separated by decades, but it is unlike *Fried Green Tomatoes* because there is no overt connection between the tale of Vito Corleone's youth and of his son Michael's problems as his father's successor. While the story of how the orphaned Vito Corleone emigrated to America and became "The Godfather" alternates with Michael's story, they are not linked by a "bridge" character.

Godfather II begins in the town of Corleone, Sicily, in 1901. Young Vito Andolini's father is murdered by the local Mafia chief for an unintended insult. Vito's older brother, Paulo, vows vengeance and is killed. Desperate to save the life of her one remaining child, Vito's mother takes Vito to the villa of the Mafia chief and begs for the boy's life, claiming that he is not bright and so could never be a threat. The Mafia chief kills Vito's mother in front of the boy. Vito Andolini manages to escape and hide until he can be smuggled away from the village and put on a ship with others emigrating to America.

When Vito arrives at Ellis Island, an impatient customs official registers "Vito Andolini from Corleone" as Vito Corleone, and that becomes his name. A physical examination given to new immigrants reveals that the boy has tuberculosis. The orphaned Vito, completely alone in the world, is put in quarantine for several months. He is nine years old.

From Vito sitting alone in a hospital room, looking out the window, the movie leaps ahead to 1958, at Lake Tahoe, Nevada, where Anthony Corleone, son of Michael and Kay, is being confirmed. Following the confirmation there is a lavish party at the Lake Tahoe family compound. It is a celebration with family and friends that echoes the opening of *The Godfather,* which began with the wedding of Vito Corleone's youngest child and only daughter, Connie.

While Michael and Kay are dancing together at the party, we learn that Kay is newly pregnant with their third child. Kay reminds Michael that he once told her: "In five years the Corleone family will be completely legitimate." She adds, "That was seven years ago." He replies softly, "I know. I'm trying, darling."

Late that night, as Kay is in bed and Michael is about to undress, Kay sleepily asks why the drapes are open. Michael looks at the windows—and instinctively falls to the floor a split second before their bedroom is sprayed with machine-gun fire from outside. Maneuvering across the floor like the heroic marine he was in the war, he pulls Kay to safety and covers her with his own body until the firing stops.

Michael realizes that for gunmen to almost succeed in killing him inside his family compound he must have been betrayed by someone close to them. As Michael suspected, the two gunmen are soon found dead, unable to tell him what he needs to know. He decides he must go to Miami to see crime boss Hyman Roth, with whom his family has been having trouble on the East Coast. Michael leaves Tom Hagen in charge of everything and slips away in secrecy, with only a bodyguard as companion. As Michael travels by train to Miami, the story moves backward in time to 1917 in New York City.

Vito Corleone is now twenty-six years old, married to a beautiful young woman he loves and the father of his first child, Santino, who is an infant. He works hard in an Italian grocery store, for a man we learn in dialogue took him in years earlier and treated him like a son.

It is at the theater one night with his boss's son that Vito first sees the evil, greedy Don Fanucci at work, threatening helpless people and taking money from them. Vito can't understand why an Italian would pick on his countrymen. He is told it is because the victims have no one to protect them. Soon Vito himself becomes a victim of Don Fanucci, when Fanucci forces the grocer to hire Fanucci's nephew. Because there is not enough work for two employees in addition to his own son, the grocer must regretfully let Vito go. The grocer is in tears, but Vito is understanding, and expresses his appreciation for all the grocer has done for him. He refuses to accept the box of food that the grocer wants Vito to take home.

Don Fanucci's demands are growing harder and harder for people to meet. Vito, the only one in the community who is courageous enough, tries to make a deal with Fanucci that will give something to Fanucci but not impoverish Fanucci's victims. It is to Don Fanucci that Vito Corleone makes the first "offer he can't refuse." Fanucci refuses. Shortly after this, during a noisy street festival, Vito kills Fanucci. He is a hero to the community, and the person to whom everyone begins to come when they have a problem they cannot solve themselves. Vito Corleone, at twenty-six, has become "The Godfather."

Godfather II alternates the early story of Vito Corleone with the story of Michael Corleone. Vito's story covers several years, and includes his return to Corleone, Sicily, some twenty-five years after his escape. He is a prosperous man now and has brought his wife, three young sons, and the infant Connie back to meet their distant relatives, and to see the town of his birth. As his family is visiting, Vito seeks out and kills the Mafia chief who murdered his father, his brother, and his mother in 1901.

Michael's story spans approximately one year (during 1958 and 1959). Over the course of the year in which Michael's story is told, the audience will see Michael in Cuba as Castro overthrows the dictator Batista. He will make the devastating discovery that the traitor is his own brother, Fredo, whose brain was impaired by a childhood illness, and he will go on to decide how to deal with this difficult situation. Before the year ends, Michael and Kay will lose the baby she carries. The emotional fireworks set off by events concerning the loss of the baby lead to the final image of the film, an emotionally wrenching visual echo of the ending of *The Godfather*. However, when the door closes on Kay in the final moments of *The Godfather*, it is to protect her from dangerous knowledge. When the door closes on her at the end of *Godfather II* it is to shut her out of Michael's life and to separate her from her children.

If you are planning to write a script that tells two stories in alternating portions, please study *Godfather II* and *Fried Green Tomatoes*. Both structures are loose, encompassing two separate stories, but the structures are not identical because their dramatic objectives are not identical.

The Searchers, released in 1956, directed by John Ford and starring John Wayne in a role that shocked his fans, illustrates a third type of loose structure. This movie covers a time span of seven years. While it only tells one powerful story, it has a subplot, or secondary story, that runs parallel to the main plot. (In *Godfather II* and *Fried Green Tomatoes,* each of the two-story pairings consists of main stories that are told in alternating segments; none of these four stories is a subplot. In *Godfather II* the separate stories are not overtly connected; in *Fried Green Tomatoes* they are connected by the "bridge character," Mrs. Ninny Threadgoode.

A subplot provides diversion, or some respite from the main action, or perhaps comic relief, but it cannot stand on its own. It depends on the presence of the main story. A subplot should not take up so much time that it competes with the main story, or dilutes the focus of the main story. *The Searchers* is an example of the perfect balance between main story and subplot. The "bridge character" between the two is young Martin Pawley.

The Searchers begins in Texas, in 1868, on the day that Ethan Edwards (John Wayne) returns home from fighting on the Confederate side in the Civil War. He is three years late, and does not explain where he has been since the war ended in 1865, except to say that he does not believe in surrender.

Ethan has come back to the ranch on which his brother Aaron, Aaron's wife Martha, and their three children live. It is unspoken but in silent moments that are drenched in subtext, it is made clear visually that at some point years earlier, before she chose Aaron as her husband, Ethan was in love with Martha and she probably was in love with him. We sense that some part of Martha's heart still belongs to Ethan, but she chose the sensible brother, not the warrior, and whatever her deepest feelings may be she will live with her choice like an honorable woman. (If you study the first ten minutes of *The Searchers* carefully you will learn how much can be said—while nothing is *said*. Watch the look that Ethan and Martha exchange when he returns; notice how, when she reaches up to get a lamp from the mantel, he takes it down and hands it to her. Watch the moment when Martha, thinking she is alone and unobserved, gently caresses Ethan's old Civil War coat.)

On his first night back we see revealed a vitally important part of Ethan's character: his viscera-deep hatred of Indians. This is clear in his hostile treatment of young Martin Pawley (who is about twenty years old at this point), and who has been brought up like a son by Martha and Aaron Edwards. The boy was found as a child by Ethan after young Martin's parents had been massacred by Indians. The reason for his coldness to Martin is that Martin is one-eighth Cherokee. (John Wayne had fought Indians in the movies before, but it was always situational, for some goal, or in self-defense or in the defense of others. Ethan Edwards's raw, pathological hatred for the Native American race in *The Searchers* was *bigotry*. John Wayne's fans did not expect this.)

The morning following Ethan's return from his wanderings after the war, a party of men, led by a captain in the Texas Rangers, arrives. This character, "Reverend-Captain Samuel Clayton Johnson" (Ward Bond), is also a preacher. Johnson announces that Aaron and Martin are needed to join their band in order to chase some suspected cattle rustlers. As the Captain is swearing Aaron and Martin in as temporary Rangers, Ethan comes into the room, strapping on his gun. Ethan tells Aaron to stay home to protect his family, that he will go in Aaron's place. Ethan suspects that the raid was not by rustlers, but possibly by a war party of Comanches. The dialogue between Johnson and Ethan makes it clear that these two men were friends at one time, but now there is hostility between them. Ethan does not respect Johnson for surrendering his sword at the end of the Civil War because Ethan does not believe in surrender.

Some forty miles away the men find the cattle have been killed by Comanche lances. It is apparent that the cattle were not killed for food. Ethan realizes that the cattle were stolen as a diversion, to draw the men away from their ranches. The two ranches that are the most likely target of the Comanche war party are the Jorgensen place and the Edwards ranch. The Edwards ranch is farthest away, so the men race back toward Jorgensen's. In a romantic subplot, the oldest Jorgensen son, Brad, is in love with Aaron and Martha's oldest daughter, Lucy, and Martin Pawley is in love with the Jorgensens' daughter, Laurie.

The Jorgensen place is untouched; the men now know that it was the Edwards ranch that was attacked. When they get back, Ethan finds the horribly mutilated bodies of Aaron, Martha, and their young son. He prevents Martin from seeing what was done to them. (I am grateful that we, the audience, were also spared the sight.) The two girls, eighteen-year-old Lucy and eight-year-old Debbie, are gone, kidnapped by the Comanches.

After burying the dead, the men set out to find Lucy and Debbie, but soon, convinced that the girls must be dead, they give up the search. Ethan has no intention of giving up, nor will Martin, who feels like a brother to the girls. Brad, who loves Lucy, insists on continuing the search with Ethan and Martin.

Some time later the tracks the three men are following split off. Ethan does not let Martin or Brad know what he suspects, and follows one set of tracks while ordering the young men to follow the other. He tells them where he will catch up with them later. When Ethan does return to Martin and Brad he is visibly upset, but won't discuss what is the matter. Martin notices that Ethan no longer has his Civil War coat, which was strapped to the back of his saddle, but Ethan won't discuss that, either.

When they find a Comanche camp in a valley below them, and Brad thinks he has spotted Lucy, Ethan is forced to tell them that what Brad saw was *not* Lucy. Ethan admits that he found the girl dead, back in the canyon. He buried her in his coat. When Brad wants to know what happened to her, Ethan refuses to tell him, and orders him never to ask for details. Brad, maddened with grief, leaps on his horse and rides into the Comanche camp, where he is immediately shot and killed. There was no way Ethan could have saved him.

Ethan and Martin continue their search for little Debbie. It goes on for *seven years.* Periodically, Ethan and Martin return to the Jorgensens, or Martin writes one of his very rare letters to Laurie. These visits and letters are the subplot scenes in *The Searchers.* Laurie loves Martin, but as the years go on and on she begins to entertain suitors, finally agreeing to marry Charlie, the most persistent of them. On Ethan's and Martin's last return before the climax of their search, Martin manages to stop Laurie's wedding to Charlie, minutes before it would have occurred.

One of Martin's letters to Laurie provides a flashback sequence. This fills in some details of Ethan's and Martin's search for little Debbie, and provides some comedy relief in the tale of how Martin accidentally acquired a fat, jolly Indian wife through a misunderstanding. It happened during a meeting in which he was trying to trade dry goods for useful information. However, the comedy soon turns dark and ugly, when the Indian woman is murdered by soldiers. Laurie is so furious that Martin had, even briefly, unknowingly, and without it being consummated, "married" an Indian woman that she vows to forget him. In spite of her resolve, she cannot.

It isn't until very near the end of the movie that we suddenly discover what had been Ethan's true intention in his refusal to stop searching for Debbie. It's a shock, and reveals the depth of Ethan's bigotry. The foundation for this shock at the climax is carefully, and subtly, laid. When we finally realize what Ethan intends to do, it is just a split second before Martin Pawley comes to the same realization. He screams at Ethan, but he is too far away to be able to stop yet another tragedy.

For the first several years of their hunt, Ethan's goal was to rescue Debbie, but once she grew to puberty he knew that she would be taken as a "wife" by Scar, the young Comanche chief he was tracking. In that time, and in that culture, a white female used sexually by Indians was as good as dead to her relatives. If she was rescued she was either insane from her ordeal in captivity, as we glimpsed in a background scene much earlier in the picture, or she became an outcast because of what was considered her defilement. Ethan, her uncle, the sole surviving member of her family, felt it was his duty, if he could not rescue her before it was "too late," to find her and *kill* her! In Ethan's mind it would have been a "mercy killing," not murder. He would have been saving Debbie from a painful life of rejection by her own people.

When, at last, Scar is defeated in battle and Ethan is able to get to Debbie, she flees from him in terror, but the now fifteen-year-old girl cannot outrun Ethan, who's on horseback. With Martin screaming in horror in the background, unable to reach Debbie in time to help her, Debbie is trapped against a rock. She is cowering in fear, unable to escape Ethan, who is looming over her.

Then, against everything that Ethan's culture taught him, contrary to the power of the hatred forged by the attitudes of the era and by his own experiences—*Ethan is unable to kill Debbie.* His humanity is stronger than his conditioning, stronger than his hatred, stronger than the obsession that drove him all those years. Instead of killing her, he lifts Debbie up, much as he did seven years earlier when she was a child and he had just returned from his travels. Then he carries her in his arms to safety.

The seven-year time span of the story and the periodic returns to the romantic subplot are the elements that qualify *The Searchers* as an example of a loosely structured film.

In my opinion, *The Searchers* is one of the masterpieces of American film literature. When it was released in 1956 it was a shock to John Wayne's fans, who never expected that Hollywood's symbol of Western heroics—who was considered more of an icon than an actor—would ever even *think* of killing a young girl!

The Searchers, without a single moment of "preaching," is a powerful indictment of the corrosive poison of bigotry, and an unforgettable tribute to the triumph of humanity over hatred.

When I first saw *Pulp Fiction,* I thought the projectionist had mixed up the reels and *that* was the reason Vincent (John Travolta) and Jules (Samuel L. Jackson) suddenly showed up in clothes they shouldn't have been wearing in that part of the movie, and the explanation for Vincent's returning to the story after he had been shot dead by Butch (Bruce Willis). It wasn't until the final scene in the coffee shop that I realized we were in the same coffee shop we had been in during the opening scene. The projectionist was innocent of blame. The filmmaker had structured this collection of linked short stories to form a *circle.* I had never seen anything like *Pulp Fiction.* I've watched this picture many times since, with great admiration for the inventiveness of the filmmaker.

There should be a warning on the *Pulp Fiction* video box: "Don't try this (structure) at home!" If you burn to break all the so-called "rules" of conventional filmmaking, then I encourage you to study how skillfully *Pulp Fiction* did it. Even if you are a writer who is most comfortable using a traditional three-act structure, *Pulp Fiction* is worth studying for the rich character details it spreads before us like a banquet. However, this was a banquet where the spread was deliberately limited. I wanted *more*—to know what happened to Butch and his girlfriend. Most of all, I wanted to know what happened to Samuel L. Jackson's character as he set off to walk the earth as a kind of wandering knight. And I wanted to see more of that incomparable problem solver, The Wolf (Harvey Keitel). I was even curious to find out if the marriage of Mia and Marsellus Wallace (Uma Thurman and Ving Rhames) would last—and if any other man would dare to give that lady a foot massage.

Pulp Fiction is an ensemble piece, and—with the single exception of The Wolf—composed of couples. (But, then again, even The Wolf got to escort a lady to breakfast after his "cleanup" of the situation in which Jules and Vincent found themselves.) Some of the couples overlap, or temporarily form separate couples. Vincent and Jules are a professional couple. Then Vincent and Mia are a temporary couple in the dance contest and during her cocaine overdose. Butch and Esmeralda, his sweet but none-too-bright girlfriend, are a loving couple. Butch and Marsellus are a temporary couple who start out trying to kill each other, but bond when they are co-captives of brutal rednecks in that terrible back room. The young woman (Honey Bunny) and the young man (Pumpkin) in the diner are madly in love, and just as madly willing to kill during a robbery if they don't get the loot they demand.

The writer and director, Quentin Tarantino, describes *Pulp Fiction* as "three stories about one story." Couples swirl through this whirlpool of plots.

Pulp Fiction begins with Honey Bunny and Pumpkin in a Denny's-type diner. This opening scene ends with Honey Bunny pulling a gun on the other diners and swearing to kill them if anybody moves!

In the next scene, we meet Vincent and Jules, heavily armed muscle men for crime king Marsellus Wallace. They are early for their appointment, so they discuss such things as what a Big Mac is called in Paris, and whether their boss was justified in throwing a man from a roof because the man gave Mrs. Wallace a foot massage. Jules and Vincent disagree about the sensual seriousness of a foot massage, and whether or not Marsellus overreacted.

During the violent and gory scene in which Vincent and Jules conduct their "business" for Wallace, they suddenly are shot at, and *should* be killed. Miraculously, the spray of bullets misses them. Because he thinks about the meaning of what happened, Jules ultimately will change the life path that he takes. *Refusing* to believe that the fact they were saved when they should have been killed is a matter of profound significance will lead to Vincent's death.

At the end of the movie structurally we are back at the beginning.

When Jules and Vincent leave the coffee shop at the end of the movie—the same coffee shop in which the story began, but at the *conclusion of the opening scene that began the movie 154 minutes earlier*—Vincent and Jules will cease being a couple and will go their separate ways, to their separate destinies. We already know what happened to Vincent, because we now understand how Quentin Tarantino, in telling this story, has bent time to his will.

I strongly suggest that if you have not seen *Pulp Fiction,* you rent or buy the videocassette to study. I also suggest you buy the screenplay, which is available in book form, published by Hyperion.

I believe that *Pulp Fiction* succeeds when it could have been a chaotic mess because the characters are so fascinating and the actors who play them are superb in the roles. There is not an uninteresting character in the movie. Whatever they are doing in the story, those of us in the audience are enthralled, wanting to know what happened next. And then what happened . . .

Now that we have discussed traditional and irregular structures, let's talk a little bit about the most successful movies and what we can learn from them.

9. What the Megahits Have in Common and What We Can Learn from Them

I've spent many years studying not only the most successful films of all time, but also the major hits of the last twenty-five years, and in this time I've developed a theory I've come to hold as true: that the megahits are all, in one way or another and regardless of how many explosions and killings they contain, love stories. By that I don't just mean stories about romantic love, about "Cupid's arrow" striking sometimes the unlikeliest of couples. That is only one powerful kind of love. *Mrs. Doubtfire* is the story of a man's great love for his children, and how far he is willing to go to be near them. The *Lethal Weapon* pictures are also "love stories" in that they chronicle the deep platonic love between two men, and the love of a happy family (the Murtaughs) for the desolate loner (Riggs) that they take into their circle. The first of the series, *Lethal Weapon,* was released in 1987, *Lethal Weapon 2* was released in 1989, and *Lethal Weapon 3* came out in 1992. According to an article in *Daily Variety* (July 3, 1997), "The first three *Lethal Weapon* films jointly grossed more than $350 million in the U.S. alone." In Michael Fleming's column in *Daily Variety* (July 8, 1997) he reports that *Lethal Weapon 4* is likely to start filming in January 1998, subject to the script being acceptable.

The Twenty Highest-Grossing Films (as of 1997)

It may well be that another film or two will have joined this exalted group by the time this is published in 1998, but according to *Video-Hound's Golden Movie Retriever* (1997 edition) and other sources, the Top 20 highest-grossing movies are, in alphabetical order: *Aladdin, Back to the Future, Batman, Beverly Hills Cop, The Empire Strikes Back, E.T.: The Extra-Terrestrial, Forrest Gump, Ghost, Ghostbusters, Gone with the Wind, Home Alone, Indiana Jones and the Last Crusade, Jaws, Jurassic Park, The Lion King, Mrs. Doubtfire, Raiders of the Lost Ark, Return of the Jedi, Star Wars,* and *Terminator 2: Judgment Day.*

If you have not seen all of the pictures on this list, I urge you to fill in the gaps in order to increase your preparation for a career as a professional screenwriter. Because they have been immensely pleasing to audiences over the years, there is something to be learned from each of them.

The love stories in the most beloved and successful pictures cover the whole spectrum of emotional needs and connections, but reduced to simplest terms they are all pictures in which the leading characters have *passion.* They care passionately about someone or something—and they will risk their lives to protect, to preserve, or to pursue the people, creatures, or things they love.

In 1982 the four top-grossing films of that year were *E.T.: The Extra-Terrestrial, An Officer and a Gentleman, Rocky 3,* and *Porky's. Porky's?*

This little movie, a crude comedy about high school kids in South Florida in the 1950s, was made for $1 million, which was a very low budget even way back in 1982. In spite of being a "period piece" and having no star names in the cast, *Porky's* went on to gross $150 million worldwide. It's easy to list what that picture *didn't* have: It didn't have fabulous stunts, great sets, stunning locations, memorable dialogue, beautiful faces, good acting, good photography, good clothes, dazzling explosions, or cascades of breaking glass.

To the audiences of all ages who flocked to *Porky's* what the picture lacked was unimportant compared to what it *did* have. There was a powerful emotional current at the heart of *Porky's*. It was about people (teenagers) who cared about each other very much. Those young people were willing to stick up for each other, to risk themselves for something more important than *themselves,* and to fight for each other against the bad guys. *Porky's* was a terrific little movie and made its investors a fortune. (It inspired two sequels: *Porky's 2: The Next Day* in 1983 and, in 1985, *Porky's Revenge.* Neither was a big success, although I'm sure they were moderately profitable, but neither picture came close to equaling the huge success of the first *Porky's.*)

The two sequels of *Porky's* had even more crude sight gags and bathroom humor, but what they didn't have was the "heart" that was in the original movie. I wondered as I watched those two sequels if it was possible that the filmmakers hadn't realized what it was that made the first picture such a hit.

We've all seen examples of pictures that probably were made because the filmmakers thought they could follow a huge success, but instead made much less successful movies because they managed to copy the wrong elements.

It's just my personal theory, but consider if *this* might have been the thought process in studio executive suites in 1965 when *The Sound of Music* was released and became an enormous moneymaker all over the world:

INT. EXECUTIVE OFFICE AT STUDIO X—DAY

STUDIO EXEC # 1
(studying report on the grosses)
Hmmmmmm. Let's analyze what elements made
The Sound of Music such a hit and duplicate them
in another movie.

STUDIO EXEC # 2
That's obvious, baby! It's a hit because it's got Julie
Andrews singing pretty songs in front of pretty
scenery!

And so in 1968 that studio released an expensive movie called *Star!*—and it was *not* a financial success . . .

The Sound of Music continued to draw in audiences wherever it played, so . . .

INT. EXECUTIVE OFFICE AT STUDIO XX—DAY

> STUDIO EXEC # 3
> *The Sound of Music* is still playing to packed
> houses all over the world—it's even a smash in
> Japan! Let's figure out what made it a hit and make
> a *Sound of Music* of our own.

> STUDIO EXEC # 4
> It's so easy I'm shocked the other guys haven't
> thought of it. We'll hire Julie Andrews, give her
> some pretty songs to sing in front of pretty
> scenery!

> STUDIO EXEC # 3
> That's it! Oh—and let's give her some better hair-
> dos, softer makeup, and some costumes that show
> off her figure. Hair, makeup and costumes—that's
> where the guys who made *Star!* went wrong.

And so in 1970 *that* studio released a new Julie Andrews musical called *Darling Lili*. It was not a financial success.

The public loved Julie Andrews in *The Sound of Music* when she played a warmhearted young woman on her way to becoming a nun, but who instead falls in love with seven motherless children and with their handsome, lonely naval captain father. The character Julie Andrews played in that movie, Maria Von Trapp, becomes an adoring mother and wife. In the dramatic climax, at the beginning of World War II, she helps her new family escape from the Nazis by leading them to safety through the mountains of Austria.

In contrast, the public did *not* embrace Julie Andrews as the very talented but icicle-hearted Broadway star Gertrude Lawrence in *Star!*, nor as a spy for the Germans in World War I, which was the character she played in *Darling Lili.*

Four hugely successful pictures released in 1996 and 1997 illustrate in their separate ways my point about the greatest hits being "love stories."

In *Twister* a female meteorologist named Jo, played by Helen Hunt, is obsessed with discovering the secret of killer tornadoes. These terrifying, destructive acts of nature can, in seconds, uproot houses and shatter lives. Jo is determined to learn enough to develop a warning system that will prevent tornado tragedies such as the one that killed Jo's father when she was a child. Jo tries not to acknowledge it, but she is also still in love with her estranged husband, Bill, which is why she keeps forgetting to sign the divorce papers he's sent her. Their shared passion for solving the mystery of one of nature's great untamed forces ultimately brings Jo and Bill back together again as a couple. There's a wonderful little moment after the characters have just barely survived a terrifying tornado attack when Bill's new fiancée, Dr. Melissa Reeves, a therapist, confesses to Bill that when he told her that he "chased tornadoes" in her heart she "thought that was a metaphor." Even though Melissa is the wrong woman for Bill, she's certainly the world's best sport, so you can't help wishing that she finds true love with someone else. In addition to the powerful bond between Bill and Jo, Jo's team of tornado chasers also love each other as an extended family, and adore Jo's wonderful aunt, a free-spirited artist who feeds them lavishly anytime they are in the neighborhood. This may not be a perfect script, but it is full of strong human feelings. You *believe* that these people will risk death to save each other, and that makes you care about them.

Independence Day features three couples who love each other— five, if you count the father and son pairing of Judd Hirsch and Jeff Goldblum and the mother and son love between Vivica A. Fox and her little boy. The three romantic couples are the handsome young president of the United States (Bill Pullman) and his lovely first lady (Mary McDonnell), who adore each other and their little girl, the divorced but still in love couple played by Margaret Colin (the president's assistant) and Jeff Goldblum, and daredevil marine fighter pilot Will Smith and his dancer love, beautiful Vivica A. Fox. The pilot and the dancer get married (with Mr. Goldblum and Miss Colin as the attendants) in a secret government bunker beneath the Nevada desert just before he takes off into space to fight the monsters who want to destroy the inhabitants of earth. The bride's adorable little boy and her golden Labrador retriever make this an instant family of four. *Independence Day* (or *ID4* as it's called in Hollywood shorthand) is filled with acts of gallantry and courage; it makes you want almost everyone to survive. Speaking personally, I would have been happy to see the sinister and spineless secretary of defense get zapped by the creature Will Smith captures with a punch in the jaw and the immortal line: "Welcome to earth!" I really wanted everyone else to live—and, to judge from the sustained cheering, the several audiences with which I saw this picture felt the same way.

Jerry Maguire, which stars Tom Cruise in the title role, is a traditional love story of the "boy meets a girl who's already in love with him—girl gets boy and then sets him free because just having him is not enough, she wants him to love her, too—boy discovers he really loves girl and wins her back" type of movie. Actually, *Jerry Maguire* is *two* love stories, which is important because the second love story has a powerful influence on the first.

The central love story is between high-energy sports agent Jerry Maguire and Dorothy, the sweet, soft-spoken, loyal single-mother bookkeeper in the sports agency where Jerry works. Dorothy is the only person willing to gamble her future on Jerry when he's fired due to a sudden and unappreciated attack of integrity.

The secondary love story is between colorful football player, Rod Tidwell (Cuba Gooding, Jr. won the Oscar as Best Supporting Actor for this role), who becomes Jerry's only client, and the athlete's outspoken and pregnant wife, Marcee. One of the most charming moments occurs in the climactic scene when Jerry, who has seen the power of real love in the relationship between Rod and Marcee Tidwell, finally finds the courage to open himself up and admit that he truly loves Dorothy. He rushes back to her, bursts into her cynical sister's Divorced Women's Support Group, and delivers a long, heartfelt speech declaring how he feels.

Dorothy responds simply: "You had me at 'hello.' "

We in the audience tend to love people on the screen who love *each other* deeply. Very powerful feelings are tapped in us; we want to spend time with those characters, and we want good things to happen for them.

The Rock is an *untraditional* love story. On the surface, *The Rock* is an action picture about a young FBI scientist, played by Nicolas Cage, and an older man—the world's greatest escape artist—who has been wrongly imprisoned for most of the last thirty years. This character, Malone, is played by the matchless Sean Connery. In order to win the freedom he should never have been denied, Connery must help Cage and a group of commandos break *into* the island fortress prison Alcatraz, from which Connery once escaped, to rescue hostages being held there.

Connery wants to live for the grown-up daughter he loves but has had a chance to know only during his brief escapes, and Cage wants to survive to marry the girl he loves, who has just told him she's pregnant. But, ultimately and most affectingly, *The Rock* is a kind of surrogate father and son love story between Connery's and Cage's characters.

In the four pictures we've just examined, and in the list of Top 20 highest-grossing films, the unifying element that they all have in common is the *passion* of the central characters. By passion, in this context, I mean the powerful desire that drives those characters to accomplish goals that look to be unachievable.

The unforgettable characters who drive these megahits understand—as writers must understand if they are to survive and to reach their potential as artists—that "difficult" is not a synonym for "impossible."

It is a very human emotion to want to be around characters (or creatures, as in *The Lion King*) who love something, and who dream big and dare even bigger. Audiences respond to the power of deep feelings year after year and decade after decade.

Now we come to another category of film I believe it would be immensely helpful for new screenwriters to study.

Remakes

It's not uncommon for studios looking for a potential hit film to "raid the vaults." That means to look through the studio's inventory of previously made films to see if one or more might be successfully remade for the present market. Remakes of successful films appeal to financing entities because:

a. The movie was successful before, so it is deemed likely to be successful again, if it is "updated" and cast with present-day stars.
b. In the original successful movie, they already have a story "blueprint" to follow.
c. A familiar title is a useful selling tool.

I want to be sure that I am clear about the reason I feel it is important for you to study remakes. I am absolutely *not* recommending that you search through a catalog of movies in order to find one that you would like to update. The obstacle for you here is that someone other than you owns the rights to the material. If you have an idea for a remake and go to the studio or film library that owns the rights to the original picture you take a great risk that the person to whom you submit your concept for a remake will simply take your idea and assign the job to someone else. It is possible that you might be able to persuade whoever owns the rights to a film you might want to remake to pay you to write the new script, but this is a *very big* gamble. What is possible, however, is that if you have impressed a studio executive or a producer with a spec script of yours, that person might think that you are the perfect writer to be given the assignment to create a new script from one of their old properties. Also, if you are at the beginning of your career they know they can hire you for a relatively modest sum and because of this you might get one of those "big chances" that happen now and then. And if it happens to you, you will be ready.

Whether or not you are given an assignment—or persuade someone to allow you—to remake an old property, you can still benefit greatly by studying original pictures and the versions that have been made subsequently. Try to determine in your careful viewing why one version of a picture was a hit and why later productions of the same story were either bigger successes or embarrassing failures. This is an invaluable exercise that will help you develop the solid knowledge of craft that will make you a better screenwriter.

On the surface, remaking a previously successful picture can appear to be a good gamble, but not all movies can be "updated" and still keep their original appeal, nor can all movies be recast with actors who have as much personal magic or chemistry together as those in the original version. It takes imagination, skill, timing, and luck to repeat or surpass an earlier success.

Here are some movies that will be useful to study. See if you can figure out where some filmmakers "went right" and others went wrong:

Sabrina, a charming "Cinderella story," was first made into a movie in 1954 and starred Audrey Hepburn, Humphrey Bogart, and William Holden. It had been a successful Broadway play, titled *Sabrina Fair,* and it was a big hit as a movie. Remade forty-one years later, in 1995, with Julia Ormond, Harrison Ford, and Greg Kinnear, it was not a success. In my opinion there were three reasons the remake of *Sabrina* did not live up to the hopes of the filmmakers. First, the character of Sabrina was turned from a 1950s Cinderella into a 1990s career woman. In the original she was a chauffeur's daughter who was sent to Paris to learn to be a cook in a millionaire's mansion. In the 1995 version she is the chauffeur's daughter who went to Paris and became a photographer. Sabrina's 1995 career got in the way of the fairy tale. Second, Julia Ormond does not have the luminous presence that made the young Audrey Hepburn a unique star. Third, Harrison Ford was playing the role of the uptight, business-obsessed tycoon. Judging by his box office track record, the public likes to see Harrison Ford in films where he is a heroic man of action, but does not seem to want to see him in more passive roles. Those are the reasons I think the remake of *Sabrina* failed to find an enthusiastic audience. What do you think?

A Star Is Born was made three times, first with Janet Gaynor in 1937, then in a musical version starring Judy Garland in 1954. In 1976, Barbara Streisand starred in the third version. When the 1954 version was released it was shortened considerably to allow the theaters to have more showings per day, and thus earn more money from box office tickets and in concession sales. More than twenty minutes of the cut footage was restored to the picture in 1997, adding three Judy Garland musical numbers and filling gaps in the story that had puzzled audiences for years. The restored version is available on videocassette. See if you can figure out why the Judy Garland version is an enduring audience favorite and what the Barbra Streisand version lacks, even though it has Streisand's immense talent and star appeal.

The Magnificent Seven, an enormous success when first released in 1960, was a western set in Mexico and produced by the Mirisch Company. While it was a new story to American audiences, actually it was a remake. *The Magnificent Seven* was based on Akira Kurosawa's 1954 masterpiece, *Seven Samurai,* which was set in sixteenth-century Japan. *The Magnificent Seven* later generated several sequels, none of which matched the success of the original American version of the Japanese classic. Since both *The Magnificent Seven* and *Seven Samurai* are marvelous pictures I urge you to see both of them to study what elements were taken from the original and transported successfully to a very different time and culture.

Jerry Lewis wrote and starred in *The Nutty Professor,* a kind of Jekyll and Hyde comedy, in 1963. When the picture was remade in 1996 it starred Eddie Murphy as the shy and lonely professor who takes the old ad line "better living through chemistry" to an eye-popping extreme. Four writers share credit for the remake: David Sheffield, Barry W. Blaustein, Steve Oedekerk, Tom Shadyac. The first *Nutty Professor* was very successful, especially with young audiences and Jerry Lewis fans. The Eddie Murphy remake was a huge success, and a personal triumph for Murphy, who played *all* of the members of his family, including both his parents, both his grandparents, and his obese teenage brother. Study both of these movies to see how the first inspired the second, and where the second departed so imaginatively from the first.

As I write this, Eddie Murphy is filming a remake of *Doctor Doolittle,* which is based on the English children's books about a doctor who talks to animals in their own languages. Murphy is playing the same title role in which the very British Rex Harrison starred in 1967 in the first filmed version. The first version of *Doctor Doolittle* was long and, in my opinion, boring. It was not a critical nor a financial success, in spite of the marvelous photography and the supporting cast of appealing animals. The filmmakers thought that with *Doctor Doolittle* they could duplicate the international success Rex Harrison had playing Henry Higgins in *My Fair Lady.* But where they went wrong was in making a Rex Harrison movie without wonderful songs and without a classic love story. Higgins and Eliza were immensely more appealing to audiences than were Doctor Doolittle and his talking parrot.

The original black-and-white version of *Invasion of the Body Snatchers,* based on a novel by Jack Finney, became an instant classic in 1956 when it starred Kevin McCarthy and Dana Wynter. It was successfully remade in color in 1978. The second version stuck pretty close to the original, but possessed some effective innovations of its own and starred Donald Sutherland, Brooke Adams, and Jeff Goldblum—and featured one of the original's stars, Kevin McCarthy, in a supporting role. See them both to learn from their contrasts and their similarities.

In 1932 Clark Gable starred in the steamy black-and-white film *Red Dust,* which was set in Indochina and in which he romanced both wild "playgirl" Jean Harlow and prim married woman Mary

Astor. Twenty-one years later, Gable reprised his role of an irresistible man in the remake of *Red Dust,* now called *Mogambo* and set in Kenya, East Africa. In *Mogambo,* he romanced Ava Gardner's "playgirl" and Grace Kelly's married woman who falls for his at-home-in-the-jungle charm. (I lived in the jungles of Kenya for three years as a wildlife photographer and for me *Mogambo, King Solomon's Mines,* and *Hatari!* feel like documentaries—but that's another story.) Both of these versions are worth seeing in order to learn how to transport the central romantic triangle to another continent and culture.

The Front Page was made four times, under three different titles. It began life as a hit Broadway comedy about Chicago newspapermen who would do anything for an exclusive, written by former newspapermen Ben Hecht and Charles MacArthur. The first filmed version was released in 1931 and starred Adolphe Menjou as the paper's stop-at-nothing managing editor, Walter Burns, and Pat O'Brien as star reporter Hildy Johnson. The simple premise of the story is that Johnson has become engaged to a nice young woman from a traditional family and resigns from the paper to live a "normal" life. Burns, desperate to keep his best reporter, convinces Johnson to cover one last story: the execution of a man convicted of murder. Burns has no intention of losing Johnson's talents, and will do everything he can think of to break up the happy couple and show Johnson where he really belongs.

A clever twist on this plot produced *His Girl Friday* in 1940. This version starred Cary Grant as editor Walter Burns and Rosalind Russell as reporter Hildy Johnson, his newly divorced ex-wife, who has become engaged to a nice man from a traditional family and quits the newspaper business to live a "normal" life. *His Girl Friday,* from a screenplay by Charles Lederer, retained the plot of *The Front Page* and added the element of romantic comedy. This version of the story is my personal favorite, even though in adding the marvelous sexual sparks between the two leading characters, the picture had to forfeit one of the great last lines from a play or movie. (For trivia lovers, here is the setup and the line. At the end of *The Front Page,* Walter Burns appears to have given up trying to keep Hildy Johnson as a reporter.

Just before he says good-bye and good luck to Johnson at the railroad station he gives Johnson his expensive watch as a reward for a job well done. Then, as Johnson is boarding the train to leave Chicago, Burns screams for the police, points in Johnson's direction, and yells: "The son of a bitch stole my watch!" And we know that once again, Johnson will be made to miss that train and that the "happy couple" isn't going to be Johnson and his fed-up fiancée, but reporter Johnson and editor Burns.)

The Front Page (back to its original title and the original two male star premise) was remade in 1974, set in Chicago in the 1920s and starred Walter Matthau as Burns and Jack Lemmon as Johnson. This version, in color, was directed by Billy Wilder from a screenplay by Wilder and I. A. L. Diamond.

The least successful of the four versions of *The Front Page* was a remake of *His Girl Friday*. It was called *Switching Channels,* was released in 1988, and starred Kathleen Turner as an anchorwoman, Burt Reynolds as her boss and ex-husband, and Christopher Reeve as the new man in her life. To see why this picture was a commercial failure you might rent both *His Girl Friday* and *Switching Channels* to compare them. For screenwriters it will be an instructive experience to see how material as good as that in *His Girl Friday* was mishandled in rewriting and casting. You don't need to see all four versions of the story, but seeing *His Girl Friday,* the Lemmon-Matthau *Front Page,* and *Switching Channels* will prove very instructive. These three pictures are excellent examples of getting it right and getting it wrong.

In 1991 Disney released one of its most successful animated features, *Beauty and the Beast.* This film (and, later, the hugely successful Broadway musical that the Disney company produced) was a remake of the exquisite 1946 French film *Beauty and the Beast,* which was based on the medieval fairy tale about the power of romantic love. Both are available on videocassette. Don't miss the French version of this movie for its enchanting visual storytelling.

The first version of *King Kong,* released in 1933 and starring Fay Wray, was a kind of beauty and the beast story. In case the audience hadn't figured it out, Robert Armstrong, the leading man, verbalized this theme with his final line: "It was beauty killed the beast." A great hit, it was remade in 1976, and was again a financial success. Jessica Lange made her movie acting debut in this production, and, sadly for the actress, received *withering* reviews. She later overcame the cruelty of the critics and proved herself to be one of America's best actresses. In 1986 a sequel was made, called *King Kong Lives,* but this production seemed to come in below the audience's radar screen and disappeared quickly. See the original version and the remake in order to learn what in this story is so appealing to audiences.

Mighty Joe Young, another "giant captured ape" picture, was released in 1949. It was a popular success with good special effects and contained what is probably Hollywood's first simian drunk scene. *Mighty Joe Young* is being remade for release in 1998.

Warren Beatty's 1979 production of *Heaven Can Wait,* starring Beatty and James Mason, was a remake of the popular *Here Comes Mr. Jordan,* which was released in 1941 and starred Robert Montgomery and Claude Rains. In my opinion, Mr. Beatty's production was one of the very few movie remakes that was superior to the original version. A bit of movie trivia: What became the Warren Beatty version was developed in the early 1970s as a proposed mixed-race starring vehicle for Bill Cosby, but that project never came together. As much as I liked the Warren Beatty version, I would like to have seen the Bill Cosby version, too. (Here's a suggestion: Because the Beatty version is almost twenty years old, why not make the Bill Cosby script with Will Smith as the star?)

In 1960, Roger Corman released the original black-and-white version of *Little Shop of Horrors,* which featured Jack Nicholson in the supporting role of an unfortunate dental patient. In the 1980s, *Little Shop of Horrors* was reconceived as a stage musical. This production was so successful that the movie version of the musical, starring Rick Moranis and featuring Steve Martin as a leather-wearing, motorcycle-riding, sadistic dentist who ultimately ends up as plant food, was released in 1986 and found an enthusiastic audience of fans. The musical version is a brilliant rethinking of the original, but both versions are very much worth seeing in order to study how the first was turned into the second.

As I was writing this book, I received a call from a friend, actress and writer Mira Waters. Mira had been reading chapters of this manuscript as I wrote them, and had been giving me reactions and suggestions. She was calling now because she had recently rented a movie called *The Associate,* starring Whoopi Goldberg. She said that she thought it illustrated some of the points I had made about creating memorable star roles and supporting characters, and asked if I had seen it. When I told her that I had not, Mira urged me to get it so we could discuss it. Respecting Mira's judgment and her enthusiasm, I went that day to my favorite video connection, Videocentre in Beverly Hills, and rented it.

I liked *The Associate* very much. I knew nothing about the movie, other than the very enjoyable 114 minutes I had just seen. I was sure it was too recent a film to be in my reference books, but I looked it up anyway and came across a listing for a French film titled *L'Associe* that had been released in 1982. From the brief plot synopsis of the French film I realized that the movie I had just seen was a loose American remake, and worth seeing to study how the same star part worked as both a male role and a female role.

Whoopi Goldberg's version did not stay in theaters very long. I began to try to figure out why this very funny movie with marvelous actors, well-written characters, and continual plot surprises had not been a huge hit. Suddenly I recalled the newspaper ad I had seen for the movie when it was released. There may have been alternative ads, but the only one I saw featured a photo of Whoopi Goldberg sitting in an executive's chair, wearing a neat pantsuit, with her feet up on top of an office desk. The title, *The Associate,* made me think it was about lawyers. Lawyers are not the most compelling subject for me. In spite of this, I remembered making a mental note to see the movie when I had time because I think anything Whoopi Goldberg does is worth a look. Unfortunately, *The Associate* vanished from theaters before I had a chance to see it. That was my loss, I learned, after Mira urged me to see it on videocassette.

There's no way I can know for certain why *The Associate* was not a big hit because I was not involved in the project. Perhaps the advertising campaign was not the right one to attract a large audience. Perhaps it was not booked in the most advantageous theaters. Perhaps the competition (movies released at the same time) was overwhelming and audiences rushed to see an "event" movie or movies on the critical opening weekend. Box office receipts on a picture's opening weekend will too often determine a movie's fate.

Or perhaps whoever made the decision thought that *hiding* the great strength of the picture, what made it special, was a good idea. The characters, their relationships to each other, and the situation were what made *The Associate* such a good movie. Whoopi Goldberg plays a brilliant financial consultant who—only because she is a woman—is denied a deserved promotion and had the credit for her accomplishments stolen by a sleazy male colleague whose major talent is his ability to lie convincingly. Miss Goldberg's costar, the wonderful Dianne Wiest (an Oscar-winner and a chameleon who looks different in every movie), played the sleazy colleague's grossly undervalued secretary. Miss Goldberg's character, defeated by her inability to crack the "boys' network" inner circle of the financial world, in desperation creates a fictional male senior partner. Thanks to the help of Miss Wiest, who leaves her contemptible boss and blossoms as Miss Goldberg's resourceful assistant, the new company soon becomes the sensation of Wall Street, until— (I would tell you more but I want you to rent this movie and see for yourself how good it is.)

I suspect that one of this movie's strengths might have been considered a liability by the men who are mostly in charge of movie studios. Beneath the details of the plot, *The Associate* is the story of two women who form a powerful bond of friendship and take huge risks together. But these women are not conventional beauties, as were Susan Sarandon and Geena Davis in *Thelma & Louise*. I think that simple fact—that the two leading women were not beautiful in the

175

"Hollywood" sense—may have had an affect on how *The Associate* was handled in its theatrical release.

My delicious fantasy is that so many people start renting *The Associate* that the men who released and distributed it are forced to wonder whether they missed a big opportunity in its theatrical release.

Sequels and Prequels

In 1989 Rick Moranis starred in *Honey, I Shrunk the Kids,* a family picture that was such a hit it was followed by a sequel in 1992 titled *Honey, I Blew Up the Kid.* (For anyone who didn't see the picture, or the ads depicting a young child the size of the Goodyear blimp, "Blew Up" in this context means "inflated.")

The Godfather, an American film many (myself among them) think is a masterpiece, was released in 1972. It starred Marlon Brando in the title role and Al Pacino as the Godfather's youngest son, Michael, who was never intended to follow in his father's footsteps but who was forced by circumstances to do just that. *The Godfather Part II,* which I think is an equal masterpiece, was released in 1974. It again starred Al Pacino as Michael, and costarred Robert De Niro as the young Godfather. The picture was structured to alternate the 1958–59 story of Michael Corleone with the much earlier story that detailed the original Godfather's youth and young manhood as he evolved from an orphaned Sicilian refugee boy, completely alone in the world, to the powerful protector of family and friends in his beloved adopted country, the land of golden promise, America. (Watching *The Godfather* and *The Godfather Part II* is likely to induce in one a powerful craving for fruit. See how many times fruit is carefully selected, admired, and then eaten in these films.) About *The Godfather Part III,* which was released in 1990, I believe that the filmmakers chose to tell the wrong story, and with—excepting Al Pacino, Andy Garcia, Talia Shire, and Diane Keaton—the wrong cast. I would have much preferred to see a story dealing with the years immediately following Michael's having Fredo killed and exiling Kay from his life. And I think the loss of Robert Duvall's character, Tom Hagen, from the third film was a major blow.

The Terminator, starring Arnold Schwarzenegger as a *very bad* cyborg from the future and Linda Hamilton as the gritty young woman he has come back to the "past" to kill, was a huge hit in 1984. It was full of the kind of entertaining violence that can be enjoyed without gagging. By the end, everyone in the movie except Linda Hamilton and her German shepherd had been killed, but the only time we saw blood was when the Terminator operated on himself. There was enough gore for three action pictures in the sequel, *Terminator 2: Judgment Day,* which starred Arnold Schwarzenegger again—this time as a good guy from the future—and Linda Hamilton, whose character by this time is the mother of a young son. *T2* (as it was called in movie industry shorthand) was released in 1991 and was a megahit. Not only did it have fabulous "morphing" special effects, but it had a story with emotional currents as powerful as its spectacular stunts and effects.

Alien, which starred actress Sigourney Weaver as Ripley, was a surprise hit with the public when it was released in 1979, in spite of the fact that this was an action picture that starred a woman, and therefore was considered a big risk. But the public—male and female— loved Ripley. By the end of *Alien,* only Ripley and her cat have survived. (A character I was very sorry to see die was the heroic Parker, played by the versatile actor Yaphet Kotto.) At *Alien'*s fade-out, Ripley and the cat settle down to sleep comfortably in a special sleeping capsule. They are scheduled to arrive back on earth in a few weeks.

The even more successful sequel *Aliens*—with more and bigger monsters for Ripley to fight—was released in 1986. It begins when Ripley and the cat wake up—fifty-seven years later—to discover that their spacecraft has gone astray, drifting for almost six decades while they slept in their capsule. By the end of *Aliens,* Ripley and the little orphaned girl she has protected so fiercely are the only survivors of their battle against the monsters. At the fade-out, they settle down to sleep for the few weeks it will take them to return safely to earth.

Alien³, released in 1992, is an oddly different movie from the first two. It begins shockingly with an event that distressed this member of the audience greatly: The new set of filmmakers *killed off* the lovely little girl Ripley fought so hard to save! And then the picture gets much grimmer from there. Something that struck me as perhaps an unfortunate coincidence was that *Alien³* had the same ending as *Terminator 2: Judgment Day,* which was released the year before *Alien³*. Just like the "good" Terminator of the second film, at the end Ripley sacrifices her own life by descending into a fiery inferno. In spite of the fact that Ripley was supposed to have died at the end of the third picture, a fourth *Alien* film was released in late 1997. This story pairs Sigourney Weaver with the younger Winona Ryder. It was not a major success. As of January 13, 1998, after forty-seven days in release, it has grossed only $46,619,841 million. (In the same forty-seven days *Flubber* sold $85,633,339 million, with many of these less expensive children's tickets.)

Rocky began as an inexpensive boxing picture produced by Irwin Winkler and Robert Chartoff, with the virtually unknown actor who had written the picture as a starring vehicle for himself in the lead. Sylvester Stallone didn't stay unknown very long, and the inexpensive *Rocky* turned into a huge hit. It received six Oscar nominations, including a Best Original Screenplay nomination for Stallone. It won three 1976 Oscars: for Best Picture, Best Director (John Avildsen), and for Best Film Editing. *Rocky 2* was released in 1979, *Rocky 3* in 1982, and *Rocky 4* in 1985. The secret of *Rocky's* success was that while it was set in and around boxing rings, the movie was not about boxing. *Rocky* was really about having a dream and finding the courage to follow it.

The first *Godzilla* film was released in 1956. It was a Japanese movie, but scenes featuring actor Raymond Burr were inserted for the American release. Burr's voice also narrated the picture on the sound track of the version released in America. Twelve subsequent pictures using the name "Godzilla" in their titles were released over the years, including *King Kong vs. Godzilla* (1963), but they were neither remakes nor sequels. Currently, the original *Godzilla* film is being remade to be released by Sony Pictures Entertainment, an American company. It is not scheduled for release until the summer of 1998, but a "coming attractions" trailer for the movie is playing in all the theaters playing the huge summer hit of 1997, *Men in Black,* which is also a Sony Pictures Entertainment release. Promoting *Godzilla* a year before it will be available in theaters establishes the film in the minds of moviegoers as a high-budget "event" film. The intention here is to build anticipation for the 1998 Godzilla to such a high level that ticket buyers will stampede *into* the theaters the way residents of Tokyo tried to stampede out of the giant reptile's path in the original Japanese *Godzilla.*

Here is a bit of movie trivia: Actor Raymond Burr had a bizarre career trajectory. In 1951 he earned admiring notices as the avenging prosecuting attorney who sent Montgomery Clift to the electric chair in *A Place in the Sun.* In 1954 he earned a kind of immortality as Jimmy Stewart's neighbor across the courtyard who murders his wife and chops her into pieces in the classic *Rear Window.* In 1956 he was artificially inserted into the Japanese-made *Godzilla,* which was not exactly a career step upward. Raymond Burr finally became a star on television, first as superlawyer Perry Mason, and later as a wheelchair-bound police detective in *Ironside.* I recount this history to illustrate that one never knows when, nor with what project, success will come. The trick to winning is staying in the game until it's your turn to win.

Sequels are generally made within a few years of the original movies that inspired them, but here are two that took a very long time between chapters of their particular stories.

In 1961 Paul Newman starred as Fast Eddie Felsen in *The Hustler,* a drama about the sleazy world of professional pool playing. It took twenty-five years before he would chalk up a pool cue again as Fast Eddie, this time in *The Color of Money,* released in 1986 and costarring Tom Cruise. As the older Fast Eddie, Paul Newman finally won a long overdue Academy Award for Best Actor.

The Odd Couple, written by Neil Simon and starring Jack Lemmon and Walter Matthau, was a huge hit in 1968. Simon wrote a brilliant sequel called *The Odd Couple II,* which picks up the story of Felix (the neat freak) and Oscar (the slob) twenty years after the first picture ended. It began filming, with Lemmon and Matthau, in June of 1997 for release in 1998. I was privileged to read the script shortly before it began filming; it's one of the best scripts I've ever read, and concludes the Felix and Oscar story in a perfect circle of an ending.

Just as it is good to study remakes, it will also be useful to study sequels and prequels in case you are ever called upon to write one on assignment, or in the event you can convince whoever owns the rights to the characters you want to explore further to let you try. Even if you never get to write a sequel or a prequel, it will be to your advantage to study what elements and what characters can successfully be carried either forward or backward in time.

Prequels are rare—probably because the original stars can't play their characters as teenagers and very young men. One of the most expensive ventures into prequels was the 1992 NBC television series *The Young Indiana Jones Chronicles.* It was a beautifully made series in every respect, but it never found the huge audience a series that expensive needed in order to survive on the network. It's my personal theory that the audience (or at least the women in the audience), knowing the character of Indy would grow up to be Harrison Ford, didn't want to spend time in Indy's childhood. (But no one asked my opinion when they were planning the show.)

It was impossible to make a sequel to the very successful *Butch Cassidy and the Sundance Kid,* which starred Paul Newman and Robert Redford in 1969, because the two star characters presumably died at the end of the picture. Imaginatively, in 1979 the studio (Fox) released a prequel titled *Butch and Sundance: The Early Days.* It starred Tom Berenger and William Katt in the roles made indelible by Newman and Redford.

In interviews, George Lucas has described his Luke Skywalker/Han Solo/Princess Laia/Darth Vader movies *(Star Wars, The Empire Strikes Back,* and *Return of the Jedi)* as a trilogy, or a three-film saga. Akira Kurosawa's 1958 film *The Hidden Fortress,* the story of a warrior who protects a princess from warring feudal lords, was an inspiration for *Star Wars.* In 1997 George Lucas began work preparing a new film trilogy that will be a "prequel saga" to the *Star Wars* series. These new films, the first of which he hopes to release in 1999, will tell the story of how Luke Skywalker's father evolved from noble Jedi Knight into Darth Vader.

Franchises

When a picture's sequel becomes hugely successful, those pictures can turn into that most financially beloved of all creative entities: the "franchise." It will be very helpful to you as a screenwriter to study franchise pictures so that you can learn to recognize—and perhaps even to create—those elements that could turn your ideas into a franchise.

There are two kinds of franchise pictures: the "character" franchise, based on the perfect combination of a character and the actor who plays him, and the "concept" franchise, in which the idea is so strong it can flourish even though the original actor or actors may be replaced.

Bruce Willis's John McClane in the *Die Hard* pictures, Mel Gibson's Riggs and Danny Glover's Murtaugh in the *Lethal Weapon* pictures, Clint Eastwood's Harry Callahan in the Dirty Harry pictures, Sylvester Stallone's Rocky Balboa and Harrison Ford in the Indiana Jones pictures *(Raiders of the Lost Ark, Indiana Jones and the Temple of Doom,* and *Indiana Jones and the Last Crusade)* are all franchise characters who have such personal popularity that it is impossible to imagine other actors playing those roles.

By contrast, some *concepts* are so strong that even cast changes do not diminish the appeal of these "concept franchises." Examples: the *Batman, Star Trek,* and James Bond pictures. While it is unimaginable that the *Lethal Weapons, Die Hards* and Dirty Harry movies could survive the loss of their stars, the *Batmans, Star Treks* and James Bond pictures have no such restrictions in their global appeal to audiences. James Bond, in fact, is the greatest franchise of all. The first James Bond movie, *Dr. No,* was released in 1962, and the eighteenth, *Tomorrow Never Dies,* was released in December of 1997. So far five different actors have starred as James Bond. In order, they are: Sean Connery, George Lazenby, Roger Moore, Sean Connery again (in *Never Say Never Again*), Timothy Dalton, and Pierce Brosnan.

Those eighteen James Bond movies do not include the film version of the first James Bond novel, *Casino Royale*. The movie version of *Casino Royale* was filmed as a comic spoof and featured actors Woody Allen and David Niven as various versions of a lampooned James Bond character. This collision of visions happened because one producer, Charles Feldman, bought the rights to *Casino Royale* and then the producing team of Cubby Broccoli and Harry Saltzman bought the rights to the other James Bond novels and stories.

From the 1930s well into the 1970s, *Tarzan* was a franchise. The movies were inexpensive to make and had enthusiastic audiences eagerly awaiting each new picture in the series.

Tarzan was a role that quite a variety of well-built actors played successfully, swinging through trees in theatrical features and in the NBC television series. Sy Weintraub, who bought the rights to *Tarzan* in the late 1950s, produced a very profitable series of *Tarzan* films in Africa, India, Thailand, and Mexico, and also produced the television series. He maintains that the best *Tarzan* story was the first one, and that in all succeeding plots "Tarzan was the one unnecessary character."

Now, make a list of the pictures discussed in this chapter and begin to outline a course of study viewing for yourself. I recommend that you begin with the megahits. When you have digested these, go on to study original films and their remakes; then concentrate your attention on the franchise pictures. All of the movies I have discussed in this chapter are available on videocassette and many play on basic cable channels. Do not watch movies that you want to study when they play on commercial networks because the frequent interruptions for commercials will disrupt your attention. Also, commercial television will sometimes delete connecting scenes that will be important for you to see in order to understand the total effect of the movie.

Understand why you are watching each of the movies you will study. If you are seeing a movie for the first time, surrender to the experience of the movie that first time. Just watch it without analyzing.

Then, after you have experienced the film once, see it again in order to study the writer's craft.

This is a large assignment, but there are no shortcuts to developing yourself into the best writer that you can become. Studying all, or most, of these movies will take some time, but the effort put in to perfect your skills can bring enormous rewards.

10. The "Pitch" and the Query Letter

In the world of the professional screenwriter it is not enough simply to be a skilled writer. One must also learn how to sell one's work. You will need to know how to sell your work in order to attract the interest of an agent, or to interest a possible buyer in your script. If you succeed in catching the interest of a buyer, that will make it much easier to get an agent.

The second most important talent, just behind writing, that a new screenwriter needs to develop is the ability to "pitch." There are two distinctly different types of pitches, the "story" pitch and the "teaser" pitch. They have distinctly different purposes. It will serve you well to learn how to perform the story pitch and to craft the teaser pitch.

In the story pitch, the writer tells a story he or she has not yet written in the hope that the person to whom the story is being told will pay the writer to write it. This kind of pitch requires that the writer be such a good performer that the producer or production executive who is listening "sees" the movie as the writer is telling the story. This requires that the writer learn to be a superb storyteller. (I will explain shortly how a writer gets the opportunity to pitch a story to someone who could pay her to write it.)

Several of the writers who have taken my workshops have later also taken acting classes. This has helped them by giving them some performance skills. Writers who have also studied acting, even for a few weeks, generally become better verbal storytellers. Acting classes also offer the additional benefit of helping writers sharpen their thinking about their characters from an actor's point of view.

Now, to the question of how a writer gets the opportunity to pitch a story to a producer or a production executive who can pay the writer to deliver the script. The answer is simple: The people who invite you in to pitch a story have already read, and been favorably impressed by, a previous script you have written. In other words, they already know you can write. Now they want to know if you are thinking about a story that they will want to commission.

Your next question is probably: "But how can I get them to read the first script so that they know I can write?" This can happen one of three ways:

1. Someone in the business has read something you have written and calls a friend to recommend that you come in for a meeting and to pitch.
2. Your agent has submitted your spec script and it was read but turned down for any number of possible reasons. Your script did, however, make a favorable impression as to your talent as a writer. Now they want to know what else you might be thinking about.
3. You don't have an agent, but you wrote such a clever teaser pitch in a query letter to that producer or production executive that he agreed to read your script. Even though he did not want to buy that particular script, he is now aware that there is a talented new writer in town, and he wants to meet you to find out what else you may have, or may want to write.

This brings us to developing the skill to write a teaser pitch that will get you through doors that are otherwise closed to you.

The Teaser Pitch

The teaser pitch is a one- to three-sentence *attention grabber* which describes a script you have already written. It is designed to make the person hearing it (or reading it in a query letter) respond with that wonderful sentence: "I want to read your script!"

The "target" of your pitch might be an agent you want to represent you, or it might be a producer, director, star, or production company executive you want to buy the material or at least read it. Remember that even if a good spec script isn't bought, it can serve as a great "audition" piece, introducing you and your skills to professionals and allowing you to be considered for writing assignments or for rewrite jobs. Good work can have more than one potential value.

We are about to learn how to create the tantalizing one- to three-sentence teaser description. You're going to be surprised to learn how easy it is, *once you master the technique of it.* Developing this skill will be more than a tool—it may prove to be essential in some circumstances.

Even when you have an agent who has agreed to represent you, that agent may need your help in framing the perfect phrases that will hook the interest of a potential buyer. Of course many agents are very good at finding the right way to present your script, but not all of them are. If this isn't your agent's strongest talent, then your clever teaser pitch will be helpful when she puts your script out on the market.

First, you must understand *what* your targets will be looking for so that you can give them the information they need in the most effective way.

When hearing a short teaser pitch or reading it in a query letter, the first thing your target will be looking for is an idea of *how* the picture could be cast. By that I mean your target will be thinking about for which star or stars this material would be suitable. Producers and production executives know that the *quickest* way to get a picture made in Hollywood is to have one of the major box office heavyweights agree to star in it. That sends a project zooming onto the "fast track."

I've worked out a formula for creating an effective two- to three-sentence pitch, and here it is:

1. In the first line, use the *name* of your star character, or characters if yours is a two-star vehicle, like the *Lethal Weapon* movies.
2. Give us some idea of what kind of trouble your lead is in, or what kind of obstacles he or she is up against.
3. If it isn't clear from the first two sentences, make sure your target knows what the genre of the script is—whether it's comedy, drama, thriller, mystery, romance, science fiction, or action adventure, or some combination, such as a romantic thriller or mystery-comedy. Your third sentence can be a witty or a memorable closing line. (I'll be giving examples of these catchy, memorable "closers" after we work on the basic teaser pitch.)

In learning how to write a teaser pitch, study movie advertisements—the ads that are devised before the releasing studios have good reviews from the critics to quote. Here are some examples of real ad copy that can easily be adapted into a pitch to sell the script. (After the good examples, I'll give you some bad examples and explain why those pitches *won't* work.)

First, here is the exact teaser text on an ad for the film *Executive Decision:*

"Five miles above the earth, an elite team of six men must make an air to air transfer in order to save 400 lives on board a 747 . . . and 40 million below."

Because the picture was about to be released and the ad included a picture of the star, Kurt Russell, there was no need to mention the star character, but suppose this script had just been written and was ready to go on the market. Here's how an effective pitch for *Executive Decision could* have read:

187

Government intelligence analyst Dr. David Grant is suddenly whisked away from a black-tie party at the U.S. embassy in Washington and flown five miles above the earth to join a Special Forces antiterrorism team. With time so short he can't even change his clothes, Grant and the team must make an immediate air-to-air transfer in order to save 400 lives on board a hijacked 747 . . .

And 40 million below.

This is what we learn in the above pitch:

The genre: action thriller.

The star role: Dr. David Grant, when not analyzing intelligence, lives the kind of glamorous life in the nation's capital that includes black-tie galas at the U.S. embassy. This emergency happens so fast there could not be enough time for the good guys to perfect a plan, and that makes the odds against their surviving their mission even greater than if they had had time to prepare. And we learn that not only are the lives of 400 innocent passengers in the 747 at stake, but so are *40 million* unsuspecting lives on the ground.

I wanted to see the movie based on that ad—and I would have wanted to read the script based on that pitch.

An ad for the movie *A Family Thing* featured photographs of Robert Duvall and James Earl Jones and the words:

"Earl and Ray just learned they are brothers. It is going to be one heck of a family reunion."

If I were marketing the script of this movie, without having the advantage of knowing Robert Duvall and James Earl Jones would be playing the parts, here is how I would have adapted that ad copy for the pitch:

A white man named Earl and a black man named Ray just learned they are brothers.

It is going to be one heck of a family reunion.

The very effective ad copy for the movie *Sleeping with the Enemy* read:

"She changed her name. Her looks. Her life. All to escape the most dangerous man she ever met. Her husband."

Here's how I would adapt that copy into the pitch.

> Twenty-four-year-old Laura Burney changed her name, her looks, and her life. All to escape the most dangerous man she ever met.
>
> Her husband.

This pitch tells us:

The genre: a woman-in-jeopardy thriller.

The star role is that of a young woman. I put in an age so that the project could be visualized as a vehicle for one of the top young female box office attractions.

Faithful, a movie released in 1995, starring Cher and Chazz Palminteri (from a play written by Palminteri), had a marvelous visual in its newspaper ad: Cher, wearing a bathrobe and bunny slippers, sits tied to a chair in front of a huge target—with the bull's-eye centered on the middle of her chest. The ad copy read:

"After 20 years of marriage, she thought she was the target of her husband's affections. She was only half right."

I didn't get to a theater to see the movie while it was playing, so all I know about the film is from that ad and from a very brief synopsis of the story. Using this little bit of information, here is an example of how the script might have been pitched before Cher was attached and the studio agreed to make it:

> Margaret is a rich, unhappy wife who decides to commit suicide on her twentieth wedding anniversary. She's interrupted by Tony, the devilishly attractive hit man her husband has hired to murder her. As Margaret sits tied to a chair, and Tony tries to get his therapist on the phone, the two make a life-changing connection.

I don't know if my version of the pitch is a perfectly accurate reflection of the movie's plot, but I do know that I would want to read that script.

That is the object of this exercise: to excite someone so that he or she will want to read your script.

Study the text in movie ads and practice adapting them into teaser pitches. Or create teaser pitches for movies that you've seen. When you've done a few of these, then start creating pitches for your own scripts, using the formula we've discussed.

To get from the theoretical to the specific, here are some examples of effective pitches. The first pitch was written by one of the most talented new writers I know, G. Wassil, and it's the pitch for his star-vehicle screenplay *Homefront*. While this particular script has not sold (as of this writing), the writer was hired for several writing assignments:

> Three tours in Vietnam and ten years as a Chicago cop didn't prepare RAZKOWSKI for his new boss.
> Nothing could have prepared *her* for Razkowski.

Think about how much we learn in those above two sentences:

Genre: It's a cop picture, so it's probably filled with action.

It has a star role, Razkowski. He's a Chicago cop and ex-military. That means tough, smart, courageous—*a part for a major male star.* And, while he's fighting crime and the bad guys, he's got to cope with a female superior officer. That suggests great conflict and probably sexual sparks, which means there's a part for an exciting actress.

The response of almost everyone who read that teaser pitch was: "I want to read that script!"

Here are some pitches developed in my UCLA Extension Screenplay Development Workshop:

Talented screenwriter Denise Snaer had sole writing credit on the produced thriller *Jamaica Beat,* but it was the teaser pitch for her next screenplay that landed Denise an agent. Here is the pitch for her romantic thriller *The Man in the Cool Suit:*

New Orleans newspaperman DASH MADISON comes to Los Angeles to track down his long-estranged father, a cop on the LAPD. But before Dash can unpack his bags he meets a beautiful woman, discovers a body in her bedroom, is suspected of murder and realizes that the need to find his father has suddenly become a matter of life and death—his own.

See how much information is conveyed in that pitch for *The Man in the Cool Suit:*

Genre: mystery thriller, which means it's probably filled with action.

It has a star role: Dash Madison. He's a newspaperman, from New Orleans (which suggests some exotic doings), and his father was a cop. The fact that he's in the bedroom of a beautiful woman he's just met suggests that he's attractive and has great sex appeal. The fact that there's a dead body in her room and that Dash becomes a suspect suggests that the lady is dangerous to him. Added to these elements is the "ticking clock" of his need to find his missing father in order to save himself.

That teaser for *The Man in the Cool Suit* tells us that it's a male-star-vehicle picture with mystery, action, romance, and a touch of the exotic. That was enough information to make the first agent who read that pitch ask to read the script. The agent then signed Denise Snaer to representation papers after reading the first ten pages of the script.

Elizabeth Powell is a young woman who writes powerful dramas that explore the darkest territory in human emotions. This is her pitch for the domestic drama *An Angel in the Family:*

Nicole Porter had survived the brutal beatings her father, Patrick, thought of as "discipline" and the death of her beloved little sister, who thought she could fly to escape her turn under the belt. Life for Nicole and her younger brother was better for the seven years their father disappeared, but now, on her 16th birthday, Nicole discovers that she's pregnant and that Patrick has come back to head their family. This time Nicole is not alone; her little sister has returned as an angel on a mission.

In the above pitch we learn that the screenplay is a drama, and that the leading characters are a sixteen-year-old-girl, Nicole, and her troubled father, Patrick. The nature of the drama suggests that Nicole and Patrick are strong acting roles.

A producer who's looking for a powerful drama, the kind that, if it works, attracts critical praise and awards, is probably going to want to read this script.

Elizabeth Powell also wrote a thriller called *Dark Flames,* a female star vehicle. This is the pitch:

Briana Reven has beauty, a glowing talent as a painter, and a tormenting secret guilt which threatens to destroy both Briana the artist and Briana the woman. Suddenly the greatest threat to Briana turns out to be Kyle Link, the brilliant teacher and tortured artist she befriends. In facing down this madman, Briana finds the courage to confront the demons of her own past.

When *Dark Flames* goes on the market, a producer looking for a female-star-vehicle thriller will probably ask to read it, because the pitch has told the producer these two pieces of essential information: who the story is about (a female artist) and the fact that she must outwit and then conquer both a dangerous man and her own past.

Richard Lorber, before he turned to screenwriting, was the author of published satires and had written successful routines for stand-up comics. When he began writing screenplays, he remained in the field of intelligent comedy, in a version of the genre I call "wit with pratfalls."

For a romantic comedy titled *Hillerman Faces North,* the pitch was:

Jack Hillerman, a Hell-raising, womanizing nuclear physicist, meets a gorgeous Russian mentalist with psycho-kinetic powers. While he's trying to prove she's a fraud, they fall in love; then she's kidnapped by Las Vegas cutthroats and he's institutionalized by a jealous psychiatrist. Reunited as fugitives, Jack discovers that when the Laws of Science collide with the Powers of the Mind, anything is possible.

This pitch tells us that it's a fast-paced, slightly mad comedy vehicle for a male star.

The script for *Hillerman Faces North* hooked an agent, but before the script went on the market, the agent suddenly retired to Las Vegas without leaving a forwarding address. (Unexpected things happen. That's one of the reasons I strongly recommend the Writer's Strength and Stamina Exercise Routine. This is a crazy business, but to succeed the writer must stay sane.)

If You Want to Pitch the Concept of Your Script

There is a variation on the teaser pitch that teases the *concept* of the story, rather than the star character or characters. This teaser technique is used only when the concept of your script is so strong and intriguing that the concept *alone* is likely to get potential agents or buyers to agree to read it.

Here are three excellent examples of the concept teaser:

The story of an eleven year old Imp in Hell who, no matter how hard he tried, could never do anything bad.
THE IMP, written by G. Wassil & Michael Connelly.

This is an absolutely enchanting script that I believe will be made when the right combination of creative elements comes together.

Here is another excellent concept pitch for drama:

What if the 15 year old daughter of the pro-life President of the United States becomes pregnant during his reelection campaign and wants to have an abortion?

It happens in *Family Secrets,* by Caroline Pfouts.

That pitch landed the author, Caroline Pfouts, an agent. The script, a drama, was widely read and came very close to being made at one company. While that has not happened (as of this writing) the script was such a good "calling card" that the writer's second screenplay, a comedy, was optioned by a producer who liked *Family Secrets* so much that he asked to see anything else she had. The second script she gave him is now in the process of being developed for production, and Caroline Pfouts is doing revisions.

The third example of the concept pitch is from comic writer Richard Lorber. The script is a sci-fi comedy called *Twenty Million Miles to Wall Street:*

A trio of humanoid extra-terrestrials kidnap a financial wizard from prison and take over Wall Street. They intend to control the world economy, hold earthlings accountable for their mismanagement of the planet, and teach us a lesson. The plan backfires when they fall victim to earthly temptations and are arrested for insider trading.

This pitch is a good example because it convinced an agent to read the screenplay and, once he read it, the agent signed Richard Lorber for representation.

The final example of the concept teaser comes from Gary E. Shrout, a commander in the United States Navy who used his knowledge of the service as a basis for a fictional screenplay he is developing. It is titled *Homeport Hollywood,* and this is the pitch:

Navy Commander Charlie Hammond had sailed the seven seas and earned a chest full of medals. Suddenly he's facing his most formidable opponent ever . . . Hollywood. Charlie's in show business now, whether he likes it or not.

Homeport Hollywood will not be finished for several months, but a producer who visited my workshop and heard the pitch asked to read the script as soon as it is ready to be submitted.

Successful writers need to have the endurance of marathon runners, not the short-distance speed of sprinters, because there are movies that make it onto the screen pretty quickly and some that take a *very long* time to be made.

An example of the latter is *One Flew Over the Cuckoo's Nest.* That project took thirteen years to journey from Ken Kesey's 1962 novel to stage play and, at last, onto the screen. Kirk Douglas, who played the leading role on stage, owned the movie rights for years but could not get the picture financed. Finally, Kirk Douglas passed the rights on to his son, actor-producer Michael Douglas, who packaged the film with Jack Nicholson to star and Milos Foreman to direct. Contrary to the many negative commercial predictions of competing studios and their expensive research firms, *One Flew Over the Cuckoo's Nest* was a great commercial success and it won 1975 Oscars for Best Actor (Nicholson), Best Actress (Louise Fletcher), Best Film, Best Director (Foreman), and Best Supporting Actor (Brad Dourif). Those same people, and the film, all won British Academy Awards in their categories the following year, in 1976.

In 1983 I read an original screenplay written by John Hill, titled *Quigley Down Under.* It had been making the rounds looking for a deal for at least seven years before it landed on my desk. I was crazy about this story of an American sharpshooter named Quigley who travels to Australia for a job that he is told consists of shooting wild dogs who are attacking sheep. When he arrives at the ranch of the man who hired him, Quigley discovers that he has really been imported to kill Aborigines. Refusing to murder human beings results in Quigley and the young woman who attaches herself to him being hunted down by the villain and his men. I thought it was a marvelous screenplay and tried to buy it to star Nick Nolte, but a deal could not be worked out. Later, my friend producer Alexandra Rose (coproducer of *Norma Rae*) optioned the script. It took her another six years to get the picture made. *Quigley Down Under,* starring Tom Selleck, Laura San Giacomo, and my favorite villain, Alan Rickman, was finally released in 1990, nearly fifteen years after it left writer John Hill's typewriter. I was pleased to see that the movie was changed very little, if there were any changes, from the script I had read seven years earlier.

Another film that almost no one among the smartest and highest-paid executives in the movie business wanted to touch was *Driving Miss Daisy.* Fortunately, the "almost"—the people who held on to their stubborn belief that the Pulitzer Prize–winning play by Alfred Uhry should be filmed—were Richard Zanuck, Lili Fini Zanuck, and David Brown at the Zanuck Company. I was having lunch regularly with Lili Zanuck in the several years it took them to get this play financed, cast, and onto the screen, and heard her many tales of turn-downs and setbacks. I marveled at and admired their refusal to take no seriously, or to let all those slammed doors shake their faith in their own taste and passion for the script. As you may know, this story has a very happy ending. The last time I checked the grosses, *Miss Daisy* (which was directed by Bruce Beresford and made for little more than the catering costs on certain major star-vehicle action films) has brought in more than $100 million domestically. 1989 Academy Awards were collected by Richard Zanuck, Lili Fini Zanuck, and David Brown as producers of that Best Picture, Jessica Tandy as Best Actress, and Mr. Uhry for Best Adapted Screenplay. (It also won an Oscar for Best Makeup.) In 1990 it won British Academy Awards in the Best Musical or Comedy category (odd, for a picture that had something important to say about race relations) for Best Picture, Best Actress (Miss Tandy), and Best Actor, the marvelous Morgan Freeman, who played the man who drives, puts up with, understands, and remains a steadfast friend to the difficult and complex Miss Daisy. How Bruce Beresford's directing was overlooked for these honors is something I cannot understand.

Closer Lines

If, after teasing the characters, the situation, and the concept, you feel a "closer" line is needed, here are some excellent examples. Not all pitches need a closer, but if you can think of a final line that is memorable and easily quotable, that can be very advantageous. A closer line is something clever or witty that follows the body of the pitch.

For the John Travolta comedy *Michael,* the ad has a picture of a man—shown only from the knees down—who's being following by a little dog. The man is wearing trousers, shoes, and a coat, and from the bottom of the coat the tips of an angel's wings are peeking out. Below the photo is this wonderful line:

"He's an angel . . . Not a saint."

I hurried out to see this movie and liked it immensely.

Another closer line to the short teaser pitch might have been:

"Michael was an angel with very earthly appetites."

I don't know what the movie *If Lucy Fell* was about because I never got a chance to see it, but I liked this line that was in the ad just below the title:

"A comedy for the romantically challenged."

In the excellent HBO Pictures production of *Gotti* (written by Steve Shagan and starring Armand Assante in the title role) the ad features a large photo of Assante, looking remarkably like the real John Gotti. Under the photo is the line:

"In the mob, there's only one thing more sacred than Family. Silence."

That line would have been a great closer for a pitch about the Gotti film, or for another movie on a similar subject.

Here is an example of ad copy that I do *not* think is effective as an ad, and that would not be at all effective if it were a teaser pitch. I am not using this to be critical of the people involved in creating the ad, only as an example of a real ad that did not attract *my* interest.

This is for a film called *The Arrival,* which I never saw.

"The greatest danger facing our world has been the planet's best kept secret . . . until now."

Even if there had not been an illustration of something that looked like a combination movie spaceship and a satellite dish, I think one could have guessed that *The Arrival* was probably about visitors from another galaxy. This sell line lacks any sense of *who* the story is about. *Who* is our hero? Whose fate will we worry about? What danger is involved? *Is* there any danger involved? Is this a drama? A comedy? If it's a thriller there is no hint of what thrills there might be in the story.

Charlie Sheen was given star billing at the top of the ad, but Sheen is a versatile actor who has played a wide variety of parts. There is no typical Charlie Sheen character, so it's impossible to tell, just from seeing that actor's name, what kind of a role he is playing. In this case, the name of the star does not supply the needed information. The result was that nothing in the ad hooked my interest.

Whether you are trying to get someone to read your script or to buy a ticket to your movie, the principle of attracting attention is the same: Give your target some *specific information* that is worded so that it excites interest.

Don't Fall into the "Synopsis Trap"

When your pitch, or your pitch in your query letter, *does* excite someone's interest, and you are telephoned by an agent or a producer, it can be such a shock that you may find it hard to think clearly. I'm going to give you a line that may be helpful in this situation.

Imagine that the telephone rings, you pick it up—and hear that an agent, a producer, or the development executive you've queried is calling you!

This person will tell you that he has read your query letter and is intrigued by your pitch. He (or his or her assistant) probably is calling to ask you to send the script. You will, of course, be delighted to do that!

However, the agent, the producer, or the development executive, after saying he got your query letter, may say:

"Tell me more about your script."

This is a trap—do not to fall into it!

What the person asking this question is *really* trying to do is to find a reason *not* to read your script—and if you are not careful, you will supply a reason by telling the story badly. The result will be that the person calling will thank you politely, but not read your script.

The most successful stories in the world can be told so badly that no one would want to read the script. Don't let your screenplay be an undiscovered jewel.

This is my suggestion as to how to handle the situation:

Prepare one more sentence that emphasizes the heart of the drama, or perhaps briefly describe an action sequence, or a comedy scene, depending on the genre of your script. Using Elizabeth Powell's screenplay *An Angel in the Family* for purposes of this example, she might describe the heart of her dramatic script with this sentence:

"It's a drama about a father who sentences himself to seven years of hell and then manages to find the strength to overcome the terrible parenting in his own background in order to win back the love of his rebellious teenage daughter." This sentence tells the person asking that the script probably contains a powerful role for a dramatic actor, which suggests potential casting. As we have learned, the agreement of a major star to appear in a film is the surest way to get that movie made.

After you have provided the person asking you to "tell me more" with one more piece of information, *then* say:

"I write much better than I explain. May I send you the script?"

In the majority of cases, the reply will be yes.

It is possible that you may also be asked this question:

"What picture is your script like?"

If your script can be compared to another, and most scripts can, you might reply:

"It's a vehicle for two male stars, with a lot of wild action and a strong emotional connection between the two of them—in the genre of the *Lethal Weapon* pictures, but with different characters." This is a comparison that is likely to appeal to the caller because those movies were enormously successful. *Never compare your script to a movie that was a financial failure.*

Or, if you've written a less violent action script for a male and female star combination you might say:

"It's in the genre of *Romancing the Stone*." (I can't think of a more recent successful example of *light* action—as opposed to *brutal* action—combined with sexual tension, romance and comedy. This is the kind of picture that, if it's good, has a big audience out there waiting.)

If you've written a more traditional romantic comedy, you might say:

"It's a male-female star vehicle in the genre of *Working Girl* or *Sleepless in Seattle*." (You will say this only if it's *true*. Never lead someone to expect one kind of screenplay and then give them another.)

My point with these illustrations is that, if you are asked, you should be prepared to liken your picture to something that's already been made, if you can do this truthfully.

If your picture is a kind of hybrid, you might say:

"It's a combination of *Liar, Liar* and *E.T.*" Or:

"It's *Home Alone* meets *Star Wars*."

If it's a drama hybrid you might say (again, only if this is true):

"It's *Indecent Proposal* meets *A Few Good Men*."

Or, if it's a low comedy with high adventure you might say:

"It's *Ace Ventura* in *Jurassic Park*."

To repeat a most important point in "selling" someone on reading your script: Be sure that you *only* liken your script to movies that have been *very successful*. I doubt that anyone is going to ask to read your script if you describe it as "a cross between *Howard the Duck* and *Ishtar*."

It's easy enough to get lists of high-grossing movies, so do a little research before you select a movie or movies to use in describing yours.

Writing Query Letters That Work

Unless you have friends or relatives in show business, or unless you have found some way to meet people to whom you can submit material, or people who can pave your way with a phone call of recommendation, you—like most newcomers—will have to sell yourself by phone or by letter.

If you are good at calling strangers and pitching your script on the phone, then by all means try that. But if you, like many writers—and I include myself in that list—would rather have a root canal without anesthetic than to try to sell yourself, then the way to bring your script to the attention of agents and/or producers or independent production companies is via a well-written query letter.

Good query letters are not hard to write, once you understand the formula. Here it is:

1. The letter must be no more than one page in length.
2. It contains three paragraphs.
3. The paragraphs are typed, preferably on white paper on a computer.
4. The sentences in each paragraph are single-spaced, but double-space *between* the paragraphs.
5. *Never* send a handwritten query letter, and *never* let it be badly typed, badly spelled, or look any way other than perfectly clean.
6. Address the letter to a *specific person* (never just to a company or to a title).
7. When you have found out the name of the person to whom you are sending the query letter, get that person's correct title (if he or she has a title) and be sure that the name is spelled correctly.

Those seven rules are really just simple common sense and not at all difficult.

Regarding rule number 1:

The reason a letter should be no longer than one page and double-spaced between the paragraphs is that a longer letter is unlikely to be read.

The fact is that the people to whom you will send query letters are very busy professionals. There is no time to read long letters from strangers. A long letter contains far more information than that stranger wants to know, and does not look as though it came from a fellow industry professional.

The first paragraph of your letter will be scanned quickly. State the purpose of the letter immediately. Even if the letter does state your business in the first paragraph, but is too long, or is not inviting to the eye by being short, the visual statement conveyed is that this is not from an industry professional. If the letter does not look like the work of someone who knows the correct way to state one's business, that suggests the writer is not a professional. Therefore, reading a script from someone who does not know how to write a letter would probably be a waste of time. Letters that are too long, or take too long to state their purpose, go directly into that waste receptacle referred to as "the circular file."

Now, here is how we break down a good query letter into those three important paragraphs:

The First Paragraph

It is important to know what to say about yourself and what not to say about yourself in your query letter. Tell them very little about your background in this first contact. The following are things that *would be* helpful to mention if any of them apply to you:

> If you are in a university writing program, or some other respected writing program or film school.
> If you've won a significant writing award.

If you are a produced playwright.

If you are a journalist.

If you are or have been in the Foreign Service or Diplo-
matic Corps.

If you have been in the Special Forces, FBI, or CIA.

If you are a songwriter with songs that have been recorded.

If you work in television or radio.

The above listed items make a positive impression in a query letter. It also helps if you live in the Los Angeles area. If you do not, I
suggest that you mention that you are planning to move to the Los
Angeles area soon, so as to be available for meetings, or that you are
often in LA.

Now here is a list of things *not* to tell them about yourself in this
first query letter:

That you are a doctor.

That you are a lawyer.

That you practice a profession other than those listed in
the "yes" list.

That you are retired.

That you "have always wanted to write."

If, for example, you are a doctor or a lawyer who has written a
script with a medical or a legal theme *do not* mention your profession
in the query letter because the person to whom you're writing is likely
to dismiss you as just another doctor or lawyer who wants to write.
Now here is the contradiction. After they read your medical or legal-
themed script and like it, then they will be delighted to know that, in
your day job, you are a doctor or a lawyer. The reason that they will
like this information *after* the fact is that your background will give
your script credibility, especially in later promotion and in publicity
material. I urge you to respect this peculiarity in Hollywood thinking.
First let them discover you as a writer, then give them a valuable piece

of information about your background; it will come to them as an unexpected bonus.

If no item on the "yes" list of things I recommend that you mention about yourself applies, then simply introduce yourself by name and then, if possible, give the person to whom the letter is addressed a sincere compliment. It *must* be sincere, or don't try this! If you have written to a director or to a producer, then compliment some picture that he or she has done that you really liked. The picture doesn't need to have been a hit. It's all right to admire a movie that was not a commercial success when mentioning it to someone involved in its making. Just don't *compare* your script to one that was not a financial success.

It is difficult to find a sincere compliment to give to an agent you are querying. I don't mean that to be unkind, it's just that so many of the clever things that agents do are done without the public knowing. However, if you read the trade papers *Daily Variety* and *The Hollywood Reporter* (and you should), you may see stories about some great deal the agent has made for a client, or some success, such as a merger or acquisition, that he has made for himself. It is appropriate to congratulate him on some announced accomplishment.

Another reason you might give to write to an agent is that you have learned that he or she represents some other writer that you admire. You can find out who represents the writers whose work you like best by calling the Writers Guild of America, West, 7000 West Third Street, Los Angeles, CA 90048, (213) 951-4000.

Paragraph One in your query letter will differ according to whether you are writing to an agent or to a potential buyer.

Paragraphs Two and Three will be identical in all your query letters.

Here is an outline for each of the two versions of Paragraph One:

Paragraph One in your query letter **to an agent** tells the recipient some relevant piece of information about yourself—*if* you can list one of the items on the "yes" list. Then say that you have just completed a screenplay and that you are seeking representation. If you have a specific reason that you are writing to that particular agent, state it here. (This is optional.)

Paragraph One in your query letter **to a producer, a director, or a development executive** at a production company is similar at the beginning, but there are significant differences. First, introduce yourself and, if possible, mention something about your background. Then state the reason that you are writing to that particular person. This is where you would give that person a compliment about a picture he has made or something that he has accomplished. The next sentence tells your target that you have recently completed a screenplay you would like to submit to him or her for consideration.

Paragraph Two contains the title of the screenplay and your teaser pitch.

Paragraph Three says simply:

If the above material interests you, I will be happy to send you the screenplay. I may be reached at—give your address and your telephone number here.

Then you conclude the letter with Sincerely yours, or Yours sincerely—or however you prefer to close a business letter.

Below is a sample query letter to an agent. The information contained has been imagined for the purpose of this demonstration; you need to supply your own equivalents.

Date

(Name of Agent)
(Name of the Agency)
(Complete Address)

Dear Mr. or Ms. (Last name),

I am looking for representation for a screenplay that I recently completed. Prior to studying screenwriting I was a crime reporter for the *Houston Chronicle*. A number of my stories have been picked up for national distribution by the Associated Press.

The screenplay I would like you to consider is titled _____ Briefly: (Put your teaser pitch here)

If the above material is of interest to you, I may be reached at (give your address and telephone here.)

Yours sincerely,
(signature here)
(name typed below signature)

NOTE: If you are enrolled in a college or university writing program be sure to say that, and/or mention some other professional experience *connected with writing* that you've had prior to creating your screenplay if you are able to do so.

Here is how Paragraph One would be altered for a query letter to a producer, director, or development executive at a production company:

Date

(Name of Producer, Director or Executive)
(Name of Company)
(Complete Address)

Dear Mr. or Ms. (Last name),

I am writing to you because your (name of picture here, or perhaps mention an interview with that person you either saw or read) had such a profound impact on my life that it inspired me to become a screenwriter. I moved to Los Angeles from Houston, where I was a crime reporter on the *Houston Chronicle,* (and enrolled at UCLA or USC or wherever writer's program, if this is applicable). Recently I completed a screenplay that I would like to submit to you.

Paragraphs Two and Three would be the same in this version of the query letter as in the first version demonstrated.

Your Script Is Ready to Go on the Market

My recommendation is that once your script is ready to go on the market you spend the first six to eight weeks making query calls—if you're good on the phone—or sending query letters to agents. The reality is that it is very difficult for an unknown writer to get an agent. If you have not been able to interest an agent in reading your screenplay within this period, my recommendation is that—while you continue to send out query letters to agents—you also begin sending them to potential buyers such as independent producers, directors (through their production companies), and independent production companies.

If a positive response to your query letter does not come quickly, keep trying. When three months have passed and you have received no response, then write a new version of your query letter and your pitch and try again. Remember, one of the secrets of winning is *staying in the game.*

Good luck, and good hunting!

11. The "Business" of Show Business

This brings us to the business of show business. Unfortunately, your first encounter with the business may be in the form of a "release." A "release" is a form of one or more pages in length designed to protect the company from subsequent law suits if the writer thinks his work has been stolen by that company. Once a writer is represented by an agent, she will never be required to sign a "release" in order to have her material read. Once a writer has made a sale she is never again in the position of being an "unknown," even though her name may not be famous. As soon as that first sale has been made a writer moves from being an aspirant trying to break into the business up to the status of a "professional."

However, until a writer secures an agent, she will, in all likelihood, be confronted by a release form. Not every independent producer requires this before someone in the company will read unsolicited work, but most do. To my knowledge, most of the established independent production companies do require a release form if the writer is not represented by an agent. No unsolicited material at all is read by the major studios. "Unsolicited material" is defined as material that does not come in via an agent franchised by the Writers Guild of America.

Some independent producers will read unsolicited material if it is sent to them through a person in the business that they know and trust. Some producers or independent companies will accept material if it comes through a respected entertainment attorney; however, few writers at the beginning of their careers can afford the fees of an important entertainment attorney.

Agents do not charge to represent a client. Their job is to sell your script and collect a 10 percent commission for doing so. They are not allowed to collect a commission larger than 10 percent for representing a script. (Here I am discussing the agent's commission for representing a screenplay; literary agents who represent books now routinely charge 15 percent commission, and 20 to 25 percent for making foreign sales for the writer client.)

Some screenwriters now have managers. If you are considering having a manager you should know that there is no cap on what a manager can charge. Whatever percentage a client pays a manager is a matter of agreement between that manager and that client.

Release forms that agentless writers are asked to sign vary considerably from company to company. Some of them are fair to both sides, but some are particularly onerous for the writer. For example, in exchange for having her screenplay read, the writer might be asked to sign away any right to legal or monetary redress, even if the material is later proved to have been stolen from that writer by the company. Another example of an unfair release is one that requires a writer to agree to a certain price that she will be paid for the screenplay if the company reading it decides to buy it! My advice is not to sign anything without a lawyer looking it over, but if you cannot afford a lawyer, then beware of clauses that seem grossly unfair. If asked to sign such a release, my suggestion is that you get on the phone to agents at midsize or smaller companies, tell them what company is interested in reading your screenplay, tell them that you don't want to sign the release they are offering you, and ask if that agent would be willing to submit the script for you. Many agents will agree to do this. If a sale results from this chain of events, pay the 10 percent commission with a smile. Don't resent the fact that the agent did not have to do the initial work, because an agent will earn that commission in protecting you in negotiating the terms of the sale.

The query letter sent to Oliver Stone's company by screenwriter Caroline Pfouts, who is also an attorney, piqued the company's interest. They asked to read her screenplay, *Family Secrets,* and sent her a release to sign. While it was not as bad as some releases, it still was not something Caroline wanted to sign, so she called an agent and explained her problem. The agent was impressed Caroline had gotten that far on her own. As soon as the agent heard Caroline's pitch for *Family Secrets* she signed her for representation. Ultimately, Oliver Stone "passed" on the script, but Caroline Pfouts had her first official agent.

Kevin Hing, a talented writer (and an impressive martial artist) who attended several of my workshops, and who is also an attorney, took the time to devise what I have come to refer to as "the writer-friendly release." He generously allowed me to make copies and pass them out to my workshop's participants. Over the years, many of the writers who received a copy of this release were permitted to substitute it for an offered release they considered unfair.

Kevin Hing has given me permission to include his writer-friendly release in this book for you to study, and for you to have something with which to compare releases you may be asked to sign. This is a simple release, fair to both the writer and to the company to whom the script is being submitted.

Please understand that by offering this exemplar release Kevin Hing and I are in no way giving any legal advice.

DATE:
ADDRESSEE:
Dear _____,
I am submitting to you herewith the following material (hereinafter referred to as the "Material."):
TITLE: _____
FORM OF MATERIAL: _____

PRINCIPAL CHARACTERS: _____

BRIEF SUMMARY OF THEME OR PLOT:

WGA OR COPYRIGHT REGISTRATION NO:_____

1. I request that you read and evaluate the Material, and you hereby agree to do so, and you agree to advise me of your decision with respect to the Material.

2. I warrant that I am the sole owner and author of the Material, that I have the exclusive right and authority to submit the Material to you upon the terms and conditions stated herein.

3. I understand that as a general rule you receive literary properties through the established channels in the industry and not through a submission such as this. I recognize that you have access to and/or may have created literary materials and ideas which may be similar or identical to the Material in theme, idea, plot, format or other respects. I agree that I will not be entitled to any compensation because of the use by you of any such similar or identical material which may have been previously created by you or may have come to you from any independent source.

4. You agree that if you use any legally protectable portion of the Material, provided it has not been obtained by you from, and independently created by, another source, you will pay me an amount that is comparable to the compensation normally paid for similar material or an amount equal to the fair market value thereof as of the date of this agreement, whichever is greater. If we are unable to agree as to said amount, or in the event of any dispute concerning any alleged use of the Material or with reference to this agreement, either party may elect in writing to submit the dispute to arbitration.

5. If an election to submit a dispute to arbitration is made pursuant to paragraph 4 above, the arbitrator shall be a

person experienced in the field in which the alleged use was made and shall be mutually selected in accordance with the roles of the American Arbitration Association.

6. I have retained at least one copy of the Material, and I hereby release you from any liability for loss of, or damage to, the copies of the Material submitted to you hereunder.

Accepted and Agreed:

By: _____   Date: _____

Remember, once you have an agent you will never have to sign a release again.

Never Lie to Your Agent

As a general rule, I do not advocate lying to anyone, but I don't believe that "improving the truth" about one's age, weight, or the real color of one's hair does any harm. What can do a great deal of harm is lying to one's agent, and I urge you *never* to do that!

Here's an example of what I mean:

Suppose that while trying to find representation you managed to get one or more production companies to read your script and they all "passed."

When you manage to persuade an agent to read your script and that agent agrees to represent it, one of the first questions that agent will ask you is:

"Where has this script been?" Translated from Hollywood speak, what that question *means* is:

"Who, or what company, has read this script?"

Be completely honest here. If one company or twenty companies have seen and rejected the screenplay your agent will need to know that. If the agent thinks your script is good, he can go back to those companies and submit it again, saying that it had been submitted earlier by the writer, but that it has since been greatly improved and he would like them to give it another look.

It is a very bad thing for an agent to submit a script to a company and be surprised to learn that it has already been there and been rejected. This not only makes the agent look and feel foolish—and justifiably angry at the writer—but it prevents the agent from giving a sales pitch that might convert the earlier rejection into a yes or at least into a meeting for you to discuss possible rewrite jobs or to pitch other material you may be working on.

Help your agent help you by *always* being completely truthful with him or her.

Tips on How to Behave in Meetings

Okay, let's briefly review matters covered so far:

You have survived my format drills, you have created vivid, appealing characters, and you have attracted an agent to your script. That agent has circulated your script among independent producers, production companies, and studio executives with whom that agent has a good relationship. No one has *bought* the script as yet, but it is on the market and under consideration. You are in the game, so to speak, and your work is being treated with respect.

Now, a production executive has read and liked your script. That company isn't interested in buying it, but the executive likes your writing and telephones you or your agent to set up a meeting with you to discuss other projects. A date and time are fixed. It is probable that your agent will accompany you to the meeting, but whether you go alone or accompanied, the next advice I'm going to give to you applies.

Arrive at the executive's office for the meeting between five and ten minutes early. Tell the receptionist that you have a (name the time) meeting with Ms. So-and-so and say, "But I'm a few minutes early."

Soon after the time set for the meeting, you will be greeted by the executive's assistant and/or secretary who has come out to the reception area to lead you back to the office where the meeting will take place. That secretary or assistant will smile and ask if you would like coffee, tea, or a soft drink or water.

I suggest that you *decline this offer.*

There are two reasons that I suggest you say a polite no. The first is that if the assistant or the secretary does *not* have to bring you something to drink you will endear yourself to that person. The second reason is that you, being understandably nervous in a first meeting, are very likely to spill the drink all over yourself or all over the executive's furniture. Not a good move.

After having endeared yourself to the staff, now you are sitting in the office of the executive for the meeting, and in no danger of spilling anything. Meetings typically begin with a few minutes of "small talk," which usually includes an exchange of industry gossip between the executive and your agent. Listen with interest, but don't intrude yourself unless you have something to contribute to the conversation or are able to make a comment that you are *certain* is amusing. After the industry gossip, attention will turn to you.

The executive will probably say something complimentary about your script and then probably will say:

"Well, tell me about self."

This is a trap. Be careful.

In my experience the best thing for you to do at this point is to give one interesting piece of information about yourself—or, if you are genuinely witty, say something funny regarding some absurdity in your personal or professional life. You can mention something funny that happened to you in the course of researching the script you are currently developing, or something interesting or funny that happened during the writing of the script they've read. Take no more than thirty to sixty *seconds* talking about yourself. (Practice with a stopwatch.) Then turn the conversation away from yourself and onto the executive. If it is possible, congratulate that person or the company on a recent success, or mention a movie they've done that you really liked. That will probably please the executive and you might hear some interesting behind-the-scenes story. Enjoy the story; people like to think they are entertaining raconteurs.

At this point the executive will probably ask you what you are working on.

If you are currently writing a new script, tell him the genre—whether it's an action picture for a male star, a thriller, a romantic comedy, etc. Then say that you have some other ideas you're also developing and ask him what he is looking for. He will probably tell you, and you may discover that you have interests in common.

If you and your agent have agreed that you will "pitch" a story to the executive, one that you would like to be paid to write, be sure that you do two very important things:

1. Before you pitch the story of that yet-to-be-written screenplay type up a detailed outline of the plot and characters and register this outline at the Writers Guild of America, West, 7000 West Third Street, Los Angeles, CA 90048. For registration purposes, label this: Outline for a Motion Picture.
2. After you have pitched the story, if there is interest in it, then "leave paper." What that important little two-word phrase means is: Leave behind with the executive the copy of the outline that you prepared and that you registered in advance of the meeting.

There are two reasons that you should always "leave paper" after a pitch:

1. The person to whom you have pitched the story will have to go one rank above him and retell the story to the top executive who can say, "Yes, call Business Affairs and make a deal to develop that pitch."
2. In the case (not common, but not unheard of) that this executive or his colleagues develop your story with someone else, the fact that you have registered the pages and left

them behind with the executive will put you on much stronger legal ground to collect compensation than if the dispute was just your word about pitching the story against that of the executive who might deny (or honestly not remember) having heard it from you.

When you have an agent you are less likely to run into such a situation, but this is not a perfect world, so do what you can to protect yourself.

I'm happy to tell you that there *will* be a time when you may feel free to ask for something to drink in a meeting with studio or production company executives:

When your screenplay is in active development and you are attending meetings with your producers and executives, and being paid to revise the script, then you will need liquid refreshment because those meetings tend to be long. I also suggest that you tape those meetings as ideas will be flying at you from every direction. When you are back at your computer making revisions it may be difficult to remember every change you were asked to make. Referring to your tape, as well as the handwritten notes you've made on specific pages, will help you do the thorough job that will help keep you employed on the project.

And, by this time, you will be a confident "pro" who has an agent and is being paid to revise a script that is heading for production—and you'll be much less likely to knock over your diet Coke out of nervousness.

One last piece of advice:

Ask for any kind of cold drink, or water, but never ask for coffee at a meeting at a production company office or at a studio. In my experience (as someone who really likes coffee) the dark liquid you're likely to get in those places will be an assault on your taste buds. Use studio coffee to wash out filters—or to throw in the eyes of AKA-toting terrorists who burst in to hijack the company in order to get a green light for their script—but don't drink it.

Your stomach will thank me.

12. Getting Past the Dreaded "Reader"

When I was at TriStar Pictures I read every script submitted to me, which meant that I had no personal life. Sometimes the "weekend stack" was so high that it was only my sense of being on a mission, on a Great Script treasure hunt, that kept me from weeping.

Remember that I had not sought out my position as a studio vice president, but had been sought out because, as a published novelist and scriptwriter, I was considered a good judge of material. Until I was behind those studio doors I had not known that executives do not typically read anything more than "coverage." ("Coverage" is an assigned reader's synopsis of the plot and that reader's comments about, and opinion of, the screenplay's concept, character development, and dialogue.) This reliance on coverage in making decisions with multimillion-dollar consequences came as a great shock to me. And, in my view, it made no sense.

My opinion of most major studio and talent agency readers is not something I am in the least bit reserved in sharing. (I have already done so in television and print interviews.) I think the majority of the little beasts should be roasted slowly on a spit. Readers are usually inexperienced and not well-paid people barely out of school. Why highly paid production executives base their opinions and recommendations on the opinions of readers astonishes me. I even knew executives who sent *writing samples* down to the bowels of the company for coverage. I can understand employing readers to write the company-required synopses for the files, but I will never believe they should be used as a first line of resistance to material.

On the other hand, I don't think that it is inconsistent to tell you that I have frequently been paid (very well) by producers as a "creative consultant"—handed a script or a book to read and asked to give my opinion as to whether or not that producer should buy the material, or asked by a producer who is creative and knows that "something is there" how I would develop the material, or fix the problems in a rewrite. I've earned my living as a novelist, producer, and screen and television writer for twenty years, so I have a rich variety of experience, a professional background on which to draw in giving opinions.

I'm not allowed to run the world and therefore cannot abolish the system of using readers, so my next suggestion is that you learn what readers are instructed to examine in scripts so as to be prepared. The only good that comes from this activity is that by reminding ourselves of what readers are required to comment upon sometimes keeps us from making mistakes in development. If we're forced to examine ourselves through their little periscopes, it can give us a fresh look at what we've written. This can be helpful to us if we learn to use their tools constructively.

Here is a sample of the instructions given to most readers when they are hired. Read it and learn how your script will be judged.

Guidelines for Coverage

Content of Forms Given to Story Analysts

I. FORMAT—COVER SHEET

Information such as *Submitted To, Submitted By, and Elements* ("Elements" means whether a producer, director, or star is attached to the project) is available on the information sheet and should be included in the appropriate spaces on your cover sheet. Otherwise, rely on the material itself for information such as *Title* (all CAPS), *Author, Pages,* etc.

1. *Rating Boxes:* All of the x's should be aligned.

   a. Idea: Judge the premise only.
   b. Story Line: Judge the mechanics of the storytelling—how well is the story put together?
   c. Characterization: Are the characters three-dimensional, well thought out, and appropriate to the genre?
   d. Dialogue: Is the dialogue interesting and appropriate for the story?
   e. Setting: Does the setting enhance the story? Is it appealing?

2. *Recommendation Codes:*

   a. RECOMMEND: This code is *rarely used* and indicates that the script needs little more than a polish to bring out its maximum potential as a film.
   b. CONSIDER: This rating indicates that the script is strong, yet problematic in some way, and merits a read.
   c. PASS: A pass indicates that the project is not recommended for development.

3. *Comment Summary:* Must be written in complete sentences, with correct punctuation, etc. It should summarize your general feelings about the script in one or two short sentences.

II. COMMENTS

- The length should be 2/3 to 3/4 of a page, single-spaced.
- Comment page should be on a separate page from the synopsis.
- A recommendation should appear at the bottom of the page.

Comments should address the strengths and weaknesses of the material, plot, characters, dialogue, structure, tone, premise, etc. Attempt to begin with an overall statement about the material, and then move on to more specific comments.

Some Specific Points to Consider:

1. *Story Line:*
   - Is the story well developed? Does it maintain its focus?
   - Is it an original idea? A new twist on an old idea? Or is it tired and derivative?
   - Is the story large enough in scope for a feature film?
   - Does the story work within its genre?

2. *Characterization:*

   Devote some space to the characterizations, the character relationships, and the consistency of the characters.
   - Are these people interesting and believable?
   - Are they clichés?

3. *Dialogue:*
   - Overall, is the dialogue special or mundane?
   - Are there long speeches which slow the action?
   - Do the characters speak with specific voices?
   - If dialects are used, are they effective?

Additional Comment Considerations:
   - References and comparisons to other films should be included if applicable.
   - Avoid using the pronoun "I."
   - Avoid your personality coming through. Clearly and concisely state your feelings—we don't need you to be witty and clever.

III. SYNOPSIS:
   - Length should be 1½ to 2 pages, double-spaced.
   - Characters should be explained when first introduced.
   - Avoid direct quotations from the script.

The synopsis is not a detailed recounting, but a storytelling. Try to capture the flavor of the story. A few well-placed adjectives and adverbs are always helpful, but don't go overboard.

Now that you know by what criteria readers are required to judge your screenplay, you can go over this form and evaluate the script yourself, in advance of submitting it. See if you can find weaknesses in any area. If you do, correct them before letting your script be judged by others.

If these instructions seem to echo the material raised in chapters 4 and 5, that is intentional. Reread the chapters on format and make sure that your screenplay is a thoroughly professional work.

One last reminder:

I cannot emphasize enough how important it is that your script be *inviting to the eye.* This means that your script has proper margins and double spaces between narrative paragraphs, and that those narrative paragraphs do not run more than four lines. That means four *lines,* not four *sentences,* if those four sentences take up more than four lines. Remember that lots of white space makes a script look like a pleasure to read, and that is the highest purpose of the first impression your script makes.

Establish your leading role or roles quickly and make them sound interesting, or intriguing, right away. A star who is considering your script must be favorably impressed by the character he's being asked to play or the chances are that he may not read further.

It is an unfortunate truth that people in the business of making movies are not looking for raw talent to develop—they are looking for *developed* talent with a script they can get made. No one on the buyer's side of the desk will care whether or not they've ever heard your name, or about your age, gender, race, or ethnicity. Only one thing matters to the people who make movies: Have you written a good script. If it doesn't look professional, they aren't likely to read far enough to discover whether or not it might be good. They don't mind dealing with unknowns—but no one wants to work with an amateur.

As the saying goes, "You never have a second chance to make a first impression."

Make sure the first impression your script makes is a positive one.

One Last Recommendation That Is in a Category by Itself

When a writer sells a screenplay or writes a screenplay on assignment, what eventually becomes of that screenplay is not within the writer's control. Generally speaking, original writers can be discarded in favor of new writers at any time, or have their original work rewritten up to—and even all the way through—a film's production. There are times when a screenwriter will be "credited" with writing a movie that was changed vastly by other people, and those others may or may not be getting a public "credit" for their work on the script. As I have said earlier in this book, if you know how to interpret writing credits they will tell you at least some of the behind-the-scenes story. Remember, if there is more than one writer who receives screen credit an ampersand (&) between the names means that those writers worked as a team. If an "and" appears between the names it means that one writer rewrote the work of the other, and it is the writer whose name is in first position (before the "and") who is deemed to have written more than the name in second position, or third or fourth.

It is agonizing for writers who are innocent of the blame to be lambasted by critics in the media for creative crimes they did not commit. In most cases there is nothing for you, the unfairly criticized writer, to do except cry, or curse, or indulge in some temporary excesses, and then go around explaining to anyone who will listen that so-and-so ruined your wonderful script. (The late great comedy writer Jack Douglas had a sign over his desk that announced: "It left here funny!")

However, there is one case in which the public was at last able to learn what the screenwriter wrote *originally,* before his script was changed by others. As far as I know, the only writer who has been able to make his original work available is Dan Gordon. The script and movie in question is *Wyatt Earp.* I think of this little peek behind the Hollywood screen as "the Writer's Triumph."

The original screenplay of *Wyatt Earp,* which starred Kevin Costner, was written by Dan Gordon. The picture that finally made it into the theaters was a materially different version of Gordon's *Wyatt Earp.* On the picture that was released, Gordon shared an "and" screenwriting credit with the film's director.

Luckily for those of us who study films and screenwriting, Dan Gordon understands contracts and Writers Guild regulations very well. He knew that he had the right to do the novel version, and the audio book version. He wrote *Wyatt Earp* for eye and ear as novel and audio versions of his original screenplay. The result is that this is the only instance of which I am aware that the audience can see a movie with an "and" between the writers' names and then read the book or hear the audio version in order to learn what the original screenwriter wanted the project to be. (I am discussing an original film here, *not* the screen adaptation of a novel. To understand how far a movie can stray from the story that the novelist *intended* to tell, I suggest one see Demi Moore's 1995 film version of *The Scarlet Letter* and compare it to the novel by Nathaniel Hawthorne.)

Novel versions, or "novelizations," of screenplays usually are written to conform to the script of the movie that will be playing in theaters, but Dan Gordon refused to do this. The result is that the novel version of *Wyatt Earp,* which is an example of really marvelous writing, launched Dan Gordon's secondary writing career as a respected novelist. The novel reflects the original screenplay, not the film that was released.

I suggest that you read or listen to Dan Gordon's *Wyatt Earp,* then rent the *Wyatt Earp* movie and judge for yourself. At the very least this will be a useful learning experience as to how a story about the same man, Wyatt Earp, can be told in different ways.

13. Surviving Rejection—"Coping" Strategies

When my first novel, *Runaway,* was being submitted by my agent to publishers, I was in that terrible state of nervous waiting that every writer understands. It's a time of bizarre behavior and irrational acts, and it requires the patience of loved ones.

One of my irrational acts was to begin searching newspapers for obituaries of writers. While I was waiting to hear from my agent, and trying none too successfully to appear sane to my husband and friends, Patrick Dennis, author of the immensely popular *Auntie Mame,* passed away. It was in Patrick Dennis's obituary that I finally found some solace.

I don't remember how this talented gentleman died, how old he was, or if the family requested a donation to a charity in lieu of flowers. What I do remember was the information that *Auntie Mame* was rejected by eleven publishers before it was bought and published by Viking. I remember wondering if Mr. Dennis's agent had submitted the book to publishers alphabetically, and whether Mr. Dennis had become deeply despondent upon receiving his rejection from Random House.

As for the fate of *Runaway:* My first literary agent submitted it to seven publishers simultaneously. Six publishers rejected it during the same week, and the agent sent me all of the rejection letters together in one horrible bundle.

There was not one encouraging word in those six rejections. (Or if there actually was some kindness, I was in too much pain to comprehend it.) Although now I don't remember which publisher it was, one of them said that my novel was "not to be confused with entertainment." I can tell you, that *hurt*. It was especially painful because *Runaway* was a gritty, graphic novel about the juvenile justice system in which young captives suffered terribly. It had its light moments, but if I had been asked to describe my intentions in writing the novel, it would never have occurred to me to say that my primary objective was "entertainment."

Two days after that dreadful bundle of rejection blows arrived, my husband and I were scheduled to go to the theater with a couple with whom we regularly went to the theater, writer Larry Gelbart and his wife, Pat (a singer and actress who, as Pat Marshall, costarred in MGM's classic college musical *Good News*). This particular night we were scheduled to see a Tom Stoppard play at the Music Center in downtown Los Angeles, and it was Larry Gelbart's turn to drive. The Gelbarts arrived at our house to pick us up, and when we climbed into the backseat of their car we realized that they weren't speaking to each other. Normally, that would have been a subject for affectionate joking, not a problem, but the only one of the four of us who had a good sense of direction and knew how to find the Music Center was Pat Gelbart, and she wasn't speaking to the driver! Somehow we made it to the theater just seconds before the play began. I don't remember which Tom Stoppard play it was, or whether or not I liked it, because when we got home there was a message on our answering machine asking me to call my agent the following day. That was all—just call him. No *clue* in his voice as to whether the news was good or bad!

I spent an agonized, sleepless night wondering why he had called. The rational part of my brain reminded me cheerfully: "They write when it's bad news and call when it's good news." But the other part of my brain whispered: "He could be calling to tell you that he's tried every publisher in New York and they've all said no so he's dropping you and the book." I watched the clock until it crawled to 6:59 A.M., Pacific time—9:59 A.M. in New York. The first moment I could call an agent's office in New York without looking desperate was 10 A.M.

The news from my agent was *wonderful!* He said that Ballantine Books, renowned for their paperback publishing, was going into the hardcover business and that my novel would be on their first hardcover list, to be published in October of 1978. They would publish it again, in paperback, a year later.

That was one of the happiest days of my life. Not only was I about to become a published novelist, but when I called the Gelbarts a few minutes later I leaned that they had happily made up and were speaking to each other again.

Like Larry Gelbart, best-selling novelist Irving Wallace was a very kind man, always generous and encouraging to new writers. I was the beneficiary of one of his most imaginative acts of kindness, which I would like to share now with you.

Just before *Runaway* was published, Irving telephoned to say he was sending me "a little good-luck present." It was something he had unearthed and he wanted to share with me: a collection of the most *terrible* reviews of works that later became great and beloved classics.

Hastily he added: "I'm not giving you this because I think *for a moment* that your book will get anything but great reviews!"

Irving is gone now, and still missed by those of us lucky enough to have known that very dear man. I do not think he would mind my sharing a few examples from the pages he sent me.

Moby Dick, written by Herman Melville in 1851, is the story of a demented sea captain's obsession with finding and killing the great white whale who ate his leg. It is, moreover, an immense parable of human life and the quest for identity. The following excerpts are from reviews that appeared unsigned:

From *Anthenaeum:* "The opening of this wild book contains some graphic descriptions of a dreariness such as we do not remember to have met with before in marine literature."

From *The Southern Quarterly Review:* [Aside from the parts where the whale is directly involved] "the book is sad stuff, dull and dreary, or ridiculous. Mr. Melville's Quakers are the wretchedest dolts and drivellers, and his Mad Captain . . . is a monstrous bore . . . His ravings . . . and the ravings of Mr. Melville himself . . . are such as would justify a writ *de lunatico* for all the parties."

Today *Moby Dick* is considered Melville's greatest masterpiece, as adventure tale, parable, and innovative novel, and it's been required reading for several generations of students.

After his epic novel *War and Peace,* Leo Tolstoy wrote *Anna Karenina,* the story of an upper-class married woman who has an affair and kills herself after society ostracizes her.

The critic Tkachev, in *The Affair,* wrote sarcastically: "Vronsky's passion for his horse . . . runs parallel to his passion for Anna . . . Such is the epic of *amours* which Count Tolstoy has created . . . where the attachments of people, cows and horses are all described with the same artistic analysis and detail."

One critic called it "sentimental rubbish," another "a melodramatic piece of nonsense," and another described its atmosphere as "genito-urinary." The anonymous critic for the *Odessa Courier* challenged readers to "show me one page, nay! one half-page that contains an idea, or rather the shadow of an idea."

According to the *Encyclopaedia Britannica,* "He [Tolstoy] is universally accepted as one of the greatest writers of fiction in the world," and "among the foremost thinkers of the 19th century."

American poet Walt Whitman published *Leaves of Grass* in 1855. He revised and added to it in nine different editions in his lifetime. The collection of poems was written in a boldly innovative free-verse style, and it championed, among other things, democracy, the American way of life, the common man, bodies, and sex. *Leaves of Grass* caused an uproar of critical debate.

Rufus W. Griswold, writing for the *New York Criterion,* could not have been more horrified. Griswold thought it "impossible to imagine how any man's fancy could have conceived such a mass of stupid filth, unless he were possessed by the soul of a sentimental donkey that had died of disappointed love. This *poet* (?) . . . just serves to show the energy which natural imbecility is occasionally capable of under strong excitement." He ended his review with a strong plea that the book be banned. Other reviews were just as bad:

From the London *Critic:* "Whitman is as unacquainted with art, as a hog is with mathematics . . . We, who are not prudish . . . declare that the man who wrote page 79 of *Leaves of Grass* deserves nothing so richly as the public executioner's whip."

Later, I learned that whenever I read Walt Whitman's reviews at one of my workshops, there was a sudden rush to bookstores and to libraries for copies of *Leaves of Grass!*

There is a certain snobbery that enters discussions about "literature" as opposed to "popular fiction." It's my belief that any work that encourages people to become habitual readers is a work well worth the paper on which it's printed.

Try to remember, when you suffer rejections or bad reviews, or when you're fired from a project, or find your screenplay has been so totally rewritten that it is almost unrecognizable to you, that many, many other writers have gone through the same agonies. One of the great Hollywood true stories is a studio executive's written evaluation of the screen test the incomparable Fred Astaire made when he came from the Broadway stage for a film role. After seeing Astaire on screen, the executive wrote: "Can't sing, can't act. Going bald. Can dance a little."

It will help to read and reread terrible reviews famous writers received, or to read the biographies of writers who suffered greatly before their eventual and long-lasting triumphs. There is comfort in learning what other people have survived.

Tell yourself that one day you will be able to laugh at this disaster, whichever one it is. The truth is that with the passage of time many awful setbacks and disappointments can be turned into amusing anecdotes. Try to remember that when you are going through the bad times.

When the worst disappointments hit, you don't necessarily have to take them well. (I only take them well in public.) You can behave badly. You can whine, cry, curse for a while, but *only* for a while. Your whining and crying gets boring for others pretty quickly, and if you keep it up even your loved ones won't want to be around you.

There are several ways to cope with the pain of rejection in the first few terrible days. Here are a few suggestions: Exercise (anything that exhausts you is good), self-indulgence (ice cream is my favorite indulgence), read books that will take your mind off yourself, go shopping, start to work on something new, do something kind for someone else. Deliver Meals on Wheels, or volunteer at a mission. Give blood. Spend two hours a week tutoring a child or an adult who's learning to read. Visit the pediatric department of a hospital, or a cancer wing—and take a look at a few very *real* problems.

And then reread the bad reviews I've quoted. You'll feel better. Eventually, the pain will recede to a faint memory.

At the beginning of your writing career you may fear that you will never get a chance to succeed because you don't know anyone who can help you, who can "open doors" for you.

The fact is that very few people are born into the entertainment industry; your problem is the problem of the vast majority of new writers. Don't just complain that you don't have any "connections"—get busy and *make* some connections.

I came to New York City from my home town in Florida at the age of eighteen because I wanted to be a writer. My assets were: $423 that I had saved working every weekend during high school and my one year at Palm Beach Junior College; determination to become a professional writer; and a stubborn refusal to believe that the gigantic odds against achieving my dream applied to *me*. I knew no one in New York, nor did I have any connection to anyone in a position to help me. I was completely and entirely on my own, with no place to go but forward.

So I found a way to make my own "connections."

I had been in New York for about six months, living in a one-room studio apartment and working at a variety of life-sustaining jobs when I read an interview with William Castle, who produced horror movies such as *The House on Haunted Hill* and *The Tingler*. He was renowned for promotional stunts: dangling skeletons over the heads of the audience, wiring theater seats to give movie-goers a little "tingle" programmed to certain specific times during *The Tingler,* and stationing nurses in theater lobbies for any patron who became too frightened during one of his films. In this interview, the producer said he was willing to look at the work of unknown writers.

I immediately sent a letter to him at his offices at Paramount Pictures in Hollywood, telling him that I had written a horror story that I would like to submit to him as a movie. (It was a lie; I had never written a horror story, but I was sure that I *could* write one if he would be willing to read it.)

A week later I was stunned to receive a telephone call from William Castle's secretary telling me that Mr. Castle would like to read my story. How soon could I send it?

"Tomorrow," I replied, foolishly. I worked all night and finished a story that I thought was great. I sent it off with deliriously high expectations.

A week later I received another call from Mr. Castle's secretary telling me that Mr. Castle was coming to New York the following Tuesday and would like to have "a breakfast meeting" with me at the Trianon Room of the Waldorf Astoria Hotel at 8:30 A.M. on Wednesday.

Certain that my writing career was about to take off like a rocket, the only thing that worried me for the next five days was that I had heard stories about "evil Hollywood producers" who preyed on innocent young girls. I spent hours coming up with the perfect excuse that I would give Mr. Castle for *not* going upstairs with him to his suite. (I was sure he had a suite and sure he would make the suggestion.) It had to be an excuse that wouldn't hurt his feelings but would keep me out of danger from this strange man, who would be the first "Hollywood" person I had ever met.

Mr. Castle was tall, built something like a bear, had close-cropped thick gray hair and a very nice smile. The Trianon Room, with its grand chandeliers, looked like the ballroom in a palace to me, who had yet to see my first real palace. We ordered breakfast, and then he turned to me and said gently:

"Linda, you wrote the worst horror story I've ever read."

At that moment I discovered that hearts can "sink" and that the pain of rejection is physical and devastating beyond words. As I fought to control my face and conceal the agony I was in, he added:

"I wanted to meet you because I like the way you put words together. You really can write, but I don't think horror is your genre. Keep at it and find out what kind of writer you are."

I don't remember anything else that was said, but afterward I realized that what William Castle had done that morning was to treat me like someone of value, as a writer worthy of encouragement. He actually respected my *talent* enough to make time in his schedule to meet me—and not once did he put a hand on my knee, look anywhere except in my eyes, or invite me up to his suite.

William Castle's respectful treatment gave me the courage to respect myself. It was a gift beyond measurable price.

I met this good, kind, happily married family man again several years later, when he was preparing to produce *Rosemary's Baby* and I was living in The Dakota, the elegant old New York apartment building in which the story was set and partially filmed. I never worked with him, but he was generous with his advice and encouragement, and he spoke highly of me to other people in the business. It was my privilege to remain friends with Bill Castle until he passed away.

My first professional "connection" in the business was made because I wrote a letter to a stranger. It's something that anyone can do.

14. The Birth of a New Major Studio
or
How Coca-Cola, CBS, and Time-HBO Got Married and Begat TriStar Pictures

Too often decisions in Hollywood as to what pictures to green-light are made on the basis of "What star can we get?" and "Who can I blame if it fails?" This chapter contains some little-known pieces of Hollywood history, vignettes that have never appeared in print before. One of them is about the founding and early days of a new studio with idealistic (and naïve) management, creative executives who were determined to choose pictures because they loved the material, who were eager to make *movies* instead of "packages." I am including it here because it is important for writers to have some idea of what goes on behind a studio's closed doors and how decisions are made. In the Byzantine world of show business what happens in a writer's professional life can be determined by friends and foes he may never meet. This chapter will illustrate what I mean.

Before the Flying Horse

In the latter months of 1982 a New York lawyer who was very astute at finance became entranced with the movie business and decided the time was right to create a new Hollywood studio. He brought together three major companies—Coca-Cola, CBS, and Time-HBO—and convinced them that backing the enterprise would be a smart investment. This studio, which would be the first new studio in decades, would be a "mini-major" in that it would not have any self-owned land beneath it, as did Fox, Paramount, Universal, Warner Brothers, and Disney with their "back lots" and extensive studio facilities, but in the quality and diversity and eventual quantity of its productions it would be a major studio.

With financing in place, the quiet search was on for a man to head the studio. (Only men were considered for this top spot.) The leading candidate was my tax attorney and friend, Gary Hendler, of the Century City firm Armstrong, Hendler & Hirsch, who was a respected figure in entertainment law. Among Gary's many clients were Barbra Streisand, Robert Redford, Sean Connery, Sydney Pollack, Elton John, Ella Fitzgerald, and Francis Ford Coppola.

Gary was in his forties, attractive, divorced, and a brilliant attorney. Among his many legal triumphs were negotiating a very favorable solution to a daunting tax problem faced by Elton John, helping Robert Redford make his dream of the Sundance Institute a reality, and helping Sean Connery prevail after millions of dollars were stolen from the actor.

At the time the new studio was being conceived, Gary had done so many innovative things as a tax attorney that he told me he was becoming bored with practicing law. Some of his clients, those who had also benefited from Gary's advice about the direction of their careers, were urging him to go into business with them and to produce their pictures, but the idea of working with just one major star was not appealing to him. He wanted a broader field of operation and was ready to take on a new challenge, but didn't know exactly what he wanted to do.

When the offer to head "Nova" (as the about-to-be-launched new studio was known at this time by the press) came, Gary had severe doubts that he wanted to run a studio. He knew that the pay and the prestige would be enormous, but if the new studio was not a success the fall from that pinnacle would be public and humiliating. We both knew executives who had been at the top of the Hollywood power pyramid, courted by everyone, and then abruptly lost their positions. Gone was the power to green-light movies, gone were the invitations to galas, gone were many of those they thought of as friends. The "apple" Gary was being offered looked delicious, but he was aware that biting into it could have disastrous consequences.

I was one of the people in whom Gary confided while he was trying to make up his mind whether or not to take the offer. It was my belief that Gary would be an excellent studio head. For several years we had discussed what worked and what did not work in movies, why some movies succeeded financially and creatively, and why others failed. Gary was a passionate reader and loved movies. He had a good story sense and great relationships with important stars and filmmakers who liked and trusted him. Yet he hesitated to put himself in so public a hot seat as that in which studio heads sit.

I worked hard to convince him to take the job. Every argument he raised, I countered. What I did not know at the time was that a close friend of Gary's, producer Dino Conte, was trying just as hard to convince Gary *not* to take the job. They were in Junior's, a delicatessen in Westwood where Gary loved the sandwiches, when Dino told him: "Don't take that job. It'll kill you." Gary told me Dino said: "Running a studio is a business of 'I, me, Caesar.' There will be so much pressure and stress on you because everybody—actors, directors, agents, producers—will be after you for what *they* want. They're not going to care about what's good for you." Dino knew that Gary was such a good lawyer because he cared so much about his clients. It was that very facet of Gary—the way he invested his emotions as well as his intellect in winning battles for friends and clients—that made Dino fear for Gary's health. Those of us who urged Gary to take the job won, but, tragically, Dino turned out to be right.

Gary Handler accepted the presidency of "Nova" (soon to be called "TriStar" in tribute to the three major entities that financed it) on

February 14, 1983. That same day he told me: "You're coming with me. I'm making you a vice president." My immediate response was: "I'm writing another novel. I don't want to be a studio executive."

Gary was a famously skillful negotiator; he did not take no for an answer. He said that he wanted me to work with him because, as a writer, I understood storytelling, and because he knew that he could trust me to give him my honest opinion, even if it meant a heated argument. (Gary told me later that Berry Gordy had seconded his idea of hiring me, and told him: "She'll watch your back.")

By the end of that Valentine's Day I was the first (and for the next four months the *only*) creative vice president of a studio with no name, no address, and no phone number. And no support staff. In spite of our having no name, address, or phone number, agents and filmmakers found us. Scripts began arriving at Gary's office and at my house at what seemed to be ten-minute intervals.

The first two *tons* of material to arrive were scripts that every other company in town had rejected, but, with the excitement of treasure hunters, we plunged into the stacks to search for undiscovered gems. We were determined that we were not going to fall for "brand-name packages," some of which had destroyed other studio regimes. Our decisions were going to be based on "What do we *love*," in spite of the fact that few studios decide what pictures to make based on what the executives actually *like*. We knew that the one thing we had to do was deliver a Robert Redford picture, because it was the Redford-Hendler relationship that had put Gary on the short list to head the new studio. We prayed Redford didn't want to do something no one on earth except his relatives would want to see. Fortunately for us, Redford wanted to do a project that we loved. It was called *The Natural,* and was from a Bernard Malamud story. We quickly found two more projects in which we were true believers.

Working at my dining-room table, still without offices and support staff, we put TriStar's first three films into preproduction. In addition to Redford's *The Natural,* which would be directed by Barry

235

Levinson, we chose Robert Benton's *Places in the Heart* and Jim Henson's *The Muppets Take Manhattan*. Both *Places* and *Muppets* had made the rounds and failed to find a home elsewhere. I've forgotten exactly who sent us the script of *Places in the Heart* but whoever it was apparently was so discouraged he or she had not bothered to have it freshly Xeroxed. There were coffee stains on the cover and dirt smudges that I jokingly referred to as "other executives' footprints" all over the pages.

Gary and I were crazy about that beautifully written script. *Places in the Heart* did not fit anybody's idea of a "commercial" movie, which is, I am sure, why it had been rejected, but it was clearly a project with which anybody would be proud to be connected. We decided this project had to be one of the new studio's initial three productions.

The choices we made in those first days were intended to send a message to the creative community that "Nova" (soon to be TriStar) was going to make high-quality projects. It was our mandate to quickly establish this new studio as a serious and potentially important force in the entertainment industry. We did not expect *Places* to make money (which, to our delighted astonishment, it did), but we *did* expect it to get critical praise and perhaps some Academy Award nominations. (Sally Field won her second Best Actress Oscar for her starring role in the picture.)

Places was our riskiest choice in those first weeks, but we assured each other that "they" (the financial powers in New York) were not likely to fire us in the first year because then "they" would look bad. This was the one brief period of time when we could choose pictures with our hearts alone, without opposition from the financial side of the company. What a happy time it was!

One of my tasks at this point was to write the synopses of our projects that Gary would present to our financial "fathers" in New York, describing those pictures in the most exciting creative terms and listing the reasons we felt certain these movies would be financially successful. The truth was that we *hoped* millions of other people would love the pictures as we did and rush to the box office to see them, but expressing our *certainty* that these first three pictures were good financial gambles was creative writing, or, to quote writer-director John Huston, "an improvement on the truth." The words must have been convincing, and Gary delivered them effectively. New York liked what Gary had to say and was supportive of our choices.

The Muppets Take Manhattan was another gamble that we won. The first Muppets movie had been a big success, but the second one was not. Neither Gary nor I had seen either of the movies, so I got prints of the two films and ran them. It was immediately obvious why one had been a hit and the other a financial disappointment. The first Muppet movie had the Muppets being true to their established characters. In other words, it was the Muppets being the Muppets. In the second movie, the Muppets were playing "roles"—and something magical was lost.

It was clear from reading the script of *The Muppets Take Manhattan* that the filmmakers had discovered the problem themselves and had corrected it. In this funny and charming script the Muppets were the Muppets again. Our Muppet picture went before the cameras on May 21, 1983. It was the same day the company finally got office space and telephones. Walter Coblenz, who had formerly headed Robert Redford's Wildwood Productions, and had just been hired as head of physical production for TriStar, was on an empty floor at 1875 Century Park East, across the street from Gary's old law office, with the telephone installers. Walter made the first outgoing call to me to say that we now had a phone number and would soon have furniture. "Come down and pick out an office," he said. (Larry Gelbart was in my new office shortly after we moved in, discussing a wonderful romantic comedy script of his. During that meeting my first salary check arrived. Larry helped me divide the amount of the check by the number of weeks since February 14 so that we could find out what I was earning as a studio vice president. I was happily surprised. Larry, being a writer, understood why it had not occurred to me to ask Gary what I was making, or even to wonder about my salary before that first check arrived, but he suggested I never let New York know that I was so indifferent to money; in Hollywood that would be heresy.)

The Muppets Take Manhattan was a critical and financial success. Gary and I were fortunate that the project was still available when we came on the scene. We wondered whether or not any other companies had taken the trouble to look at the first two pictures before making a decision, instead of rejecting the project because of the disappointing returns on the second picture.

Here are two little behind-the-scenes vignettes about *Places in the Heart*. The moral of this first story is: Don't believe someone who says "Pictures don't lie." I was a photographer, and I know that pictures *can* be unreliable witnesses.

It was my habit to see all the dailies of our pictures. When they began coming in from the Texas location of *Places* I was horrified at how bad Sally Field looked. Let me say immediately that Sally Field is, in person, a very attractive woman, and in 1983 she was beginning the years of her peak attractiveness. But cameras were not always her friend. In the scenes we were getting she looked so *un*attractive that I was afraid people would be turning to each other in their seats and asking, "What's wrong with Sally Field?" instead of paying attention to the story.

A call to the production office on location produced the information that her regular makeup man was on another movie and had not been available. We arranged that the makeup man be "ransomed" from the other production and flown to Texas immediately, and that the first few days of her scenes be reshot. It was worth the added expense, because soon Sally Field looked as pretty in the dailies as she needed to be in the early part of the story, before she becomes a young widow and is forced to go to work picking cotton in the fields in order to save her home.

Let me add, Robert Benton is the most responsible of filmmakers, in addition to being such an artist. In spite of the reshooting, and the fact that he (knowingly) shot a script that was longer than the film that could be released, he still managed to come in slightly under schedule and slightly under the budget he was given. The second behind-the-scenes story I want to share with you about

Places illustrates how crucial a release date can be to a movie's success.

There were two other "farm" movies being made at the same time as *Places: Country,* starring Jessica Lange, and *The River,* starring Sissy Spacek and Mel Gibson. Even though all three stories were different, we did not believe that the marketplace could support three farm pictures in the same year. We determined that we *had* to be first in release, and, thanks to Robert Benton, we were. The theory proved to be sound, and *Places in the Heart* was successful, both creatively and financially.

While Gary and I had three major movies in preproduction before TriStar had offices, it was another *year* before New York designed official stationery for us.

The Natural was our first release, the film with which we launched TriStar Pictures. Gary Hendler and Robert Redford had been attorney and client so long that the joke was Redford was waiting at the gates of Harvard Law School for Gary to graduate. Because of this long and close relationship, Gary asked Redford to keep within the picture's approved budget; that was important to Gary on this first release. Redford promised to do so. It is well known that Robert Redford is a fine actor and director. He is polite in working relationships and was open to suggestions and comments. But he did not keep his promise about staying within the approved budget. Because of Gary's long association with Redford, and because Gary had relayed to the company's financial backers Redford's promise to stay within the approved budget, the result of that promise not being kept was a professional embarrassment for Gary. His rivals and enemies saw this as the first tiny crack in Gary's "white knight" armor. They took note of it for future use.

About the time we moved into offices, Gary brought his friend and client, the director Sydney Pollack, into the company as a creative consultant. Gary achieved a level of comfort by having Sydney to call upon for advice, but it did not turn out to be a perfect alliance for Gary. Sydney, perhaps in a zealous attempt to be helpful, made quite a few development commitments that Gary then had to stand behind and, in some cases, defend to New York. He told me that these commitments amounted to several million dollars in development fees that did not result in movies being produced. Bad gambles in the spending of development money is unfortunately normal in long-established major studios, and in some rich independent production companies, but putting a lot of projects into development before they were thoroughly thought out and discussed was very much contrary to how Gary had intended TriStar to operate.

One project that was put into development in this manner was an idea pitched in one sentence by an Academy Award–winning screenwriter. The writer was given $350,000 (a big fee in 1984) to write the screenplay. When the script was delivered, the story only covered *half* of the one sentence that was pitched. The result of that gamble was an expensive script that was never made. It was a considerable embarrassment for Gary, at a time when the honeymoon with the financial end of the company in New York was over.

Anyone who has ever worked in film production knows that sooner or later you are going to run into big trouble. It's then that an executive needs good friends. Dino Conte was a very good friend to Gary Hendler. He had produced pictures with Sean Connery, Meg Ryan, Eddie Murphy, Nick Nolte and Richard Gere, Kim Basinger, and others. Another good friend was Walter Coblenz.

Agent Michael Ovitz, head of Creative Artists Agency (CAA), convinced Gary to green-light a picture about robots and heat-seeking bullets that had been written by and would be directed by Ovitz's client, Michael Crichton. The movie was called *Runaway,* and starred Tom Selleck and Gene Simmons of the rock group Kiss. We were well into production in Canada when a possible directors' strike loomed. Historically, the directors had not been a guild that was inclined to strike, but there was always a first time. If the Directors Guild called a strike while we were in production with a major film it would be a catastrophe for us. Walter Coblenz advised Gary about a plan to shoot first and second unit simultaneously, and flew to Canada to help implement it. As it turned out, at the last minute the directors did not strike, but Gary told me that those actions saved the production close to a million dollars on the budget.

A few months later we ran into an unexpected problem on *Berry Gordy's The Last Dragon.* The use of clips from several Bruce Lee movies was vital to Berry's production, which was a comedy with music that centered on a black martial artist named Bruce LeRoy. One clip was two and a half minutes of sound and picture and another thirty seconds of just sound from Bruce Lee's biggest movie, *Enter the Dragon,* which was a Warner Brothers 1973 release. We also needed a very important twenty-second scene from a Bruce Lee picture produced by Raymond Chow. The final clip we needed was from another Bruce Lee movie, the rights to which were controlled by Mike Medavoy, who was then at United Artists. Many films have used clips from other movies. It is generally a simple matter of paying the company that owns the movie from which you want a clip a fee, which is usually nominal. Companies, as a rule, cooperate with each other in such matters as it is probable a return accommodation will be needed one day.

Mike Medavoy could not have been more helpful when we approached him about what we needed. His response was: "Use as much as you want. No problem."

This was not the case with certain executives at Warner Brothers. The person we approached to get the footage from *Enter the Dragon* first quoted a price that was higher than expected, but we agreed. Then the price went up. Then it went up again. Again we agreed to pay it. Then the answer came that, paraphrased, meant "No to you at any price."

Because Gary and a Warner Brothers executive were not on the best terms, Gary thought the refusal was "personal, not business"—to paraphrase a line from *The Godfather.* Then we encountered our next obstacle, which was Raymond Chow. Raymond controlled a twenty-second clip that was the most necessary to our picture of all of the clips, but he would not give us that clip unless we managed to persuade Warner Brothers to give Raymond something that *he* wanted, but that he had been refused! This was the moment Gary chose to go off on a sailing vacation in the Caribbean, where he would not be reachable by phone for two weeks! He left, telling me to explain to Berry Gordy—who was deep in production in New York—that we hadn't been able get the clips so he would just have to rewrite the script. "He'll be okay about it," Gary said.

I knew that Berry (who, at this point, had been my closest friend for twelve years) would *not* be "okay about it." And if I told him that Gary had gone off sailing, leaving Berry in this creative fix, it would at least seriously damage, if not end, their own friendship. I had introduced them to each other several years earlier and did not want that to happen. In desperation, I called Dino Conte for help. He listened to the problem, said, "I'll see what I can do," and hung up.

The next day, thanks to Dino, we got our three minutes of *Enter the Dragon* sound and picture, Raymond Chow got whatever it was he wanted from Warner Brothers, and, as promised, he then gave us the crucial twenty seconds we needed from him. And Berry Gordy was spared having to rewrite a picture in the middle of a very complicated production.

Before my years at TriStar Pictures I had thought that the enemies of a studio executive were competing studios. It was a few months before I realized that Gary's strongest opposition might be under our logo on the opposite coast. Unfortunately, Gary did not believe my suspicions that there were forces within the company that wanted the "fun" of Gary's job, the "glamour" of choosing the pictures and dealing on a day-to-day basis with stars and star filmmakers. Gary, who knew how hard a job he had, would not believe that his position as head of TriStar Pictures was in jeopardy, nor that certain of his own colleagues would work behind the scenes for his ouster.

Few writers, directors, and actors know that their dreams and hard work can end in terrible disappointment through no fault of their own. An intramural power struggle in a company can have a devastating effect on the fate of a picture that's on the release schedule of a studio in turmoil. Very few writers, in particular, understand the part that a studio's distribution of their film plays in its commercial success or failure. Not even Gary understood, until it was too late, how much his professional fate was in the hands of the people who booked into theaters the pictures he green-lighted. The choice of how many theaters, where they were located, when the picture was booked, and against what competition in the marketplace, and the relationships with the most important theater chains, were vital to a picture's ultimate commercial fate. The motion picture business is in the most basic sense a distribution business, but distribution was an area of the business in which Gary was a novice. And it was a subject he was not given time to master.

A treasured friend of mine, Leo Greenfield, who had once headed domestic distribution at two major studios, Warner Brothers and Disney, had taught me enough about the art of distribution so that I was very worried about the fate of some of the movies that were identified as "Gary's." One was an inexpensive little "bubblegum" musical that starred TV daytime drama superstar Mary Beth Evans, and had a terrific soundtrack album. The album was produced by Michael Lloyd, winner of an Academy Award, a Golden Globe and four Grammys. I was concerned when I saw a report that listed the theaters in which it was playing. They did not strike me as being in the right areas for the intended audience, so I drove out to visit several of them to see for myself. The theaters I visited were in places I would have been afraid to drive at night. One theater manager, who showed me the gun he wore under his jacket, could not understand why he had been sent a "date movie" when his theater regularly booked Charles Bronson action pictures or "slasher flicks."

Another picture I believe did not have wholehearted company support was Alan Parker's film *Birdy*, which starred Nicolas Cage and Mathew Modine and was adapted from a novel by William Wharton into a beautiful screenplay by Jack Behr and Sandy Kroopf. When I read the script I thought it was marvelous, but I also knew that we were under pressure at that point to choose big, obviously commercial productions. I was not in favor of our doing *Birdy* at this time, but Gary said yes to it and it went into production. From the moment it was on our schedule it was our movie, and I was among its enthusiastic champions. The dailies were extraordinary in every way. I have seldom seen a movie that was better written, directed, or acted. The happiest part of my day during this period was seeing the *Birdy* dailies. I thought we had an award winner on our hands, and a picture that was so good it might well be a commercial success.

Birdy won the 1985 Cannes Film Festival Grand Jury Prize, but, in spite of glowing reviews, it was not a financial success. I don't believe that it was given an opportunity to find the audience that might have embraced it and turned it into a commercial hit. A picture like that needed to be handled like the rare gem that it was. My hope is that now that Nicolas Cage has become a superstar *Birdy* will be rereleased in a manner that allows it to gain the huge audience it deserves to have.

Gary Hendler didn't quite make it to his second anniversary as president of TriStar, but he extracted a handsome settlement of his contract and took some promising projects with him that he could choose to produce himself or in partnership with others. True to what had happened to other studio heads who vacate their offices, many people in the industry turned their backs on Gary. One who did not was Frank Mancuso, then president of Paramount Pictures, now chairman of MGM/UA. Frank was an acquaintance of Gary's, someone Gary (and just about everyone else in Hollywood) liked and respected, but they were not close friends. Nevertheless, Frank was determined to be helpful to Gary in any way that he could. He knew that it was important for Gary to get a project going quickly and offered to let Gary make a picture at Paramount. Gary was not ready to put a picture together that quickly, but I know how much Frank Mancuso's kindness and generosity meant to him because Gary mentioned it while he was reminiscing during the last weeks of his life.

When Gary left TriStar I thought that I, as one of his "people," would be fired the moment he was gone. When I wasn't, and the weeks went by, I began to think that a miracle had happened and I would be one of the rare vice presidents allowed to remain when the president who hired them had been removed. I was wrong. Arnie Messer was TriStar's head of business affairs and one of the people in the company I liked the most. His office was near mine and we had many enjoyable talks about movies. Also, we had survived the incomparable experience of driving with Marcello Danon, producer of *La Cage aux Folles*, with whom I was working on developing an American version of that film. Marcello, who spoke thirty-eight languages, of which English was his poorest, was charming on foot but a madman behind the wheel of a car. He was convinced that red lights, stop signs, and speed limits were simply suggestions to be ignored. Arnie and I bonded after being passengers in Marcello's car, the way survivors of other near-death experiences bond.

One day after my second anniversary with the company Arnie came into my office, which was not unusual, and then closed the door, which was *very* unusual. Gently, he told me that my time at TriStar was over. (I think he said something kind and flattering, but I was too stunned to hear that.) In shock, I asked: "You're *firing* me?" He replied: "Oh, no. Firing would mean that you did a bad job, and you did a wonderful job. We're letting you go."

I made some joke about this happening *after* I had learned to pronounce and spell the name of the man just named to be Gary's successor, Jeff Sagansky (whom I had not met at that time). What I was trying to do was use humor to keep myself from bursting into tears until after Arnie left my office. I think I just barely managed it. He had a tough job that day and did it as well as anyone could have. Arnie Messer is now one of the founding partners of Phoenix Pictures, and remains an executive and a gentleman of whom I am very fond.

I had never been "let go" from anything before. I cried for about twenty-four hours, virtually nonstop. (I had a longhaired dog at the time, a shepherd-collie-husky named Sitka, who thought he was getting a bath that night.) The next afternoon Dino Conte called to say hello. I was still crying. Gruffly, he told me to stop it. "Don't you realize, you've been set free! You're a writer. Go write!"

Producer John Veitch (his latest release is the exquisite film *Fly Away Home*) called as soon as he heard about the "sweeping management changes" at TriStar. Even though we knew each other only through meetings to discuss material, John did an incredibly kind thing. He offered to let me produce a movie *he* was about to produce—in other words, he would step aside and let me take the job in his place. Although deeply touched by his gallantry, I declined. But I will never forget the generosity of John Veitch.

I took Dino's advice and started back on the novel I had begun before TriStar Pictures was formed, but it wasn't long before Rod Amateau, a producer-director-writer with whom I had worked closely on one of our productions, invited me to share a screenwriting assignment with him, and to coproduce the movie with him. We had very little time to do it: just eight months from assignment to in-the-theaters. (Working with Rod was a joy. Not only is he a consummate professional in many areas, but he is the best joke teller I've ever met.)

As soon as principal photography on that movie was completed, Dino Conte asked to see the script. He read the first paragraph of the narrative—actually, just the first *sentence,* he told me later—closed the cover, and at that moment hired me to write a screenplay for him. He quoted a price which was more than fine with me and told me to write him a short outline of the script.

A few days later I gave him a nine-page story outline. He *hated* it! He complained that I'd turned the wrong character into the hero. I visualized my screenplay assignment flying out the window, but then he opened the top drawer of his desk and pulled out the first check in my series of payments. I was dumbfounded that I still had the job.

"You're a good writer," he growled. "You just have to be watched."

In spite of the kind offers of Frank Mancuso, Gary Hendler did not live long enough to produce a picture of his own. He was struck suddenly with a particularly vicious type of cancer and died within a few months of the diagnosis. There is a school of thought within the medical profession that believes certain cancers are triggered by stress.

As Dino Conte had predicted, the stress on Gary during his two years at TriStar had been terrible.

There was little hope of Gary's recovery, but he fought hard until his very last day. His most selflessly devoted nurse was his daughter, Susan. During the months of his illness, Gary Hendler—former studio head, once an important entertainment attorney—was unable to do anything for other people, which had made him "invisible" to some people in the business. Among his most stalwart Hollywood friends, those who loved him and didn't care whether or not he was powerful in the entertainment industry and who remained on call for anything Gary might need day or night, were Berry Gordy (who put his own business affairs on the far back burner in order to supervise and closely monitor Gary's medical treatment), Dino Conte, Sean Connery, Barry Hirsch (Gary's former law partner), Michael Ovitz, Carl Pollard (owner of the Minnesota Twins), and Ron Meyer, who was then a partner with Mike Ovitz in Creative Artists Agency and is now president of Universal Pictures.

Sean finally left Los Angeles only because he was legally compelled to start a picture in Europe that could not be postponed any longer. Gary made him go. Hours before he died, in our last conversation, Gary gave me the gift of asking me to look after his daughter, Susan.

TriStar Pictures has remained in business through several regimes. Now it is under the umbrella of the Sony Corporation. Coca-Cola is no longer one of the company's financial fathers. I still smile when I remember that an announcement of a visit to Los Angeles by Roberto Goizueta, CEO of Coca-Cola, would trigger a frantic search of the office closets to find the large silver-framed picture of himself that Roberto had presented to Gary, but which Gary set out on view only when "Don Quixote," as Gary referred to Roberto, was due in town.

Some talented creative executives emerged from TriStar, among them Jeff Sagansky, Casey Silver, who heads Universal's Motion Picture Group, and many others.

247

The two-plus years I spent at TriStar gave me a rare perspective into the profession of screenwriting. I had been a published novelist, then a studio vice president, then a working screenwriter and producer. The experience of having been on both sides of the desk—the buyer's side and the seller's side—is what led to my invitation to teach the course in screenplay development at UCLA Extension, and which led, ultimately, to the writing of this book.

15. Recommended Reading and Viewing

The following are books that I recommend screenwriters read for what can be learned about storytelling, character development, and dialogue:

Adventures in the Screen Trade, by William Goldman (Warner Books, 1983), is full of wonderful advice from a fine screenwriter. This man is generous enough, and loves his art and craft enough, to share his hard-earned wisdom with others. Read this book more than once.

Max Perkins—Editor of Genius, (E. P. Dutton, 1978) a biography by A. Scott Berg. Maxwell Perkins was one of the great literary editors of all time, the man who discovered and guided to their pinnacles such writers as Fitzgerald, Hemingway, Thomas Wolfe, Marjorie Kinnan Rawlings, and James Jones, to name a few. Fortunately for Scott Berg, and for us, Perkins had a hearing problem, so he dispensed most of his advice to his writers in the form of letters to them. These letters survived to help all of us who read this book. When *Max Perkins* was first published, I bought so many copies to give to friends that I began to wonder if the IRS would let me list Scott Berg on my tax form as a dependent. This book is still in print and it's also available in many libraries.

Rewrites, a memoir by Neil Simon (Simon & Schuster, 1996), covers a period of sixteen years in his professional and personal life. It begins in 1957, when, desperate to get out of creating sketches and jokes for television, he sat down to write his first Broadway play. It concludes with the death of his first wife, Joan, in 1973. This book is a marvelous course in good writing, and it has the additional pleasure of "introducing" us to a very special woman, Joan Simon. (To women who buy this book my suggestion is: Don't read it while wearing mascara.)

Who the Devil Made It, by Peter Bogdanovich (Alfred A. Knopf, 1997), is a priceless collection of interviews director Bogdanovich conducted with sixteen of the most important directors in the history of moviemaking. The only thing that matches Peter Bogdanovich's passion for films is his ability to draw the secrets of great filmmaking from great filmmakers. A little-known color in Peter Bogdanovich's artist's palette of talents is that he is a very fine actor. As a director, I have seen him give, practically line by line, film performances for which the actors on screen were later praised highly.

Making Movies, by Sidney Lumet (Alfred A. Knopf, 1995), describes how this director chooses what project to direct, prepares it with the writer, chooses the actors, rehearses them, and then directs the motion picture. This is a very valuable up-close look at the creative process of an extraordinarily talented man.

Monster, by John Gregory Dunne (Random House, 1997), is his account of the eight years and multiple drafts it took to bring the Robert Redford–Michelle Pfeiffer movie *Up Close and Personal* to the screen. The author also shares information about other projects that he and his wife, Joan Didion, worked on separately and together during this period. This is an accurate look at the adventures of writers who work on assignment.

The Deal, by Peter Lefcourt (Random House, 1991), is classified as a novel, but I found it virtually a documentary detailing how independent producers and studios operate—and how movies get made. It's hilarious, but the comedy is based on some realities of the movie business.

A Cast of Thousands (Pocket Books, 1993) is a novel by award-winning screenwriter Steve Shagan which details the inner workings of Hollywood in all of their hilarity and madness. This novel is full of the marvelous dialogue for which screenwriter Steve Shagan is celebrated. Among Steve Shagan's screenplay credits is *Save the Tiger,* which gave actor Jack Lemmon what is probably his finest dramatic role, and the 1973 Oscar for Best Actor. Shagan was nominated for an Academy Award that year, and won the Writers Guild Award for Best Original Screenplay of 1973.

Stein on Writing, by Sol Stein (St. Martin's Press, 1995), is written to be understood, and the author conveys his knowledge with wit and simplicity. While it is not targeted to screenwriters, what Sol Stein says about good writing, and his examples of how to achieve it, are well worth study by screenwriters—especially his chapter titled "The Secrets of Good Dialogue."

The Artist's Way, by Julia Cameron (G. P. Putnam's Sons, 1992), really is what its subtitle proclaims: "A Spiritual Path to Higher Creativity." This book will be especially valuable to the person who yearns to write but does not yet have the self-confidence to follow that dream.

Blueprint for Writing, by Rachel Friedman Ballon, Ph.D. (Lowell House, 1994), is subtitled "A Writer's Guide to Creativity, Craft & Career." The author is a gifted communicator who conducts regular seminars and workshops nationwide and from her home base in Los Angeles.

When Women Call the Shots, by Linda Seger (Henry Holt & Co., 1997), is subtitled "The Developing Power and Influence of Women in Television and Film" and contains illuminating interviews with Richard and Lili Zanuck, Sherry Lansing, Nora Ephron, Meg Ryan, Roger Corman, and others. What these prominent members of the entertainment community have to say is well worth hearing.

To Be Loved (Warner Books, 1994) is the autobiography of Berry Gordy. The founder of Motown, the writer and producer of the songs that formed for several generations "the sound track of our lives" (to quote Dick Clark), tells a story rich in drama and filled with marvelous dialogue. Berry Gordy has an incredible—almost a *"phono-graphic"*—memory, and that memory was supplemented with thirty-five years of meetings and creative sessions he audiotaped and stored in his archives. Berry Gordy tells his fascinating and entertaining story the way he wrote his songs—in wonderful *scenes* that make a reader feel she's right there in the room. Reading this book would benefit a screenwriter because it demonstrates how to write excellent dialogue in the distinct and individual voices of a variety of characters. Also, the dramatic episodes he relates in telling his story are models of beginning, middle, and end storytelling.

Trophy Wife, a novel by Kelly Lange (Simon & Schuster, 1995), is of value because of its lively dialogue exchanges and the author's sharp eye for character-revealing details. It is also instructive to observe how the major characters are altered by the circumstances of the plot. Newswoman Kelly Lange has used her skills as a journalist to create first-rate mystery fiction.

Rage of Angels, by Sidney Sheldon (William Morrow & Co. 1980), is virtually a course in how to develop interesting characters, create tension, and keep the story going in an upward dramatic spiral until the climax and resolution. Sidney Sheldon is a master at creating fully detailed characters, especially women. He pushes his leading ladies into "hot water" and then increases the "heat" at such a rate the reader can't put the book down. It's no mystery that he's listed in the Guinness Book of World Records as "The Most Translated Author of All Time," with nearly 300 *million* books in print around the world. (Before he became a novelist, Sidney Sheldon was an Academy Award–winning screenwriter and an Emmy-winning television writer.)

Aaron Spelling: A Prime-Time Life, by Aaron Spelling, with Jefferson Graham (St. Martin's Press, 1996), is an inspirational personal story, but it is also full of tips on how to create compelling characters and drama.

Because I've lived in African jungles I'm not the easiest person to frighten, but there are two novels I found so scary that for only those two times I did not want to be alone in the house while I read them. The first was William Peter Blatty's *The Exorcist,* which I read in manuscript form before it was published in 1972. I was all alone in a very isolated and unprotected old house! The second was Stephen King's *Salem's Lot* (Bantam, Doubleday, Dell, 1975), which made me go through the house frequently with two large dogs, turning on lights, checking doors, windows, and the burglar alarm system. I recommend that screenwriters read these two novels to learn how to build tension and spring terrifying surprises in their scripts.

For lessons in marvelous "speakable" dialogue that is perfectly crafted to their specific characters, please read novels by the following authors:

Joseph Wambaugh—read as many of his wonderful cop novels as you can, but at the very least please read *The Choirboys* (Delacorte Press, 1975) for its extraordinary dialogue and character development.

Ed McBain—any or all of his 87th Precinct novels. They are called "police procedurals" because the stories are full of the details of how a police department in a major city (a fictionalized version of New York City) works.

John D. Macdonald and **Ross Macdonald.** John D.'s Travis McGee and Ross's Lew Archer mystery novels are full of human feelings and the small but vivid details that make characters impossible to forget.

Elmore Leonard—the offbeat (and often bizarre) characters in his books are so vividly alive that they manage to be believable. And Leonard's dialogue is often laugh-out-loud funny.

Donald E. Westlake—his novels are filled with good dialogue and imaginative characters. If you've never read Donald E. Westlake, please start with *Trust Me on This* (Warner Books, 1988), which describes the inner workings of a powerful tabloid newspaper, and *The Ax* (Warner Books, 1997), which details how one "downsized" corporate middle manager deals with eliminating the competition for the new job he needs desperately.

The Last Good Kiss, by James Crumley (Random House, 1978), is a novel that page by page is just wonderful writing in every respect. I recommend that any writer who is *not* in Alcoholics Anonymous read this novel. The reason that I don't suggest recovering alcoholics read *The Last Good Kiss* is that on virtually every page characters are drinking, *thinking* about drinking, *talking* about drinking, *recovering* from drinking too much, or feeling that they *need* a drink.

16. The First Act of *Marabunta*

Wink Roberts and I wrote *Marabunta* as a theatrical feature and our agent submitted it "wide," that is, to twenty-four motion picture companies simultaneously. Fastened by brads into the script, preceding the text, were copies of actual photographs Wink had found of the lethal South American soldier ants the screenplay describes and some of the incredible things they do.

It was seeing those pictures that finally convinced me to write the script with Wink, something I had been saying no to for almost two years, since he first proposed the idea that we write a thriller about these terrifying and mysterious creatures. Tired of waiting, but still sure that he would eventually persuade me to work with him on it, Wink had gone ahead and written a first draft of the script.

Also attached to the script were *real*—albeit dead—soldier ants which had been encased in green-and-amber plastic and attached to metal key rings. Wink and his lady love, screenwriter Barbara Wadkins, had spent several hundred dollars buying these killer ant key rings in South America. The producers who turned down the script nevertheless kept the key rings.

Not long after the scripts were sent out, our agent notified us that he had made a deal with a company called The Producers Entertainment Group, headed by Irwin Myers and Rhonda Bloom, which had produced, among other pictures, the Tina Turner story, *What's Love Got to Do with It?* TPEG believed that they could set the picture up at Fox—as a television movie.

What Wink and I did not know at the time, but what the producers and our agent *did* know, was that suddenly "bug pictures" had become a hot trend and several were already in various stages of development at the studios.

We also learned that, ironically, our *Marabunta* had not been submitted to TPEG, but rather to producer Mike Levy, who was at that time sharing office space with TPEG because his own new offices were not ready yet. TPEG's young development executive, Kirt Eftekhar, had heard about our script from Mike Levy's assistant. Kirt read it, liked it, and took it to his bosses, producers Irwin Myers and Rhonda Bloom. I'm recounting the circuitous route *Marabunta* took from my computer and Wink's to the screen in order to illustrate a principle in which I believe strongly: Never ask a potential buyer to send your screenplay back. When asked by a writer in my workshops when they should ask that their scripts be returned my answer is: "Never." Let those to whom the script has been submitted keep the copies. Good agents don't ask for a rejected screenplay to be returned. They know that a screenplay that is in circulation has a better chance of being "discovered" than scripts that are returned. The twisted path that *Marabunta* took from creation to purchase is indicative of the unpredictability of Hollywood.

TPEG made a very agreeable deal with us, and then quickly put us into development at Fox TV. This meant that *Marabunta* was now "in contention" to be made as a Fox Tuesday Night Movie for the 1998 season.

Working with the best studio development executive I have ever met, Fox TV's Deborah Service, our script quickly became better and better. Three of Deborah's ideas are dramatized in Act One. At her suggestion the picture opens with the shock of what happens to the young honeymooning couple. The next big surprise is the skeleton we came to refer to as "Deborah's moose." Deborah also wanted what she called "an ordinary kitchen-ant moment." Her request inspired the scene with the cookie cabinet in Sheriff Croy's office.

It wasn't long after our rewrites were turned in that *Marabunta* was given the official green light by Fox and moved from in contention into preproduction, with a start date for filming of June 9, 1997. Within an astonishingly short five months of making our deal with TPEG for *Marabunta,* Eric Lutes (from *Caroline in the City*), Mitch Pileggi (from the *X Files*) and Julia Campell were hired to play Jim Conrad, Jeff Croy, and Laura Sills, and the picture began shooting on location in Utah.

After our deal was made and we were given the green light to proceed to production, Wink had to lend his own precious key ring (the last one left) to the special-effects people who were creating the computer-generated and the plastic "practical" ants. They even made "stunt ants" on springy legs for close-ups when ants were crawling over an actor's face.

The fact that *Marabunta* was written as a theatrical feature and was then converted to a TV Movie of the Week is unusual, because TV movies are usually bought based on a concept (or a book or newspaper headlines) and *then* they are written. In fact, had Wink and I pitched our soldier ant story to Fox TV the studio might have bought it, but it's unlikely they would have allowed us to write it. This is because, at the time, we were feature film writers, not credentialed TV movie writers. Now, because we were paid to transform our theatrical feature into a TV movie, we are also considered to be TV movie writers.

Ironic as it may be, this is show business and *things happen however they happen.* That's just the way it is. Expect the unexpected. In the words of Helene Hanff (author of two of my favorite books, *84 Charing Cross Road* and *Underfoot in Show Business*): "Everything that happens is unexpected."

Converting our theatrical feature version of *Marabunta* into a network television movie turned out to be relatively easy. For one thing, the story had no nudity or strong language. We had to cut two or three brief, but expensive, scenes because they would have busted the budget, and in cutting them we learned that the story was actually better for the cutting because it was now tighter and it brought the star into the story a page sooner. We also had to rewrite one action stunt because the budget did not allow us to blow the door off a 4X4.

"You can scratch that 4X4, you can dent it, you can get it dirty," we were told, "but you can't blow the door off because then we'll have to *buy* the vehicle!"

Other rewriting had to be done because it was not possible to secure certain locations we thought we would be able to use. Different locations required different action scenes and altered dialogue. For me, that's "the fun stuff." It's like getting the chance to redecorate your house, once you thought you'd furnished all of the rooms. The arduous part is building the house in the first place.

A network television movie is written in either seven or eight acts that must last for a specific number of minutes per act. Commercials are then inserted into these breaks. Because a thriller such as *Marabunta* is filled with action sequences, many of which provided perfect hooks for the end of an act, we did not have to twist the story artificially to conclude each act on a note of suspense in order to keep the attention of the audience.

Now, here to study is Act One of *Marabunta*. I think it may be helpful to you to note how the major characters—Jim Conrad, Laura Sills, Sheriff Jeff Croy, and his son, Chad, are introduced into the story, and how they are described. Analyze the dialogue to observe how each exchange between the characters either provides the audience with information about the characters or advances the plot.

Every scene in the script has a *purpose* for being there. For example, in the breakfast scene between Sheriff Croy and his young son, Chad, we see the affection between them and we learn that they are struggling to continue something resembling a normal life since the death of the boy's mother. We also learn that father and son plan to go climbing together on the coming weekend and that the climbing paraphernalia is in Croy's 4X4. This bit of information explains the presence of the gear when, much later in the script, that equipment will be vital to the outcome of the story.

As a practice exercise, note in each scene the lines that reveal information about our main characters, or demonstrate their personalities, or give us information about the foe they are about to face: the deadly soldier ants.

This picture is scheduled to air as a Fox TV Tuesday Night Movie in spring, 1998. As I write this, Fox plans to change the title, but has not decided on a new one.

Marabunta

by Wink Roberts & Linda Palmer

SHOOTING SCRIPT

Start Date: June 9, 1997
Location: Utah
Starring: Eric Lutes (Conrad)
Mitch Pileggi (Croy)
Julia Campbell (Laura)

ACT ONE

FADE IN:

1 EXT. MOUNTAIN PICNIC AREA—AFTERNOON (EARLY
FALL)

It's a spectacularly beautiful early Fall afternoon. In this lush green
picnic area at the edge of the woods we hear the SOUND of little
forest creatures: the melodic chirping of birds, the soft croaking of
frogs, the rattling of branches and the whispering of tall grasses.

This gentle symphony of Nature is shattered by the SOUND of a
MOTORCYCLE as it roars into view and stops. The cycle has
Washington plates and is ridden by GLENN and SARAH, an at-
tractive young couple. As Glenn turns off the engine:

                    SARAH
     I'm cold, Glennie. It's our honeymoon, we're sup-
     posed to spend it in bed.

                    GLENN
                (taking out camera)
     Just let me finish up the roll. I want to capture you
     in this fabulous light.

Reluctantly, Sarah acquiesces. Glenn grabs her hand before she can
change her mind and they take a narrow path that leads into the
woods.

                GLENN (CONT'D)
     You'll be rewarded for this.

                    SARAH
                (sexual innuendo)
     I like the sound of that.

2 EXT. FOREST—AFTERNOON

As Glenn and Sarah hurry along the path, the gentle sounds of nature begin to disappear.

REVERSE ANGLE

POV FROM SOMETHING CONCEALED

This SOMETHING watches Glenn and Sarah kiss and caress as they come nearer and nearer. Suddenly the young couple stops. They stare in awe at what they see just ahead of them.

POV GLENN AND SARAH

A STRANGE SILENCE surrounds a sloped mound of earth and twigs climbing 15 feet high, 20 feet wide at the base, tapering up to an altar-like top.

> GLENN
>
> That's fantastic!

> SARAH
>
> What is it?

> GLENN
>
> I don't care—look at the way the afternoon sun hits the top.

> SARAH
>
> You don't want us to climb up there?!

> GLENN
>
> The light'll be great on your hair. Come on.

> SARAH
>
> Aw, Glennie.

They begin to climb up the side of this strange mound. When they reach the top they see a flat "roof." Glenn positions Sarah with the light haloing her hair and starts shooting rapidly.

> GLENN (CONT'D)
> God, you're beautiful!
>> (then:)
> Damn—end of the roll.

> SARAH
> Great. Let's go back.

> GLENN
> Just one more roll. Honey, it'll be a magazine cover!

Before Sarah can protest, Glenn hurries back down the slope.

3 EXT. MOUNTAIN PICNIC AREA—AFTERNOON

Glenn runs to his bike and presses the rear button, causing the rear seat to pop up. He takes a package of film from a photographer's bag.

> SARAH'S VOICE (O.S.)
>> (calling, frightened)
> Glenn!

> GLENN
> Just a second.

He begins to load the camera. Suddenly he hears Sarah SCREAM!

4 EXT. FOREST—AFTERNOON

Glenn bolts toward the mound and sees Sarah, visible only from the waist up, SCREAMING in terror. She's desperately trying to climb out, but she's sinking into the top of the mound!

                            SARAH
        Help! Help me!

Glenn drops his camera, clawing for purchase as he frantically scales
the mound. He reaches Sarah and grabs her hands just as the
screaming girl's head is about to disappear below the surface!

                            GLENN
        Sarah! Hang on!

Glenn leans over the edge, trying to brace himself to gain leverage—
but in trying to pull Sarah out, Glenn leans over too far toward her
and falls in! The young honeymooners disappear into the depth—
and SUDDENLY we hear SCREAMS of terror turn to SCREAMS
OF AGONY . . . and the SCREEN GOES BLACK.

        ON BLACK SCREEN

Bleed in a strange SOUND—something like . . . CRUNCHING
. . . but not quite like any crunching we've ever heard. It's a little
softer, a little more insistent . . . and it should stir the hairs on the
back of our necks and chill our blood . . .

Title: "MARABUNTA" on BLACK SCREEN

Begin MAIN TITLES in white on BLACK SCREEN. This
CRUNCHING—a spooky, creepy sound we will never forget—
is underscored with eerie, haunting strains of MUSIC . . .

FADE IN

Our impression is that we are in a jungle, observing: ECU of TWO
TARANTULAS—surely the ugliest spiders ever created—as they
EAT a small bug. Then CAMERA MOVES to:

ECU of a PRAYING MANTIS COUPLE—mating. The mating
ritual ends as the Female suddenly BITES THE HEAD off her mate!

CONRAD'S VOICE (O.S.)
That's it, lady—take what you want and then
throw us guys away.

CAMERA PULLS BACK TO REVEAL we are *not* in a jungle,
but:

5 INT. NATURAL HISTORY MUSEUM—ENTOMOLOGY
LAB—MORNING

The pair of Tarantulas and the Praying Mantis and her late mate are
actually in glass cases filled with the replicated terrain we mistook
for a scene from Nature. The cases rest on a worktable in this lab.
Reverse on the lab's glass door reads: "JAMES CONRAD, M.D.,
Ph.D., Director of Entomology."

DR. JIM CONRAD, wearing surgical gloves, has been watching
the Tarantulas and the Praying Mantis. Conrad is the antithesis of
the stereotypical nerdy scientist: he's good-looking, athletic, and
has an irreverent sense of humor. Conrad reaches into the case to
remove for study the body of the late mate.

CONRAD
(to the Mantis)
I'm going to put an ad for you in the Personals:
"Young widow, hot to mate again. You won't be
my first love, but I'll be your last."

He puts the headless body into a plastic container and sets it aside.

Around Conrad we see that this lab contains row upon row of
stacked shelves above a work station on which stand clear glass jars
filled with assorted INSECTS soaking in Formaldehyde.

ON THE WALLS, meticulously displayed in glass cases, are rare
butterflies (some of extraordinary SIZE and BEAUTY) and beetles
of various sizes. Other cases house a wide array of exotic bugs.

267

Mounted above the door to the lab is a BASKETBALL HOOP.

Conrad strips off his gloves and picks up a Nerf basketball. Now facing the hoop, he's concentrating, attempting a three pointer into the hoop above the door. He shoots and—swish!

CONRAD (CONT'D)
Jim Conrad for three! Yes!! At the buzzer!!!

The laboratory door opens. His graduate student lab assistant, FRAN, enters, ducking automatically. It's clear she's done this before. Conrad goes for another shot, but this time misses.

CONRAD
How are we for time?

FRAN
You'll never make it, Dr. Conrad.

Conrad takes some bits of meat from a sandwich on the table and feeds them to the pair of Tarantulas.

CONRAD
I will if you let me drive your car.

FRAN
(horrified)
Absolutely not. I've only had it for a week!

Conrad gently taps the glass to attract their attention, gives them more food.

CONRAD
(re Tarantulas)
Take care of Bill and Hillary. I think she's pregnant.

                    FRAN
      Congratulations.

Conrad makes a quick tour of the lab, picking up papers, glancing
at them, stuffing them into various file folders which he hands to
Fran—as Fran, receiving the folders, simultaneously takes items
out of her purse and hands them to Conrad.

                 FRAN (CONT'D)
      Here's the key to your apartment. I watered your
      plants. Here's your plane ticket. Your bag's in my
      trunk.

He hands her some loose papers and more file folders.

                    CONRAD
      If Dr. Mason calls, what are you going to tell him?

                    FRAN
      He'll have your article on the Rove Beetle by the
      tenth.

                    CONRAD
      If Barry Richards calls—

                    FRAN
      You've decided not to sell the beach house after all.

                    CONRAD
      If Danielle calls—

                    FRAN
      You died in a freak lawn chair accident.
                 (looks at her watch)
      You're absolutely not going to make that plane,
      Dr. Conrad.

A devilish glint lights Conrad's eyes. He holds out his hand.

                    CONRAD
          Car keys.

6 EXT. SCENIC VIEW OF ALASKA FROM THE AIR—DAY
SUPER ON SCREEN: "GOODNEWS BAY, ALASKA"

7 EXT.—HAZARD'S HELICOPTER SERVICE—DAY

BOB HAZARD, an outdoorsman supreme, and dressed to prove
it, exits the hangar and approaches Conrad's Airplane.

                    HAZARD
          Hey, Bugman.

Conrad turns from the plane, holding his duffel bag and back-
pack.

                    CONRAD
          How you doing, Bob? It's great to see you.

                    HAZARD
          So how come you're three years late for our fishing
          date?

Conrad keeps up with Hazard as they walk around the structure
toward the back.

                    CONRAD
          I'm in bugs—our busy season is twelve months a
          year. Tell me about this secret new spot of yours
          where the salmon'll jump onto our lines.

Hazard reacts to the mention of salmon the way a dog reacts to a
fresh, juicy bone.

                            HAZARD
Lake Wanaka, just outside Burly Pines. Nobody's
there this time of year.

                            CONRAD
Sounds perfect.

Hazard stops near several helicopters. Painted on the side of the
choppers is: "Hazard's Helicopter Service." Hazard indicates that
Conrad is to put his duffel into the newest Copter nearby.

                            HAZARD
                          (re Copter)
Bugman, meet my new baby.

                            CONRAD
She's gorgeous.

8 EXT. ALASKAN COAST / ROCKY BEACH—DAY

We see the rugged Alaskan Bay below. We NOTE IN PASSING
some stray ACACIA LOGS that lie rotting on the rocky beach.
(The CAMERA should plant this sight in our consciousness, but
the significance of this glimpse will be revealed later.)

Hazard's Copter flies at low altitude just above the steep, jagged
CLIFFS that isolate the rocky beach below.

9 INT. COPTER—DAY

Conrad, in the seat next to Hazard, looks down at the beach.

10 EXT. ALASKAN COASTLINE—DAY

The Copter banks hard ninety degrees to the East and flies in-
land.

11 INT. COPTER—DAY

CONRAD

I'm impressed. Last time I was here you had one copter—now you've got a fleet.

HAZARD

And a bill from the IRS for back taxes, and an ex-wife who hates my guts.

Conrad smiles sympathetically and looks out the Copter.

CONRAD
(looking down)
How much farther to Burly Pines?

HAZARD

Five minutes by air, couple of years by foot.

12 EXT. ALASKAN WILDERNESS—DAY

The Copter flies over this desolate territory. No people, no buildings, roads, airports—just RIVERS, small LAKES and a thick, succulent FOREST so dense that from the air it looks like a carpet of green.

The Copter flies over a pristine lake that has a boat dock and a few small boats anchored alongside.

CONRAD'S VOICE

That Burly Pines?

13 INT. COPTER—DAY

HAZARD

Shady Lake. Lots of tourists come up during the summer for the great fishing, but they've gone since Labor Day.

Conrad watches out the window for signs of life. Suddenly the cloud cover ahead disperses and Conrad sees:

14 EXT. VOLCANO—DAY

Off in the distance, a gigantic VOLCANO looms. A thin vapor trail rises from its center.

> CONRAD'S VOICE
> That volcano looks active.

> HAZARD'S VOICE
> Mount Wupache? Naw, she just burps once in a
> while.

15 EXT. ABOVE BURLY PINES—DAY

As the Copter BUZZES closer, Conrad sees a nearly completed gigantic DAM. Rustic homes dot the landscape near the lake and the forest.

16 INT. COPTER—DAY

> HAZARD
> Burly Pines gives "nowhere" a good name.

> CONRAD
> Why does anybody live there?

> HAZARD
> Jobs building the new Dam. And it doesn't get
> dark until midnight. You can fish 18 hours a day.

17 EXT. AREA ABOVE LAKE WANAKA—LATE AFTERNOON

The Copter safely touches down on the hillside.

Conrad and Hazard climb out of the Copter and shoulder back-packs to which fishing poles are strapped, and start off into the woods beside the lake.

                    HAZARD
     My secret fishing area's too dense to land any
     closer, but we're not far away.

Hazard removes a can of bug spray, gives himself several squirts and offers it to Conrad.

                    CONRAD
     No thanks. I never met a bug I didn't like.

                    HAZARD
     Suit yourself.

18 EXT. FOREST—LATE AFTERNOON

Conrad and Hazard are making their way through the forest, moving around the lake. Conrad pours on bug spray as he fights off mosquitoes.

                    CONRAD
     I forgot how much I love Alaska.

                    HAZARD
     Don't wait another three years to come back. Life's
     too short to work all the time.

They walk along the path that parallels the lake when they see a fallen tree—and a large FORM (that we will shortly realize are MOOSE ANTLERS) protruding upward from the far side.

                    CONRAD
                  (whispering)
     What's that?

HAZARD

Looks like a moose—must be asleep.

Hazard and Conrad maneuver very cautiously forward and Hazard quietly slips a revolver from his pack.

CONRAD

You're not going to shoot him!

HAZARD

Hell, no—but we might need to scare him off if he decides to charge us.

Conrad and Hazard reach the downed tree. Still the antlers have not moved. Very carefully they shift into position to see the animal. Their eyes mirror their shock:

ANOTHER ANGLE, revealing

MOOSE ANTLERS—and a STRIPPED CARCASS. The bloody skeleton lies on its side. A short crossbow ARROW lies on the ground between bones in the large animal's rib cage.

CONRAD

Wolves?

HAZARD

An' mountain lions an' buzzards—looks like everything had a go at the big guy.

HUNTER # 1'S VOICE

Hey!

Conrad and Hazard turn to see TWO HUNTERS, dressed in camouflage attire and carrying CROSS-BOWS, appear from the dense forest. They're sweating and puffing, as though they've trudged a long way.

                    HUNTER # 2
                 (to Conrad & Hazard)
            Hey! That's our moose!

The two Hunters stare down at the skeleton in shock.

                    CONRAD
            Why'd you leave him for scavengers to eat on for a
            week?

                    HUNTER # 1
            Like hell we did!
                        (retrieves arrow)
            These're ours. We've been tracking him.

                    HUNTER # 2
            We wounded him two hours ago.

Hazard and Conrad exchange puzzled looks.

19 EXT. CAMPSITE BESIDE LAKE WANAKA—EVENING

Conrad and Hazard, bundled against the cold evening air, sit
beside their fishing poles. Their fishing lines have been cast
out into deep water—but it's obvious they have caught no
salmon.

Conrad, cold and hungry, is carefully cutting a candy bar exactly
in half with his hunting knife.

                    CONRAD
            "The salmon'll jump right onto our lines," you
            said. Where are they?
                        (hands half the candy bar to Hazard)
            Here, make it last.

HAZARD

Two weeks ago there were so many salmon you
could practically walk on 'em.

CONRAD

Looks like they swam for the border.

HAZARD

Maybe we just need different bait.

CONRAD

In the morning you get different bait—I'm going
to get some food.

20 EXT. MURDOCK'S TRADING POST—MORNING

Murdock's old lakeside store has a weather-faded sign that reads:
"Murdock's Trading Post." An American Flag flies from a tall pole
near the door and a small sign in the window tells us that Murdock's is also the local Post Office.

Conrad and Hazard, dirty, hungry and tired, approach Murdock's.
The only visible sign of life is a HUSKY dog (Blue) on the porch
of the Trading Post. She's whining.

As they approach the entrance, the Husky becomes excited. Her
whining intensifies and she scratches at the door to be let in. Hazard greets the dog and gives her an affectionate scratch on the head.

HAZARD

Hi, Blue.
(to Conrad)
Murdock's dog. He should be open by now.

Conrad pets Blue as Hazard tries the door and finds it locked.
Blue's whining has become more urgent.

CONRAD
(to the dog)
What's going on, girl?

Hazard knocks loudly on the door as Conrad peers in through the window. The dog jumps up on her hind legs, as though also trying to see in.

HAZARD
Hey, Murdock!
(to Conrad)
Something's not right.

CONRAD
It looks like a real mess in there.

Hazard forces the old door open a bit with his shoulder. As he opens it the rest of the way, it CREAKS loudly.

21 INT. MURDOCK'S—MORNING

Conrad and Hazard enter the Trading Post to see: the place has been trashed! Blue streaks past Conrad and Hazard, racing toward the back of the Trading Post.

HAZARD
What the hell—?

Shelves of canned food, bear traps and guns have been knocked over, glass display cases toppled and smashed. Game trophies are askew on the walls.

CONRAD
Look.

Hazard's eyes follow Conrad's down to the wooden floor to see a dark smear of dried liquid. From the back room, Blue starts barking loudly.

HAZARD

Is that blood?

Conrad doesn't reply. He starts back in the direction of Blue's frantic barking. Hazard follows.

The door to Murdock's office is standing partway open.

22 INT. MURDOCK'S OFFICE—MORNING

Conrad cautiously leads the way into the office to see — the back of a man's head.

His long black hair—indicative of his Native American heritage—hangs down a foot below his shoulders and drapes the back of the chair. The rest of Murdock is blocked from view by his high-backed chair. Blue is on the other side of the chair, out of sight of Conrad and Hazard, whining piteously.

CONRAD

Mr. Murdock?

Hazard approaches the back of the chair, reaches out to touch Murdock's shoulder when—"Murdock" TUMBLES forward and crashes to the floor.

The eyes of Conrad and Hazard widen in horror: Trent Murdock is no longer a man—he's a SKELETON in clothing, completely picked clean of flesh! His hair, separate from his skull, remains hanging over the back of the chair.

CONRAD (CONT'D)

First that moose—now a man . . . What's loose up here?

HAZARD
(grabbing phone, punches number)
Sheriff Croy, this is Bob Hazard . . .

23 EXT. ROAD—MORNING

The Sheriff's 4X4 racing over the road, SIREN BLARING. A Deputy's patrol car follows closely.

24 EXT. MURDOCK'S TRADING POST—MORNING

The two official cars speed up to the front of the Trading Post and skid to a stop. SHERIFF JEFF CROY gets out. He's a good man, tough, smart, no-nonsense, in his 40s.

DEPUTY DAVE BLOUNT jumps out of his patrol car. He's a man in his 20s with small, mean eyes. In contrast to the sheriff's well-worn, comfortable clothes, Blount's deputy's uniform is im-maculate and military-looking.

Conrad and Hazard meet Croy and Blount at the entrance to Murdock's.

> SHERIFF CROY
> Where is he?

> HAZARD
> Inside. Damndest thing you ever saw.

Conrad extends his hand to Sheriff Croy; Croy takes it.

> CONRAD
> Jim Conrad.

> SHERIFF CROY
> Sheriff Croy. This is Deputy Blount.

25 INT. MURDOCK'S OFFICE—MORNING

Sheriff Croy kneels beside the clothed skeleton of Trent Murdock as Blount peers down over Croy's shoulder.

Conrad—opposite Croy—examines the floor around Murdock's chair while Hazard stands slightly to one side, out of the way. Blue is lying nearby, quiet and grieving for her dead master.

                    BLOUNT
    Jeez . . .

                    HAZARD
                 (to Conrad)
    What do you think—one of those flesh-eating
    viruses?

                    BLOUNT
    What are you asking him for?

                    HAZARD
    He's a scientist. From Los Angeles.

Suddenly, from the front of the store—

                    LAURA'S VOICE
    Hello . . . ? Mr. Murdock . . . ?

Sheriff Croy is up instantly, turning toward the door—

                    SHERIFF CROY
    Stay out of here!

Conrad stands up to see LAURA SILLS, in her 20s, athletic and pretty, dressed in jeans, sweater and a jacket, stop in the doorway to Murdock's office.

                    LAURA
    What's happened?

SHERIFF CROY
Don't come any closer, Laura.

Sheriff Croy moves so that he's blocking her sight of Murdock.

LAURA
Why—?

SHERIFF CROY
Trent Murdock's dead.

LAURA
What happened to him?

SHERIFF CROY
I'm still investigating.
                    (to Blount)
I don't want people wandering in here!

Blount, not happy to leave the scene, grudgingly goes out.

SHERIFF CROY (CONT'D)
Is there something you wanted, Laura?

LAURA
Mr. Murdock had some fish for me. My biology
class was going to dissect them, but that's not important now.

Sheriff Croy gently steers Laura to the open office door. We
see Blount tacking yellow crime scene tape across the front entrance.

SHERIFF CROY
No sense depriving the kids. I'll have somebody
bring the fish over to you tonight.

LAURA

Thank you, Sheriff.
                    (to Hazard)
Goodbye, Bob.
                    (to Conrad)
Goodbye . . . ?

CONRAD

Jim Conrad.

LAURA

You look so familiar.

HAZARD

He writes books nobody can understand.

LAURA

James Conrad? Are you the entomologist?

CONRAD

Guilty.

LAURA

I knew I'd seen your face. Your picture's on the
back of *The Unseen World*. It's not very good.

CONRAD

Well it got some pretty good reviews.

LAURA

I meant the picture. But I bought a second copy
for the school library.

CONRAD

You doubled my sales. Thanks.

SHERIFF CROY

Laura, we've got to get back to the station.

LAURA

Let me know if there's anything I can do.

26 EXT. ROAD LEADING TO BURLY PINES—DAY

Sheriff Croy's 4X4 leads a two-vehicle procession toward town. Croy is at the wheel, Hazard beside him. (Note: there's a FIRE EX-TINGUISHER attached to the roll bar. Also in the vehicle is a rolled-up AREA MAP stuck in among the paraphernalia carried by a small-town Sheriff.) In the back of the 4X4 is a body bag containing Trent Murdock's remains. Murdock's Husky, Blue, lies across the bag, quietly grieving.

Following is Deputy Blount's patrol car. Blount drives; Conrad's in the passenger seat.

27 INT. BLOUNT'S CAR—DAY

CONRAD

Been a strange 24 hours. What's going on up here?

BLOUNT

You tell me—ain't you the scientist?

CONRAD

An entomologist. We know just enough to know how little we know. Like what's here in Alaska that could reduce a man to a skeleton without remov-ing his clothes? Like what stripped a moose clean in two hours—what drove the salmon away?

BLOUNT

Thanks for the interest, but I think we can handle this ourselves.

28 EXT. SHERIFF'S STATION—DAY

The 4X4 and the patrol car pull up in front of the Sheriff's Station on the main drag of this small town.

A Native American (GRAY WOLF MURDOCK, brother of the dead man) stands at the door of the Sheriff's Station. Gray Wolf is tall, well-muscled, the construction foreman of the local dam project.

Next to him is MARGIE McNALLY, Croy's secretary. She has a gentle manner, a sweet face.

Croy and Hazard get out of the 4X4 as the Husky jumps out, goes over to Gray Wolf and rubs against him. Conrad and Blount exit the patrol car.

> GRAY WOLF
> I want to see my brother.

29 INT. BACK ROOM AT SHERIFF'S STATION—DAY

There's a long worktable and a full-size refrigerator against the back wall. There are shelves full of reference books and paperback mysteries next to stacked cardboard boxes full of old files.

The closed body bag lies stretched out on the worktable. Conrad looks at it, thinking, as Croy speaks to Gray Wolf.

> SHERIFF CROY
> I don't know how to prepare you for this—

> GRAY WOLF
> Just let me see.

Croy moves to the worktable. He unzips the body bag to chest level. Gray Wolf keeps his steely composure as he stares down at the clothed skeleton of his brother.

                    GRAY WOLF (CONT'D)
                         (to Croy)
              What did this to my brother?

                    SHERIFF CROY
          We're not really sure, Gray Wolf. Maybe some
          animal . . .

                    GRAY WOLF
          Show me the animal that shreds a man's flesh to
          the bone and then puts his clothes back on!

Conrad leans in for a closer look and sees something. He quickly reaches into the bag with a tissue and retrieves a tiny sample.

                    SHERIFF CROY
          Conrad! Don't touch anything. The Coroner won't
          be here until tomorrow.

Gray Wolf looks at Croy.

                    SHERIFF CROY (CONT'D)
          Don't tell anybody what you've seen until we
          figure out what happened. I want your word, Gray
          Wolf.

Gray Wolf nods.

                    GRAY WOLF
          I would like to be alone with my brother.

There are three desks in this office. The largest and messiest belongs to Sheriff Croy. The neatest is Blount's. The only desk with a computer is Margie's.

Blue is whining at the closed door to the back room. Margie looks at the Husky sympathetically.

MARGIE
Poor doggie. Would you like a cookie?

Without waiting for Blue to answer, Margie goes to a cupboard above the electric coffee maker. Just as Conrad and Sheriff Croy come in from the back room Margie opens the cupboard and—

MARGIE (CONT'D)
Eeeeccccckkkkkkk!

SHERIFF CROY
What's the matter?

MARGIE
Look—ants!

CONRAD
Get away from there!

Conrad practically knocks Croy over dashing to the cupboard to see what Margie's found. Margie is surprised at Conrad's behavior.

In the cupboard: A line of tiny, everyday kitchen ants, swarming all over a package of cookies. Ants have ravaged through bags of flour and sugar and boxes of crackers, ruining everything.

MARGIE

It's just some ants. I'll get rid of them.

Margie takes a piece of paper and tries to slip it under the line of ants.

SHERIFF CROY

What are you doing?

MARGIE

Moving them outside.

BLOUNT

Jeez!

Blount goes to the small supply closet, grabs a bottle of disinfectant and opens it. To Margie's horror, he goes to the cupboard and starts splashing it over the ants.

MARGIE

What are you doing?!

BLOUNT

Disinfectant. I like 'em to suffer.

MARGIE

Blount, you're disgusting!

Gray Wolf Murdock comes out of the back room and closes the door.

GRAY WOLF

Tell me when I can come for him.

SHERIFF CROY

Sure, Gray Wolf.

Gray Wolf gives Blue's collar a gentle tug and the Husky follows him out.

SUDDENLY there's a RUMBLING SOUND and the floor beneath their feet rolls slightly as the shelves rattle and several books fall to the floor!

                              MARGIE
            Oh dear Lord!

Margie, Hazard and Croy reach out to steady themselves. Conrad keeps his balance, seeming to ignore the minor 'quake.

The RUMBLING and the SHAKING are over in a few seconds. Croy checks the phone—still working—and checks the locks on the gun case as Conrad helps Margie pick up the books that dropped from the shelf.

                          SHERIFF CROY
            That wasn't so bad.

                              MARGIE
            But we're getting more and more of them.

                              CONRAD
                          (deadpanning)
            What? Did I miss something?

                              HAZARD
            He lives in L.A.

Margie laughs nervously.

                        HAZARD (CONT'D)
            I want to check on the helicopter.

Hazard exits. Conrad carefully holds the tissue with the sample he found on Murdock's bones.

> CONRAD
> I want to make some tests . . . Is there some place I can stay tonight?

31 EXT. ROAD LEADING TO CABINS—DAY

Sheriff Croy's 4X4 negotiates the bumpy road toward a cluster of rustic rental cabins at the edge of the woods.

Off in the distance behind the cabins we see the Volcano rising above the trees. The wisps of steam coming from it are visible in the fading light.

> SHERIFF CROY'S VOICE
> You can use Zack Henry's cabin. He only comes up from Seattle during hunting season. Place is stocked with food, if you know how to use a can opener.

32 EXT. CABINS—DAY

Sheriff Croy's 4X4 drives up to the door of cabin # 4 and stops. Conrad gets out and pulls his duffel bag from the back seat.

> CONRAD
> Thanks, Sheriff.

At that moment, the door to cabin # 3 opens—and Laura Sills comes out, carrying a paper bag of recyclable trash and heading toward the nearby locked trash bin. She sees Sheriff Croy and Conrad and smiles.

> SHERIFF CROY
> Brought you a neighbor, Laura.

CONRAD

Hi, neighbor.

LAURA

Hello, Dr. Conrad.

CONRAD

Jim.

SHERIFF CROY
(to Conrad)
I'll pick you up in the morning. 'Bye, Laura.

LAURA

'Bye.

Sheriff Croy drives away. Laura disconnects the chain from the trash bin and starts to lift her trash.

CONRAD

Can I help you?

LAURA

I've got it. Thanks.

Laura tips the trash into the bin, reconnects the chain and starts back toward her cabin.

CONRAD

I need a hot shower.

LAURA

I'm sorry—there isn't any. I just did my laundry.

CONRAD

That's okay. Cold showers build character.

Conrad takes the key Sheriff Croy gave him and fits it into the door of cabin # 4. The lock turns, but instead of entering the cabin, he stops to look at Laura.

Laura enters her cabin and turns quickly to catch Conrad looking at her. She smiles and closes her door.

> CONRAD (CONT'D)
> (to himself)
> I think I'm going to like it here . . .

33 INT. CONRAD'S SHOWER—DUSK

Conrad is having a cold, cold shower—and hating it. As Conrad turns off the water he hears the O.S. sound of someone KNOCK-ING on the door.

34 INT. BEDROOM-LIVING ROOM OF CABIN—DUSK

Conrad, a towel around his waist, passes through this one-room cabin on his way to answer the KNOCKING at the door. The cabin is sparsely but adequately furnished with all the basic necessities.

Conrad opens the door to see—Laura.

> LAURA
> I thought maybe you could use a hot meal.
> (re his towel)
> We usually dress for dinner.

35 INT. LIVING-DINING ROOM IN LAURA'S CABIN—NIGHT

Laura's cabin is neat and attractive. The living-dining area is filled with healthy indoor plants, books, Native American rugs and artifacts. There's a fire in the fireplace and a dozen trophies on a shelf.

Laura and Conrad have finished dinner. There's a fruit bowl with oranges, bananas, and grapes on the table; Conrad's eating the grapes. Laura pours coffee and hands a cup to Conrad.

> LAURA
> Jim, how was Trent Murdock killed?

> CONRAD
> I'm sorry, but Croy asked us to keep it under
> wraps until we know more.

> LAURA
> Croy's a rarity: a smart and honest cop. Poor guy,
> his wife died a few months ago.

They take their coffee cups and move to the sofa in front of the fire. Conrad looks around.

> CONRAD
> (re the trophies)
> Looks like you're really good at something.

> LAURA
> Marksmanship. My dad taught me to shoot when
> I was twelve.

> CONRAD
> He was a hunter?

> LAURA
> A New York City Police Captain.

CONRAD

How did a big-city woman come to live in a small
town in Alaska?

LAURA

She got tired of big-city men.

CONRAD

You know Los Angeles is really just a collection of
small towns.

As Conrad hoped, this makes Laura smile.

LAURA

Now what's a world-famous entomologist doing in
Burly Pines?

CONRAD

Hazard and I have known each other since college.
I needed to get out of L.A. for a while, so I came
up for the salmon fishing.

LAURA

Didn't I read this in an old novel—a famous scientist goes fishing, stumbles on a mystery and screws
up his vacation.

CONRAD

I haven't written it off as a complete disaster.

Laura is pleased at Conrad's subtle flirtation, but deftly changes the
course of the conversation.

LAURA

Seriously, what do you think happened to Murdock?

CONRAD

I have a theory . . . If we were in a warmer place
I'd be more sure what killed Murdock. But the
only explanation I have right now is impossible
because the ground up here is too cold.

LAURA
(gets up)
I want to show you something . . .

36 EXT. BURLY PINES SCHOOL—NIGHT
(ESTABLISHING)

The town's school is located in one small brick building.

37 INT. LAURA'S CLASSROOM—NIGHT

Laura shows Conrad the pictures and graphs on the walls. There's
a microscope on Laura's desk. She unfolds a long sheet of graph
paper, shows it to Conrad.

LAURA

As a science project, we've been keeping track of
the accelerated earthquake and geothermal activity in the area. The most fascinating thing we
discovered is the underground temperature
change.

CONRAD
Tell me.

LAURA

Mount Wupache has been dormant for two thousand years. But lately the local sulfur springs have
increased in size and the earthquakes are more frequent.

                    CONRAD
        So the volcano woke up.
                    (re microscope)
        You have a clean slide?

Laura takes one from a box in her desk and hands it to him. Conrad reaches into his pocket and removes the sample he took from Murdock, puts it on the slide and under the lens of the microscope as they talk.

                    LAURA
        What are you looking at?

                    CONRAD
        Something I found on Murdock . . . Please, go on.

                    LAURA
        We've been using a thermo-coupler in the ground.
        The Anchorage Seismic Laboratory agrees with
        our findings: the temperatures and the geothermal
        activity are steadily increasing.

                    CONRAD
                    (still peering into microscope)
        Then the earth is warming beneath the town.

                    LAURA
        It's like the tropics down there now. That's proba-
        bly what drove the salmon away.

He straightens up from the microscope and looks at her, his eyes full of ominous portent.

                    CONRAD
        I'm afraid we've got a bigger problem than missing
        fish . . .

CAMERA PANS DOWN beneath Laura's first-floor classroom, and continues on down, down, beneath the basement, into the bowels of the earth until we see:

38 INT. ANT TUNNEL—NIGHT

An ANT TUNNEL beneath the school, filled with SOLDIER ANTS, moving rapidly and with purpose. This is a complex, highly sophisticated civilization of connecting tunnels and nests, an ANT WORLD populated by millions of intelligent, deadly creatures, existing below the surface of our own world.

We hear that frightening CRUNCHING noise, and it is a sound that turns our blood to ice . . .

                                            FADE OUT:

END ACT ONE

A Few Final Words

I hope you feel this book has been helpful to you, that it has given you a clearer understanding of what it takes to be a successful screenwriter. As we conclude our journey, please remember this:

The first impression that a writer makes, with skillful use of words and confident command of craft, and the first impression that a character makes, with what he or she says or does, should grab the reader's interest. Otherwise, there might not be a second chance—at least not with that particular project.

Opportunities for a writer to be "discovered" are precious. Don't waste them by showing a script before it has been perfected to the best of your ability *at that time*.

I have never known of a script that did not go through anywhere from some to many revisions once a director came on board and actors were cast. That is part of the collaborative process of moviemaking, and the writer is part of the creative team.

What I am talking about here is resisting the impulse to show your work while there are still things in it that *you* know you can do better. If producers or production executives eager to find a "hot" script (and almost all of them are) have heard your premise and liked it, they may try to persuade you to show it to them before you think it's ready by saying:

"Let me look at it. I can see the potential in a script even if it's in rough shape." Sadly for the writer who falls for this line, that is very seldom true. So I encourage you to submit your work *only* when it is ready to be read, and then be prepared to see it through many revisions. You may have some frustrating days, but you will be a working writer and you can be very proud of that.

Finally, I would like to stress how important it is for you as an artist to keep writing day after day or night after night, on whatever schedule you can make. This is the obligation you owe to your talent.

A blessing in my life is the friendship of one of the finest dramatic writers I have ever known, the multi-award-winning S. Lee Pogostin. Near the end of my time at TriStar Pictures, Lee and his wife, Betty, gave me an IBM Selectric III typewriter. But the gift came with a catch, which was spelled out in code on the brass plaque that was attached to the side. Translated, it read: "Lee Pogostin loves Linda Palmer, but only if she writes every day."

Writers *write*. No matter what.

I wish you all hard work and good luck! Now, go to your keyboards. I look forward to seeing your movies.

FADE OUT